Jim Hooper
665 Louise CT Campbell

Microprocessing Fundamentals

Hardware and Software

Edward V. Ramirez
Grumman Aerospace Corporation

Melvyn Weiss
Hughes Aircraft Company

McGRAW-HILL BOOK COMPANY

GREGG DIVISION

New York Atlanta Dallas St. Louis San Francisco
Auckland Bogotá Düsseldorf Johannesburg
London Madrid Mexico Montreal
New Delhi Panama Paris
São Paulo Singapore
Sydney Tokyo
Toronto

Sponsors: George Horesta and Mark Haas
Editing supervisor: Alice V. Manning
Design supervisor: Karen T. Mino
Art supervisor: Howard Brotman
Production supervisor: Kathleen Morrissey
Cover photographer: Martin Bough/Studios, Inc.

Library of Congress Cataloging in Publication Data

Ramirez, Edward V
   Microprocessing fundamentals.

   Includes index.
   1. Microprocessors. I. Weiss, Melvyn, joint author.
II. Title.
QA76.5.R299 1980   001.6'4'04   79-17922
ISBN 0-07-051172-1

Microprocessing Fundamentals: Hardware and Software

1 2 3 4 5 6 7 8 9 0 DODO 7 8 6 5 4 3 2 1 0 9

Contents

Preface

This book provides an introductory treatment of the microprocessor. Major topics covered are the basic elements of a microprocessor, programming fundamentals, the microprocessor interface, and microprocessor applications. With the growing number of microprocessors entering the field, an attempt was made to use a generic microprocessor rather than emphasizing any particular one. While this book does not contain any specification sheets or analyses of present-day microprocessors, it will provide you with a sound background in microprocessor fundamentals. The subject matter does not require any background in digital technology; however, a basic knowledge of this subject may be beneficial.

Chapter 1 deals with the basics of digital technology and should be helpful to readers who are unfamiliar with digital techniques. Chapter 2 reviews the basic elements of digital computer systems, stressing the fundamental operations that must take place at the functional level. In Chap. 3 you are introduced to microprocessor concepts. Chapter 4 is devoted to technology and the functional operation of solid-state memories.

Chapter 5 covers programming fundamentals with the concepts of instructions and addressing modes being presented. The "generic instruction set," a group of 30 basic instructions, is described, with illustrative examples to help you to understand the concepts of addressing modes and instructions. An understanding of the generic instruction set will provide you with the knowledge to program any available microprocessor.

Chapter 6 is devoted to software, with machine, assembly, and high-level languages described. The procedure describing how software is developed and the tools for accomplishing this are included. Chapter 7 introduces flowcharts and describes, step by step, the program instructions required to implement the numerous flowcharting examples.

An insight into microcomputers and bit-slice microprocessor units is presented in Chap. 8. Chapter 9 discusses interfaces, an important aspect in understanding microprocessors. Data transfer techniques and input-output devices are major categories within this chapter. Chapter 10 is devoted to application and selection of microprocessing systems.

This book is intended for the two-year college student, the hobbyist who wishes to understand the inner workings of a microprocessor, and the engineer or manager who wishes an entry-level text on microprocessors.

As a text for classroom use, the material is intended to be covered in a one-semester course in an electrical technology or computer engineering department. The book is also suitable for self-study, since it presents the fundamental aspects of microprocessors, which are then reinforced by problems at the end of every chapter. The chapters are written so as to provide a balanced treatment between hardware and software.

We would like to thank Jim Becker, Bart Collins, and Lenny McDonough of Grumman Aerospace and Walter Flattau of Sperry Gyroscope for helping review the manuscript. Their valuable suggestions are greatly appreciated. Finally, we dedicated this book to our families for their encouragement, loyalty, and patience during this period.

Edward V. Ramirez

Melvyn Weiss

Introduction
Evolution of Microprocessors

The development of microprocessors in the 1970s represents a significant advance in electronics. The microprocessor's popularity stems from many factors, such as its small size, its low power needs, its small parts count compared with hard-wired logic, and, perhaps most important of all, its low cost. Because of the microprocessor's small size and low cost, consumers and small businesses can now have in a handful of chips as much computational power as computers that in 1970 were affordable only to big users of data processing systems.

In the early 1960s a single transistor used for digital logic circuitry sold for an average price of about 5 dollars. In the late 1970s the same 5 dollars could purchase a single microprocessor chip; however, this chip had 10,000 transistors and included all the necessary resistors and intracomponent connections—a truly remarkable technological achievement.

To a large extent we owe the successful development of microprocessors to the needs of the military and the space program, which led manufacturers to develop miniaturized electronic circuits known as *microelectronics*. The need was for systems with reliable performance, low power dissipation, light weight, and small volume. These goals required small circuits. Semiconductor manufacturers were able to increase the circuit density of a basic chip by using simpler processes and by reducing the pattern mask sizes. This trend toward higher-density packaging continued through the 1960s. However, the success of microprocessors is really attributable to the commercial market, whose demands have created a high level of production and a subsequent reduction in the selling price of microprocessors.

A microprocessor can be defined as a single integrated circuit consisting of thousands of digital gates which perform the arithmetic, logic, and control functions of a general-purpose computer. It is a member of the family of large-scale integrated circuits, which reflect the present state of a trend toward miniaturization that began with the development of the transistor in the late 1940s.

As the semiconductor industry continues to make lower-cost chips with more functions, it is only natural for it to attempt higher levels of circuit integration. Microprocessors require external input-output circuits and external memory to functionally operate as computers. The trend is to incorporate these circuits into the same chip as the microprocessor, thereby forming a computer on a single chip. This configuration is called a *micro-computer*. Integrated into an area of less than 40,000 square mils (mil^2) are a memory, input-output interface circuits, and the arithmetic, logic, and control functions of a microprocessor. As new classes of these devices become available, the use of microprocessors and microcomputers will broaden.

In the mid-1960s, when medium-scale integration (MSI, with 50 to 400 transistors per chip) technology appeared, it was widely used to make smaller computers than those that had previously existed. Minicomputers, as these computers were called, were intended for a specific, limited market. Minicomputers were designed to capture (as they in fact did) the low end of performance, such as controller functions, data acquisition, and displays formerly handled by large computers.

Minicomputer advantages included fast processing rates, relatively short word lengths, and versatile input-output structure. Also an important factor in the "mini" success was the small physical size achieved by the use of MSI. Large computers, called *main frame* units, using MSI parts soon followed. Cost was probably the most important factor in the success of the minicomputer. In the mid-sixties minicomputers were selling for about $25,000; by the late 1970s they were selling for under $10,000. This low price, coupled with modest performance, guaranteed minicomputers a place in the computer market.

The data processing spectrum is so wide that microprocessors and microcomputers have also captured part of the available market and even created new markets. The microprocessor will capture many of the low-end applications presently being performed by minicomputers.

Another trend being observed is in the increased level of complexity found in newer microprocessors. Circuits such as timer/counters and drivers, normally found external to the chip in older microprocessors, are now being integrated into the chip. When the first microprocessor was developed it was a 4-bit unit with modest density. Other units developed since have increased bit length and density. By the late 1970s most microprocessors were using 8 bits per word, with newer units having 16 bits per word. It is reasonable to forecast that with the emphasis presently being placed on 8-bit microcomputers and 16-bit microprocessors, dramatic price reductions for single-chip 16-bit microcomputers will be a reality.

Basic Digital Techniques

The microprocessor is a product of large-scale integration (LSI) technology, which uses digital techniques for its input, output, and internal structure. This chapter presents a review of number systems and digital integrated circuit (IC) building blocks.

The decimal number system which we use has as its base 10, since each digit position can contain any number from 0 to 9, a total of 10 different numbers. Early attempts to design decimal computers provided little fruitful result, as it is difficult to reliably represent 10 different states. A more satisfactory approach utilizing only two levels was adopted, with logic 1 representing one level and logic 0 representing the other level. In order to understand the binary system, it is first necessary to fully understand the familiar decimal (base 10) number system.

1-1 DECIMAL NUMBER SYSTEM

The number 4385 is read as "four thousand three hundred eighty-five"; we start with the most significant digit at the extreme left. A method of writing 4385 is

$$4385_{10} = 4 \times 10^3 + 3 \times 10^2 + 8 \times 10^1 + 5 \times 10^0$$

The digit position at the extreme right is the one of least value. The value of each digit position to the left increases by a power of 10.

When we add two numbers in the decimal number system, the rules are to first add the least-value digits and then the next higher-value digits, etc.

4

Should the sum of any two digits exceed 10, a carry is generated into the next higher digit position. For example,

$$086$$
$$+057$$

The addition is performed as

$$6 + 7 = 3 + \text{``carry 1''}$$
$$8 + 5 + 1 \text{ (previous carry)} = 4 + \text{``carry 1''}$$
$$0 + 0 + 1 \text{ (previous carry)} = 1 + \text{``carry 0''}$$
$$\text{Answer} = 143$$

In subtraction, the subtrahend is subtracted from the minuend. The subtraction rules state that if the minuend digit is less than the subtrahend digit then the base 10 is added to the minuend and the next subtrahend digit to the left has a "borrow 1" added to it. For example:

$$86 \text{ minuend}$$
$$-57 \text{ subtrahend}$$

The subtraction is performed as

$$6 - 7 = 10 \text{ (1 borrow)} + 6 - 7 = 16 - 7 = 9$$
$$8 - 5 = 8 - (5 + \text{``borrow 1''}) = 8 - 6 = 2$$
$$\text{Answer} = 29$$

A more significant method of subtracting is the 9's or the 10's complement system.

The 9's and 10's Complements

Nine's and ten's complements can be used to convert subtraction operations to additions.

To convert to the 9's complement, each decimal digit is subtracted from 9. For example, Find the 9's complement of 37, 45, and 29.

$$
\begin{array}{ccc}
99 & 99 & 99 \\
-37 & -45 & -29 \\
\hline
62 & 54 & 70
\end{array}
$$

9's complement of 37 = 62

9's complement of 45 = 54

9's complement of 29 = 70

In 9's complement subtraction, the subtrahend is complemented and then added to the minuend. The carry generated from the highest digit position is not used to form a new digit position but instead is added to the sum under the original digit position.

EXAMPLES

Subtract 17 from 84   Subtract 3 from 75
9's complement of 17 = 82   9's complement of 03 = 96

```
              84                                          75
          +  82                                      +  96
            ⌐166                                        ⌐171
carry    ↳  1              carry          ↳  1
            ———                                         ———
             67                                          72
```

To convert to the 10's complement system from the 9's complement, 1 is added to the 9's complement value.

EXAMPLE

Determine the 10's complement of 12, 44, and 73.

9's complement of 12 = 87, 10's complement of 12 = 88
9's complement of 44 = 55, 10's complement of 44 = 56
9's complement of 73 = 26, 10's complement of 73 = 27

In 10's complement subtraction, the subtrahend is first converted to its 10's complement and then added to the minuend. The resultant carry generated from the highest digit position does not form a new digit position but instead is ignored.

EXAMPLE 1

Subtract using 10's complement arithmetic

$$\begin{array}{r} 86 \\ -57 \\ \hline \end{array}$$

$$\text{subtrahend} = 57$$
$$\text{9's complement} = 42$$
$$\text{10's complement} = 42 + 1 = 43$$

$$\begin{array}{r} 86 \\ +\ 43 \\ \hline 129 \end{array}$$

Ignore carry

Answer = 29

EXAMPLE 2
Subtract using 10's complement arithmetic

$$456$$
$$-308$$

$$\text{subtrahend} = 308$$
$$\text{9's complement} = 691$$
$$\text{10's complement} = 691 + 1 = 692$$

$$456$$
$$+\ 692$$
$$1148$$

Ignore carry

$$\text{Answer} = 148$$

1-2 THE BINARY NUMBER SYSTEM

Digital systems, in contrast to analog systems have only two states, On and Off. These two conditions can be represented by the opening and closing of a switch or in common transistor-transistor logic (TTL) by the 1 state (4 V $\pm$ 1 V) and the 0 state (0.2 V $\pm$ 0.2 V). The logic 1 state is frequently specified as 2.4 V minimum and the logic 0 state as 0.8 V maximum. Since a digital system has only two states, it can be readily represented by the binary system, which has only two notations, 0 and 1. The binary system is the base 2 system, in contrast to the decimal system, which is the base 10 system. The principle behind representing any decimal number in binary is positional notation. That is, all digit positions to the left of the point, which in the binary number system is called the binary point, have ascending powers of 2. The first, or least significant, digit to the left of the binary point has a 2^0 value. The next digit to the left has a 2^1 value or weight assigned to its position. Each subsequent position to the left has its weight value, in powers of 2, increased by 1 over the previous digit. A four-digit number will have the digit weight assignment $2^3 2^2 2^1 2^0$, where any digit if it is 1 will assume the weight of its position. The binary number 1010110 can be converted to its decimal equivalent value as follows:

$$1010110 = 1 \times 2^6 + 0 \times 2^5 + 1 \times 2^4 + 0 \times 2^3 + 1 \times 2^2 + 1 \times 2^1 + 0 \times 2^0$$
$$= 1 \times 64 + 0 + 1 \times 16 + 0 + 1 \times 4 + 1 \times 2 + 0$$
$$= 86_{10}$$

Table 1-1 represents the equivalent binary numbers of decimal numbers 0 through 15. A table of powers of 2 is found in Appendix A. Note that the

TABLE 1-1

DECIMAL NUMBER	BINARY EQUIVALENT	DECIMAL NUMBER	BINARY EQUIVALENT
0	0000	8	1000
1	0001	9	1001
2	0010	10	1010
3	0011	11	1011
4	0100	12	1100
5	0101	13	1101
6	0110	14	1110
7	0111	15	1111

number 15 has 1s in all digit positions. This implies that with four digits the highest value that can be represented is 15. This can be expressed mathematically as

$$\text{Highest decimal value} = 2^n - 1$$

where n is the number of binary digits. With eight digits, the highest decimal number that can be expressed is 255; i.e., $2^8 - 1 = 256 - 1 = 255$.

Bits and Other Terms

A *binary digit* (a 1 or a 0) is called a *bit.* A group of 4 consecutive bits within a computing system is called a *nibble,* while 8 consecutive bits make up a *byte.* Most microprocessing systems have an 8-bit internal structure, where transfers between the elements are done in parallel and with 8 bits. The term commonly used to describe a group of 8 bits that function together as a unit is the *word.* A word in a typical microprocessing system is a byte (8 bits); however, in larger systems a word can be 16 bits. Large data processing systems use words of 32 or 64 bits. This represents 4 to 8 bytes, or twice this number of nibbles.

In any data word organization, the bit furthest from the least significant bit (LSB) is called the most significant bit (MSB). In computer terminology both the LSB and the MSB digits are usually specifically referred to as such.

Binary Code Applications

Suppose it is necessary to represent the numbers 0 through 9 (10 characters) and the uppercase and lowercase alphabet (52 characters) in binary codes; this would require a total of 62 characters. Since $2^5 < 62 < 2^6$, a minimum of 6 bits is required. These 6 bits form a word, with each word capable of

TABLE 1-2 Binary Representation of the Character Code

B5 (MSB)	B4	B3	B2	B1	B0 (LSB)	WORD NUMBER	CHARACTER
0	0	0	0	0	0	0	A
0	0	0	0	0	1	1	B
0	0	0	0	1	0	2	C
⋮	⋮	⋮	⋮	⋮	⋮	⋮	⋮
0	1	1	0	0	1	25	Z
0	1	1	0	1	0	26	a
⋮	⋮	⋮	⋮	⋮	⋮	⋮	⋮
1	1	0	0	1	1	51	z
1	1	0	1	0	0	52	0
1	1	0	1	0	1	53	1
⋮	⋮	⋮	⋮	⋮	⋮	⋮	⋮

defining a character. The binary format of these characters could be as shown in Table 1-2, with B0 through B5 representing the 6 binary bits. When this binary format is transmitted to an 8-bit microprocessor, each byte represents a character plus 2 spare bits, bits B6 and B7. These spare bits may be used to verify that no bits were lost in the transmission to the microprocessor and to tell the microprocessor that the transmitted character is valid.

A self-checking scheme which can enhance the validity of the transmitted data can be implemented by the use of *parity*. Parity is a method by which the total number of binary 1s (or 0s) is always even or always odd—no matter which character is transmitted. When the sum of the binary 1s in a word is odd, this is called *odd parity*. If the sum is even, this is called *even parity*. Table 1-3 shows a revised word structure using the entire 8 bits. The microprocessor using this word structure can test bit B6 to see if the character is valid, and after determining validity it can verify proper transmission.

Positive Logic vs. Negative Logic

A common misconception is that negative logic refers to negative voltage. This is not true. Positive logic in TTL means simply $4\text{ V} \pm 1\text{ V} = \text{logic 1}$ and $0.2\text{ V} \pm 0.2\text{ V} = \text{logic 0}$. In negative logic $4\text{ V} \pm 1\text{ V} = \text{logic 0}$ and $0.2\text{ V} \pm 0.2\text{ V} = \text{logic 1}$. In positive logic the word True refers to $4\text{ V} \pm 1\text{ V}$ and False $0.2\text{ V} \pm 0.2\text{ V}$, while in negative logic the word True means $0.2\text{ V} \pm 0.2\text{ V}$ and False means $4\text{ V} \pm 1\text{ V}$. If an interface is TTL and uses negative logic, a True signal will be $0.2\text{ V} \pm 0.2\text{ V}$. Figure 1-1 shows positive-logic and negative-logic waveshapes.

TABLE 1-3   Binary Representation of the Character Code Using B7 as Parity (Odd) and B6 as Validity*

PARITY (ODD) (MSB) B7	VALIDITY B6	B5	B4	B3	B2	B1	(LSB) B0	WORD NUMBER	CHARACTER
0	1	0	0	0	0	0	0	0	A
1	1	0	0	0	0	0	1	1	B
1	1	0	0	0	0	1	0	2	C
⋮	⋮	⋮	⋮	⋮	⋮	⋮	⋮	⋮	⋮
1	1	0	1	1	0	0	1	25	Z
1	1	0	1	1	0	1	0	26	a
⋮	⋮	⋮	⋮	⋮	⋮	⋮	⋮	⋮	⋮
0	1	1	1	0	0	1	1	51	z
1	1	1	1	0	1	0	0	52	0
0	1	1	1	0	1	0	1	53	1
⋮	⋮	⋮	⋮	⋮	⋮	⋮	⋮	⋮	⋮
1	1	1	1	1	1	0	1	61	9

*1 = VALID
0 = INVALID

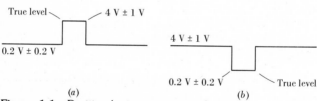

Figure 1-1   Positive logic vs. negative logic. (a) Positive logic; (b) negative logic.

Decimal-to-Binary Conversion

A method of determining the binary equivalent of a decimal number is to successively divide by 2 and use the remainders as the answer, the first remainder being the LSB, and so on.

EXAMPLE

Determine the binary equivalent of 57_{10}.

$$2\overline{)57} \quad \dfrac{28}{} \quad R = 1 \text{ (LSB)}$$

$$2\overline{)28} \quad \dfrac{14}{} \quad R = 0$$

$$\begin{array}{r} 7 \\ 2\overline{)14} \end{array} \quad R = 0$$

$$\begin{array}{r} 3 \\ 2\overline{)\ 7} \end{array} \quad R = 1$$

$$\begin{array}{r} 1 \\ 2\overline{)\ 3} \end{array} \quad R = 1$$

$$\begin{array}{r} 0 \\ 2\overline{)\ 1} \end{array} \quad R = 1 \ (MSB)$$

Therefore the answer (from bottom to top) is 111001.

Binary-Coded Decimal (BCD) System

A *binary-coded decimal* (BCD) number is a 4-bit word in binary format that represents a decimal number. The decimal number 495, for example, is expressed in BCD format as 0100 1001 0101.

$$0100_2 \times 10^2 + 1001_2 \times 10^1 + 0101_2 \times 10^0 = 4 \times 10^2 + 9 \times 10^1 + 5 \times 10^0$$

$$400 + 90 + 5 = 495$$

Table 1-4 shows a more complete analysis of the BCD representation of the decimal number 495.

TABLE 1-4   BCD Representation of Decimal 495

Weight	800	400	200	100	80	40	20	10	8	4	2	1
BCD	0	1	0	0	1	0	0	1	0	1	0	1
Decimal		400				90				5		

The BCD numbering system can be extremely useful when a digital system has to provide an interface to a decimal display. Most decimal displays require a BCD input. A BCD-to-decimal decoder is discussed later in this chapter.

Octal Representation

It can be difficult to remember binary numbers that contain many bits. The 8-bit binary number 01011100 is difficult to remember. However, the number can be broken up into three groups, starting with the LSB, and then individually evaluated:

01 011 100

1   3   4

It can be written as 134_8 or 134 octal. The decimal equivalent is

$$1 \times 8^2 + 3 \times 8^1 + 4 \times 8^0$$
$$= 64 + 24 + 4 = 92_{10}$$

Decimal-to-Octal Conversion   The conversion from decimal to octal is similar in technique to that from decimal to binary shown previously. The number is divided by the base of the system to which you are converting.

$$8\overline{)92} \quad\quad R = 4 \text{ (LSB)}$$
with quotient 11

$$8\overline{)11} \quad\quad R = 3$$
with quotient 1

$$8\overline{)\ 1} \quad\quad R = 1 \text{ (MSB)}$$
with quotient 0

Therefore $92_{10} = 134_8$

The octal representation of numbers is useful in defining microprocessor instructions or operation codes. As an example, the Intel 8080 microprocessor instructions for Halt and Jump are 166_8 and 303_8, respectively.

Fractional Numbers

How are numbers less than 1 represented in binary? In decimal notation a point (the decimal point) is used to separate the whole number from the fraction. In binary, the first position to the right of the point (called the binary point) has a weight of 2^{-1}, or 0.5; the second position, 2^{-2}, or 0.25; the third position, 2^{-3}, or 0.125; etc.

Binary-Fraction–to–Decimal Conversion   A binary fractional number is converted to a decimal fraction by multiplying the first bit to the right of the binary point by 2^{-1}, the second bit by 2^{-2}, etc.

EXAMPLE
Convert 0.10101000 to a fractional decimal number.

$$0.10101000 = 1 \times 2^{-1} + 0 \times 2^{-2} + 1 \times 2^{-3} + 0 \times 2^{-4} + 1 \times 2^{-5}$$
$$+ 0 \times 2^{-6} + 0 \times 2^{-7} + 0 \times 2^{-8}$$
$$= 0.5 + 0 + 0.125 + 0 + 0.03125 + 0 + 0 + 0$$
$$= 0.65625$$

Refer to Appendix A for a complete table of powers of 2.

Decimal-Fraction-to-Binary Conversion   A decimal fraction is converted to a binary fractional number by successively multiplying the *fraction* (to the right of the point) by 2 and using the *integers* (I, to the left of the point) produced by the multiplication as the result. The first integer is the MSB.

EXAMPLE
Convert 0.65625 to a binary fractional number.

$$0.65625 \times 2 = 1.3125 \quad I = 1 \text{ (MSB)}$$
$$0.3125 \times 2 = 0.625 \quad I = 0$$
$$0.625 \times 2 = 1.25 \quad I = 1$$
$$0.25 \times 2 = 0.50 \quad I = 0$$
$$0.50 \times 2 = 1.00 \quad I = 1$$
$$0.00 \times 2 = 0.00 \quad I = 0 \text{ (LSB)}$$

Therefore the answer (from top to bottom) is 0.101010.

Binary Addition

Binary addition works on the same principle as decimal addition. The sum operation is initiated in the rightmost position and possible carries are propagated to the left. Each digit of the addend is added to the corresponding digit in the augend. The result is the sum, possibly including a carry. Binary rules of addition are:

AUGEND	ADDEND	SUM	CARRY
0	0	0	0
0	1	1	0
1	0	1	0
1	1	0	1

EXAMPLE
Add the following two binary numbers and verify your results.

$$
\begin{array}{ll}
101\ 0110 & \text{Augend} \\
+\ 011\ 1001 & \text{Addend} \\
\hline
1000\ 1111 & \text{Sum} \\
0111\ 0000 & \text{Carry}
\end{array}
$$

Answer: 1000 1111

To verify:

$$
\begin{array}{rl}
101\ 0110 = & 86_{10} \\
011\ 1001 = & 57_{10} \\
\hline
& 143_{10}
\end{array}
$$

$$1000\ 1111 = 1 \times 2^7 + 0 \times 2^6 + 0 \times 2^5 + 0 \times 2^4 + 1 \times 2^3$$
$$+ 1 \times 2^2 + 1 \times 2^1 + 1 \times 2^0$$
$$= 1 \times 128 + 0 + 0 + 0 + 1 \times 8 + 1 \times 4 + 1 \times 2 + 1 \times 1$$
$$= 143_{10}$$

Binary Subtraction

As in decimal system arithmetic, each digit in the subtrahend is subtracted from the corresponding digit in the minuend. The result is the difference, possibly requiring a borrow. When the minuend is less than the subtrahend, then the base number (2) is added to the minuend and the next subtrahend digit to the left has a "borrow 1" added to it.

The binary rules of subtraction are

MINUEND	SUBTRAHEND	DIFFERENCE	BORROW
0	0	0	0
0	1	1	1
1	0	1	0
1	1	0	0

EXAMPLE
Subtract 0011 from 1101

1101	Minuend
0011	Subtrahend
1010	Difference
0010	Borrow

Expressed differently:

$$1 - 1 = 0 + 0 \text{ borrow}$$
$$0 - 1 = 1 + 1 \text{ borrow}$$
$$1 - 0 = 1 - (0 + 1 \text{ borrow}) = 1 - 1 = 0 + 0 \text{ borrow}$$
$$1 - 0 = 1 + 0 \text{ borrow}$$

Answer: 1010

Sign-Magnitude and 2's Complement Systems In the example of subtraction just shown, the results conveniently were positive. The question arises, "How are negative numbers represented?" An extra binary bit directly to the left of the most significant, or extreme left, bit can be used to define the sign of the number. This method is called the *sign-magnitude system*. If this extra bit is a 0, then the number is positive; if it is a 1, the number is negative.

EXAMPLE

$$+2 = 0 \quad 010$$
$$-2 = 1 \quad 010$$
$$+5 = 0 \quad 101$$
$$-7 = 1 \quad 111$$

Although this is rather easy to understand, it doesn't work too well with computers.

EXAMPLE
Find the sum of +3 and −5.

$$+3 = \quad 0 \ 011$$
$$+ \ (-5) = \quad 1 \ 101$$
$$0 \ 011 + 1 \ 101 = 10 \ 000 \ (\text{overflow})$$
$$= +0$$

Clearly the wrong answer. This addition caused an overflow beyond the capability of the number system (3 bits + sign) and a result of 0 instead of −2, or 1 010. Unless the sign bit is isolated from the magnitude, the sign-magnitude system really works only for positive numbers. It can, however, work for negative numbers too if we change the negative numbers to the 2's complement number system. The 2's complement system is identical to the binary system for positive numbers. Negative numbers are represented by taking the inverse of the positive number and adding a 1. When a binary number is inverted (all 1s become 0s and all 0s become 1s), the new number is in its 1's complement form. Adding a 1 to a number in 1's complement produces the 2's complement number. To represent −10 in 2's complement form the following format should be used.

$$+10 = 0 \ 1010$$
$$\text{sign bit} \ \Big\lessgtr$$
$$\text{Inverse (1's Complement)} = 1 \ 0101$$
$$\text{(add one)} + \quad \underline{\qquad 1}$$
$$-10 \ \text{in 2's Complement} = 1 \ 0110$$

Microprocessors use 2's complement arithmetic, so that an 8-bit microprocessor will represent a negative number by making the extreme left bit, or bit 8, a 1. The result of an arithmetic operation performed by an 8-bit microprocessor, for example, will allow for only a 7-bit result, since the most significant bit is used for sign identification. Note that 0s are inserted to the left of the most significant bit that describes the positive number, while 1s are inserted to the left of the most significant digit that describes the negative number. Therefore the number −10 becomes 1 1110110.

Table 1-5 shows the difference between the sign-magnitude, 1's complement, and 2's complement systems. Note that all positive numbers are represented the same way in all three systems.

TABLE 1-5

VALUE	SIGN MAGNITUDE	1's COMPLEMENT	2's COMPLEMENT
0	0 0000000	0 1111111	0 0000000
+1	0 0000001	0 0000001	0 0000001
−1	1 0000001	1 1111110	1 1111111
+2	0 0000010	0 0000010	0 0000010
−2	1 0000010	1 1111101	1 1111110
+5	0 0000101	0 0000101	0 0000101
−5	1 0000101	1 1111010	1 1111011
+7	0 0000111	0 0000111	0 0000111
−7	1 0000111	1 1111000	1 1111001
+10	0 0001010	0 0001010	0 0001010
−10	1 0001010	1 1110101	1 1110110

Returning to our previous example, adding +3 and −5 and using 2's complement arithmetic,

$$
\begin{array}{r}
+3 = 0\ 0000011 \\
+\ (-5) = 1\ 1111011 \\
\hline
1\ 1111110
\end{array}
$$

The result gives us a sign bit of 1, which means a negative number whose value is in 2's complement form. Table 1-5 shows that this value is −2.

EXAMPLE
Subtract 2 from 13 using 2's complement arithmetic.

$$
\begin{array}{r}
13 = 0\ 1101 \\
+\ (-2) = 1\ 1110 \\
\hline
0\ 1011
\end{array}
$$

The result is positive and the value is simply 1011, or 11_{10}, since positive numbers are the same in both the sign-magnitude and 2's complement systems.

To obtain the value of a negative number in 2's complement form, simply perform another 2's complement, ignoring the sign bit.

EXAMPLE

What is the value of the number represented in 2's complement as 1 1110?

$$1110 = 0001, \text{1's complement}$$
$$= 0010, \text{2's complement}$$
$$0010 = 2$$

Hence the value is −2.

The Hexadecimal System

Perhaps the most widely used number code is hexadecimal, or base 16, as shown in Table 1-6. The hex system, as it is commonly called, partitions the binary digits into groups of 4 bits. Letters A through F are used to correspond to the decimal numbers 10 through 15. The hex equivalents of 0000 to 1001 are the conventional digits 0 to 9. A composite table showing the hex, binary, and octal notation for the decimal numbers 0 to 16 is given in Table 1-6.

TABLE 1-6   Number Systems Conversion Table

DECIMAL	HEXADECIMAL	BINARY	OCTAL
0	00H	00000	000
1	01H	00001	001
2	02H	00010	002
3	03H	00011	003
4	04H	00100	004
5	05H	00101	005
6	06H	00110	006
7	07H	00111	007
8	08H	01000	010
9	09H	01001	011
10	0AH	01010	012
11	0BH	01011	013
12	0CH	01100	014
13	0DH	01101	015
14	0EH	01110	016
15	0FH	01111	017
16	10H	10000	020

There are recommended rules in using hexadecimal notation; these have been developed to make hex clearly recognizable and to reduce potential errors. These are:

1. All numbers must start with a digit. A 0 is inserted if the number starts with a letter.

2. The number must end with the suffix H.

EXAMPLE

5C hexadecimal is written 5CH

A4 hexadecimal is written 0A4H

Hexadecimal-to-Decimal Conversion The decimal equivalent for 0A4H is

$$0 \times 16^2 + 10 \times 16^1 + 4 \times 16^0 = 164_{10}$$

The decimal equivalent for 5CH is

$$5 \times 16^1 + 12 \times 16^0 = 92_{10}$$

The usefulness of a hexadecimal number should now be quite clear. In 8- or 16-bit data words only two or four hexadecimal digits are required, while three or six octal digits are necessary. The binary number 10101100 is partitioned as

$$1010|1100$$
$$= 0ACH$$

This allows for a simpler and less error-prone method during manual entry and display.

Decimal-to-Hexadecimal Conversion Decimal-to-hexadecimal conversion can be performed by the previously described methods.

EXAMPLE

Convert 92_{10} to hexadecimal.

$$16\overline{)92} \quad \begin{matrix} 5 \\ \end{matrix} \quad R = 12 = C$$

$$16\overline{)5} \quad \begin{matrix} 0 \\ \end{matrix} \quad R = 5$$

Therefore $92_{10} = 5CH$.

Hexadecimal-to-Octal Conversion Some microprocessors utilize hexadecimal notation in specifying memory locations, while others utilize octal. To facilitate the conversion from one system to another, see Appendix B, where 256_{10} locations are translated from one system to another. As an example, 0A4H uses row A and column 4 to derive the value of 244_8.

Hexadecimal Addition In hexadecimal addition a carry is generated when the sum exceeds 15_{10} or 0FH.

EXAMPLE

$$4 \ A \ 4 \ 1 \ H$$
$$+ \ 0 \ B \ 9 \ 2 \ F \ H$$
$$\overline{1 \ 0 \ 3 \ 7 \ 0 \ H}$$

$F + 1 = 16_{10} = 0 + 1$ carry

$4 + 2 + 1$ carry $= 7$

$A + 9 = 19_{10} = 3 + 1$ carry

$B + 4 + 1$ carry $= 16_{10} = 0 + 1$ carry

$0 + 1$ carry $= 1$

Result: 10370H

EXAMPLE

$$2 \ C \ E \ A \ 5 \ H$$
$$+ \ 4 \ B \ F \ 8 \ 9 \ H$$
$$\overline{7 \ 8 \ E \ 2 \ E \ H}$$

$5 + 9 = E$

$A + 8 = 18_{10} = 2 + 1$ carry

$E + F + 1$ carry $= 30_{10} = E + 1$ carry

$C + B + 1$ carry $= 24_{10} = 8 + 1$ carry

$2 + 4 + 1$ carry $= 7$

Result: 78E2EH

Hexadecimal Subtraction   In subtraction, a borrow is required when for any digit position the minuend digit is less than the subtrahend digit. A borrow in hexadecimal requires that 16_{10} be added to the minuend digit and a "borrow 1" be added to the left adjacent subtrahend digit.

EXAMPLE

$$1 \ 0 \ 3 \ 7 \ 0 \ H \qquad \text{minuend}$$
$$- \ 0 \ B \ 9 \ 2 \ F \ H \qquad \text{subtrahend}$$
$$\overline{4 \ A \ 4 \ 1 \ H}$$

$0 - F = (16 - 15 + 1 \ \text{borrow})_{10} = 1 + 1$ borrow

$7 - (2 + 1 \ \text{borrow}) = 7 - 3 = 4$

$3 - 9 = (3 + 16 - 9 + 1 \ \text{borrow})_{10} = A + 1$ borrow

$0 - (B + 1 \ \text{borrow}) = 0 - C = (16 - 12 + 1 \ \text{borrow})_{10} = 4 + 1$ borrow

$1 - (0 + 1 \ \text{borrow}) = 1 - 1 = 0$

The result is 4A41H.

1-3 DIGITAL INTEGRATED CIRCUIT DEVICES

This section deals with the fundamental digital integrated circuit (IC) devices. A knowledge of these is necessary for a better understanding of how the microprocessor functions within a microcomputing system. The digital IC devices covered include:

- Gates
- Inverters
- Buffers
- Flip-flops
- Latches
- Decoder/demultiplexers
- Multiplexer/data selectors
- Tri-state devices

Gates

A gate is a circuit that performs one of several specific functions. A gate is named for the function it performs, the most common gates being the AND, OR, NAND, NOR, and EXCLUSIVE OR gates. Gates have several inputs but only one output, and a gate's function determines what relationship the output has to the inputs.

The simplest method of describing how a gate or any basic IC functions in a digital system is to translate its operation into a truth table.

Truth Tables

A truth table shows the relationship of all possible outputs of a digital IC device to all possible inputs. A truth table will help describe the function or the logic operation of the device. Manufacturers' IC specification sheets will often describe a device, with a short explanation of how the device operates and a detailed truth table.

The AND Gate

An AND gate has two or more inputs and one output. An output of logic 1 will be generated when all inputs are logic 1. When any input is logic 0, the output is logic 0. A circuit with two inputs will have four possible states that can produce outputs. The truth table and symbol for a two-input AND gate are shown in Fig. 1-2.

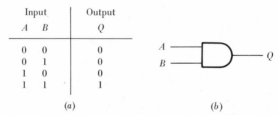

Input		Output
A	B	Q
0	0	0
0	1	0
1	0	0
1	1	1

(a)   (b)

Figure 1-2 The AND gate. (a) AND truth table; (b) AND symbol.

The OR Gate

An OR gate has two or more inputs and one output. The output of an OR gate is logic 1 when any of the inputs is at logic 1. The truth table and symbol for a two-input OR gate are shown in Fig. 1-3.

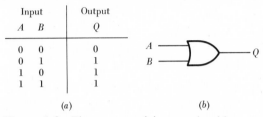

Input		Output
A	B	Q
0	0	0
0	1	1
1	0	1
1	1	1

(a)   (b)

Figure 1-3 The OR gate. (a) OR truth table; (b) OR symbol.

The Inverter

An inverter is a single-input device which simply complements, or "NOTS," the input condition. A logic 0 at the input, for example, will produce a logic 1 output. The truth table and symbol for an inverter are shown in Fig. 1-4. Note that the symbol has a bubble to indicate inversion.

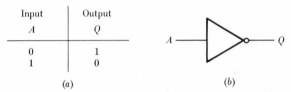

Input	Output
A	Q
0	1
1	0

(a)   (b)

Figure 1-4 The inverter. (a) Inverter truth table; (b) inverter symbol.

NANDs and NORs

Logically a NAND gate is an AND gate followed by an inverter, and a NOR gate is an OR gate followed by an inverter. The truth tables for two-input NAND and NOR gates and their corresponding symbols are shown in Figs. 1-5 and 1-6, respectively.

Input		Output
A	B	Q
0	0	1
0	1	1
1	0	1
1	1	0

(a)   (b)

Figure 1-5 The NAND gate. (a) NAND truth table; (b) NAND symbol.

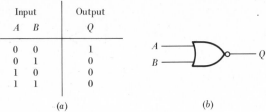

Input A B	Output Q
0 0	1
0 1	0
1 0	0
1 1	0

(a)　　　　　　　　　(b)

Figure 1-6　The NOR gate. (a) NOR truth table; (b) NOR symbol.

In manufacturing digital IC devices, it is easier to fabricate NAND and NOR gates than AND or OR gates.

The EXCLUSIVE OR Gate

The EXCLUSIVE OR gate is a two-input gate in which the output is logic 1 when the inputs are logically different and logic 0 when the inputs are logically the same. Another name for the EXCLUSIVE OR gate is a *digital comparator,* as the circuit enables 2 bits of different words to produce an output when the bits are not equal. A set of EXCLUSIVE OR circuits is used for *every* 2 bits of the word being compared. The truth table and the symbol for an EXCLUSIVE OR gate are shown in Fig. 1-7.

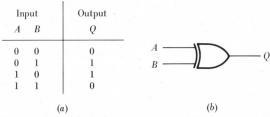

Input A B	Output Q
0 0	0
0 1	1
1 0	1
1 1	0

(a)　　　　　　　　　(b)

Figure 1-7　The EXCLUSIVE OR gate. (a) EXCLUSIVE OR truth table; (b) EXCLUSIVE OR symbol.

The Buffer

The *buffer* is an IC device that provides no change in logic at the output but does provide a high input load impedance, a low output impedance, and therefore good output drive capability. It works the same way as an emitter-follower circuit. How is it used? The output of an MOS microprocessor, for example, has very poor drive capability when driving a TTL device. By inserting a buffer between the output of the MOS microprocessor and the input of the TTL device, we can solve the problem. The buffer provides an input load the microprocessor can handle and an output drive that is TTL-compatible. The truth table and the symbol for a buffer are shown in Fig. 1-8.

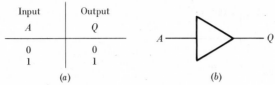

Input	Output
A	Q
0	0
1	1

(a)   (b)

Figure 1-8 The buffer. (a) Buffer truth table; (b) buffer symbol.

The *JK* Flip-Flop

A *JK* flip-flop is an IC device that will output information on the Q and $\bar{Q}$ lines that depends on the states of the J and K inputs at a specific time. That specified time is usually represented by the positive- or negative-going edge of a clock pulse, as shown in Fig. 1-9.

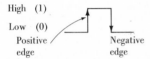

High   (1)
Low   (0)
  Positive   Negative
  edge   edge

Figure 1-9 Positive- and negative-going edges of a clock pulse.

There are two types of *JK* flip-flops: *edge-triggered* and *master-slave,* as shown in Fig. 1-10*a* and *b*. In *edge-triggered* flip-flops the J and K inputs determine the Q and $\bar{Q}$ outputs at either the positive or the negative edge of the clock pulse, depending on the flip-flop specification. In master-slave flip-flops the J and K inputs are entered into the flip-flop when the clock pulse reaches the logic 1 voltage level and are transferred, or "slaved," to the output when the clock pulse changes from a logic 1 to a logic 0 level. In a master-slave *JK* flip-flop care must be taken not to let the J and K inputs change while the clock is high or "$+V$." This limitation of the master-slave *JK* flip-flop has led to wider use of the edge-triggered *JK* flip-flop. The truth table and symbol of the *JK* flip-flop are shown in Fig. 1-11*a* and *b*.

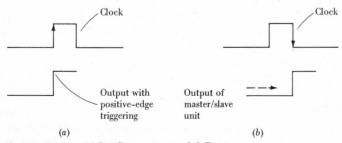

Clock   Clock

Output with   Output of
positive–edge   master/slave
triggering   unit

(a)   (b)

Figure 1-10 *JK* flip-flop outputs. (a) Positive edge-triggered; (b) master-slave.

Inputs		Output	
J_n	K_n	$Q_{n+1}*$	Remarks
0	0	Q_n	No change
0	1	0	Reset
1	0	1	Set
1	1	$\overline{Q}_n$	Toggle

J_n, K_n, and Q_n are values of J, K, and Q, respectively, prior to the clock; Q_{n+1} is the value of Q after the clock edge.

*Clock must be present for table to be valid.

(a)   (b)

Figure 1-11 The JK flip-flop. (a) JK flip-flop truth table; (b) JK flip-flop symbol.

The J and K inputs of the flip-flop can be at either a 1 or a 0. The outputs Q and its complement $\overline{Q}$ follow the truth table function. When both the J and K inputs are 1, then the outputs will switch to their opposite states. This is called *toggling*. If the output has been 1 it will go to 0, and if it has been 0 it will toggle to 1.

The JK flip-flop responds to two input signals that are not synchronized (asynchronous) with the clock. They are the Preset (PR) and Clear (CLR) signals. Either signal can occur at any time, depending on the system. Their effects are shown in the expanded truth table (Table 1-7). The active state (when the signal occurs) is 0 for each input. Both signals have overriding powers: when either occurs, it will force the outputs to a specified condition of the truth table regardless of the existing state or value of the J and K inputs. The J and K input states are commonly called, under these circumstances, "don't care" states, symbolized by X in the truth table.

Note that in the table both the prior and after clock states (Q_n and Q_{n+1}) are specified. A K_n signal in conjunction with the clock will cause no effect to the output if Q_n is at a 0 state.

The D Flip-Flop

A D flip-flop is similar to a JK flip-flop except that it replaces the J and K inputs by one input D, the data input. A truth table for the D flip-flop and its symbol are shown in Fig. 1-12a and b.

A 1 on the data input in conjunction with the clock (D flip-flops are available with either edge triggering) will cause a set output condition of a 1. A 0 on the data input at the clock time will reset the output. Hence, the Q output will assume the state of D at each clock pulse. The Preset and Clear signals function as in the JK flip-flop. A 0 on the preset input will control the flip-flop and cause it to set, while a 0 on the clear input will reset the D flip-flop.

TABLE 1-7   Expanded Truth Table for the JK Flip-Flop

INPUTS				OUTPUT			
CLR	PR	J_n	K_n	Q_n	Q_{n+1}^*	$\overline{Q}_{n+1}^*$	Remarks
1	1	0	0	0	0	1	NC
1	1	0	1	0	0	1	NC—flip-flop had been reset
1	1	1	0	0	1	0	Set
1	1	1	1	0	1	0	Toggle
1	0	X	X	0	1	0	Set—Preset signal takes over
0	1	X	X	0	0	1	NC—flip-flop had been reset
1	1	0	0	1	1	0	NC
1	1	0	1	1	0	1	Reset
1	1	1	0	1	1	0	NC—flip-flop had been set
1	1	1	1	1	0	1	Toggle
1	0	X	X	1	1	0	NC—flip-flop had been set
0	1	X	X	1	0	1	Reset—Clear signal takes over

where J_n, K_n, and Q_n are values of J, K, and Q, respectively, prior to the clock pulse, and Q_{n+1} is the value of the output Q after the clock pulse edge
X denotes don't care conditions
NC = no change

*Clock must be present for table to be valid except when CLR or PR are 0.

Inputs			Output		
CLR	PR	D	Q_n	Q_{n+1}^*	Remarks
1	1	0	1	0	Reset
1	1	1	0	1	Set
1	0	X	0	1	Set–preset signal takes over
0	1	X	1	0	Reset–reset signal takes over

Q_{n+1} is the value of Q after the clock edge.

Q_n is the value of Q prior to the clock.

*Clock must be present for table to be valid.

(a)

(b)

Figure 1-12   The D flip-flop. (a) D flip-flop truth table; (b) D flip-flop symbol.

The Latch

The latch is an integrated circuit device that transfers input data to the output during a clock transition. After the clock transition, the latch holds or stores that output data whether or not the input data changes. A latch generally contains a number of D-type flip-flops. A typical 4-bit latch is shown in Fig. 1-13.

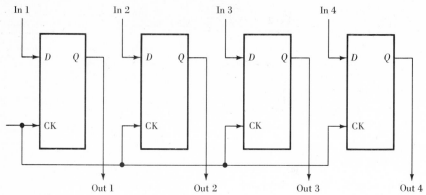

Figure 1-13 A typical 4-bit latch.

The Decoder/Demultiplexer

A decoder/demultiplexer is an IC device that selects one or more outputs in a prescribed manner from a combination of input signals. Decoders have a few input lines which are decoded to generate many output lines; n input lines can have 2^n possible unique output lines. Special-purpose decoders, such as a BCD-to-decimal decoder, will have a BCD four-line input and generate 10 unique output lines representing 0 through 9. The output lines are typically in the 1 state when they are quiescent and in the 0 state when they are active. As an example, suppose BCD 7 (0111) is the input to the decoder; then output lines 0, 1, 2, 3, 4, 5, 6, 8 and 9 are at logic 1 and line 7 is at logic 0. A typical two-line to four-line decoder truth table and configuration are shown in Fig. 1-14a and b.

The Multiplexer/Data Selector

The multiplexer/data selector acts in the opposite sense from a decoder/demultiplexer. It utilizes many inputs and produces a single output. A four-line to one-line multiplexer has two address lines which are decoded

Inputs		Outputs			
In 2	In 1	Out 0	Out 1	Out 2	Out 3
0	0	0	1	1	1
0	1	1	0	1	1
1	0	1	1	0	1
1	1	1	1	1	0

(a)

(b)

Figure 1-14 A two-line to four-line decoder and truth table. (a) Truth table; (b) symbol.

In 4	In 3	In 2	In 1	Select 2	Select 1	Output
X	X	X	0	0	0	0
X	X	X	1	0	0	1
X	X	0	X	0	1	0
X	X	1	X	0	1	1
X	0	X	X	1	0	0
X	1	X	X	1	0	1
0	X	X	X	1	1	0
1	X	X	X	1	1	1

X = Don't care.

(a)   (b)

Figure 1-15 A four-line to one-line multiplexer/data selector. (a) Truth table; (b) symbol.

internally to select the one input line that will produce the output. A typical multiplexer truth table and configuration are shown in Fig. 1-15a and b.

Tri-State Devices

As discussed previously, an IC device generally has two types of output states: logic 1 and logic 0, with a 1 representing one voltage and 0 another voltage. A tri-state device provides yet another state, the *high-impedance,* or *open,* state.

A mechanical tri-state device has been with us for many years. It is the relay, such as the one shown in Fig. 1-16. When the control voltage energizes this relay, the output follows the input. However, when the control voltage is absent, the relay is deenergized and the output is open.

Electrically, tri-state devices have three states: the normal, low-impedance logic 1 and 0 states and a third, a high-impedance state. This third state

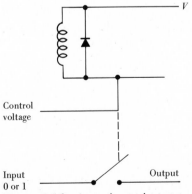

Figure 1-16 A mechanical tri-state device.

Input A	Control input	Output Q
0	0	1
1	0	0
0	1	High impedance
1	1	High impedance

(a)

(b)

Figure 1-17 A tri-state inverter. (a) Symbol; (b) truth table.

prevents the output of the device from supplying (being a *source* of) or receiving (being a *sink* of) current. The output is inhibited by a control input signal. Buffers and inverters can be designed as either tri-state devices or two-state units. A truth table of a tri-state inverter is shown in Fig. 1-17.

One of the most important applications of tri-state devices is in the *bus system* of a microprocessor. The bus system is a switching network that permits information to be transmitted between several locations. Buses can be bidirectional or unidirectional. Consider a bidirectional data bus to a microprocessor system (see Fig. 1-18) where input and output of each I/O unit are tied together using tri-state buffers. When control line 1 is at logic 0, the data from I/O 1 is transmitted to the microprocessor. Control line 1 at a logic 1 enables the same I/O device to receive data from the microprocessor. Control line 2 operates in the same manner with I/O 2.

PROBLEMS

1. a. Convert 67 to the 10's complement system.
   b. Subtract 67 from 91 using 10's complement arithmetic.
2. a. Convert the binary number 11110010 to its decimal equivalent.

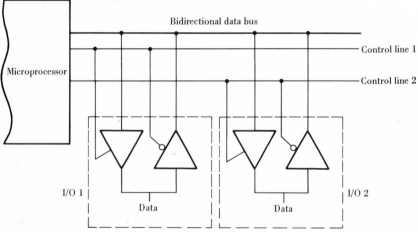

Figure 1-18 A bidirectional microprocessor bus system.

    b. In a sign-magnitude system where an MSB of 1 represents a negative number, determine the decimal equivalent for the binary number in Prob. 2a.

3. Convert the decimal number 100 to:
   a. Binary
   b. Octal
   c. Hexadecimal
   d. BCD

4. Add the following binary numbers:

a.	10101001	b.	00011110	c.	11111000
	+01111010		+00011110		+00001111

5. Generate the 2's complements of the following numbers and give their decimal equivalents:
   a. 00000001   b. 00011001   c. 00101010

6. Determine the original value of the following numbers, which are in 2's complement notation:
   a. 10101010   b. 10001001   c. 11001101

7. Convert to hexadecimal:
   a. 256_{10} c. 1024_{10}
   b. 255_{10} d. 01110001_2

8. a. Convert to hexadecimal:
       076_8
   b. Convert to octal:
       0BCH

9. Perform the following hexadecimal operations:

a.	00FFH	b.	32ABH	c.	0A0AH	d.	0A32BH
	+0111H		+7115H		+0A0AH		−0463FH

10. Using positive logic, determine what type of gate (NAND, NOR, EXCLUSIVE OR) is described.
    a. A logic 1 input always causes the output to go to logic 0.
    b. When both inputs are the same, the output is always logic 0.
    c. A logic 0 input always causes the output to go to logic 1.

11. Explain the operation of a buffer. How is it used?

12. Explain the differences between a *JK* master-slave flip-flop and a *D* flip-flop.

13. Which two inputs of the *JK* and *D* flip-flops are not synchronized with the clock (are asynchronous)?

14. A latch is generally composed of what type of flip-flop? An octal latch consists of how many flip-flops?

15. Define *multiplexer* and *decoder*.
16. What are the main advantages of tri-state devices?

REFERENCES

1. Bartee, Thomas C.: *Digital Computer Fundamentals,* McGraw-Hill Book Company, New York, 1977.
2. Lee, Samuel C.: *Digital Circuits and Logic Design,* Prentice-Hall, Inc., Englewood Cliffs, N.J., 1976.
3. Richards, R. K.: *Arithmetic Operations in Digital Computers,* Van Nostrand Company, Inc., New York, 1955.

Computer Fundamentals

The underlying principles necessary for gaining an understanding of micro-processors are closely related to the fundamentals of digital computers and general-purpose processors. This chapter will be devoted to the basic definitions and functional use of the main elements of the computer.

2-1 THE MEMORY SYSTEM

Memory Hierarchy

The memory system of a computer consists of storage elements used to retain information. One kind of basic element used for storage is the inte-grated-circuit solid-state memory consisting of many flip-flops, each retaining 1 bit of information. Other forms of storage units are floppy disks, magnetic tapes, bubble memories, and magnetic-core devices. All of these forms are used in computer systems to read and/or write information. Those memo-ries which are fast enough to interact with the microprocessor and have *parallel* organization and interface are called *prime* or *main storage devices.* In this group are solid-state circuits and magnetic-core memories. Floppy disks, magnetic tapes, and bubble memories are inherently slower devices which, because of their *serial* organization and interface, cannot maintain pace with the computer. Their role is that of secondary or auxiliary storage (such as preloading the main memory before making the system opera-tional), or that of a storage base for data which is not to be retrieved during "real time" (actual time when the computer is executing the program). The

31

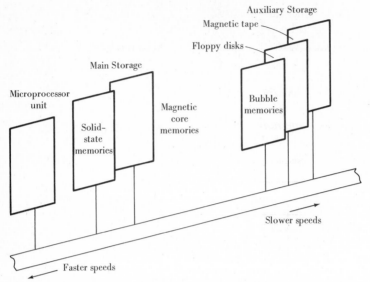

Figure 2-1 Hierarchy of memory devices in microprocessor systems.

partitioning of memory into main and auxiliary storage units is called *memory hierarchy*. A diagram of this partitioning is shown in Fig. 2-1.

The Memory Element

Memories consist of storage devices or elements with each device containing one bit. If a memory consisted of 32 flip-flop devices, then each flip-flop would be capable of being set or reset. Storing data (either a 1 or a 0) in a flip-flop memory element is equivalent to writing into the memory. Sampling or extracting the state of the flip-flop is the equivalent of reading out from the memory. Thus the Write and Read operations are the equivalent of storing data and extracting data, respectively.

Sequential and Random-Access Memories

There are several approaches used in reading from or writing into memories. Some memories are organized so that if, for example, word 8 were to be read out, words 1 through 7 must first be read out or extracted. This form of memory is called *sequential,* or *serial,* since one word follows another in a fixed order when reading or writing functions are performed. The bubble memory, magnetic tape, and floppy disk are all forms of sequential memories. Extracting data is commonly referred to as *accessing memory,* and by its nature accessing sequential memories is a very slow operation requiring access times in the millisecond region. Consequently, sequential memories have been relegated to the role of secondary memories.

The alternative to sequentially accessing memories is to allow the memory to be accessed randomly. Randomly accessing a memory permits any word in a memory device to be read out within a specific time independent of what word has been previously read out. Assuming a Read access time of 750 nanoseconds (ns), for example, if it were necessary to read out words 8 and 12, only a total time of 1500 ns would be required: 750 ns to read out word 8 and an additional 750 ns to read out word 12. Since the process of reading or writing is purely random but selectable, this form of memory is called *random-access memory,* or RAM.

Figure 2-2 illustrates both the sequential memory and RAM. The simpli-

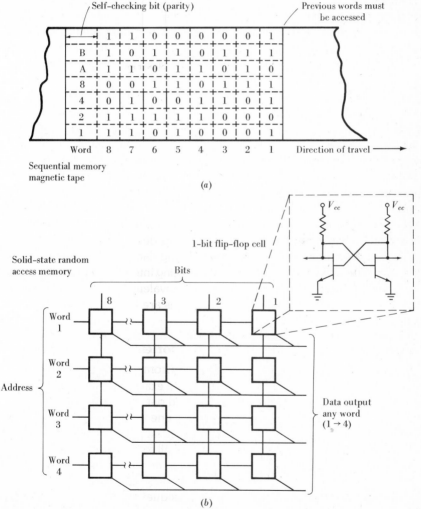

Figure 2-2 Comparison of sequential and random-access memories.
(*a*) Sequential memory—magnetic tape; (*b*) random-access memory—solid state.

fied diagram shows that by selecting or addressing any one of the four words of RAM, all the bits which make up the word are read out.

Functional Use of Memories

There are four different types of information that are typically stored in a main memory. These consist of:

- Instruction words
- Constants
- Data words
- Temporary storage

Instruction Words The instruction words are commands in the form of a byte or multiple bytes which tell the microprocessor which operation to perform (such as Add, Subtract, etc.). A group of instructions is called a *program,* and programs are pre-stored, or written into the memory before the memory is actively integrated into the computer system and made operational. The programs can be implemented in one of two ways. If the instructions are well defined, if the program has been successfully running and verified, and if no further changes are considered at any time, then there is no need to select a memory system with Write capabilities. A memory system with only Read capability is called a *read-only memory* (ROM); it should be chosen for this application. These memories are custom-designed to meet the specific requirements of a particular system, since they contain unique programs dedicated to performing specific tasks. Closely related to this technology are *programmable read-only memories* (PROMs) and *erasable programmable read-only memories* (EPROMs). Chapter 4 will discuss these technologies in detail.

The alternative technique for implementing instructions is to use a memory that contains both Read and Write capability, even though the Write capability in this application is not needed. This form of memory is simply called a *read-write* (R/W) *memory* or, by a misnomer, a RAM. (There has always been misleading terminology in this area. Both read-write memories and read-only memories are RAMs, since the access time to any location in either memory is constant.)

Data Words *Data words* are memory words whose contents represent numerical data used to solve equations or control functions. Data words are stored in the data memory when the microprocessing system has separate memories for data and instruction. When there is only one memory to contain both instructions and data, then a RAM is used, since the data words require Read-Write capability.

Consider an example which illustrates the utilization of the various forms of memory. A microprocessor is used to solve the equation of a falling body,

$$S = V_0 t + \tfrac{1}{2} g t^2$$

where S is the distance, V_0 is the initial velocity, g is gravitational force, and t is time. The terms V_0 and t are variable: they can change under different conditions, such as different initial values or different increments of time. This means that S is a variable also. Thus V_0, t, and S are all data words; g, however, is a constant. If the equation were to be solved for a 3-second fall in increments of 1 second, then we would have 3 data words for S, 3 for t, and 1 for V_0, or a total of 7 data words. This example illustrates that data words must be stored in a type of memory which can be altered, such as a read-write memory. Data words generally have their initial values pre-stored and are later updated when more current information becomes available.

In many applications which time-share the instructions and data in a RAM, it is good practice whenever possible to put the instructions and data into separate areas. That is, instructions should be sequentially stored and data words blocked off into another area. This will help reduce the common occurrence which develops during software testing of programs whereby instructions are destroyed when the program area in which they are stored is inadvertently written over.

Even though there is no guarantee that instructions cannot be erased by placing them into the read-write memory, it may nevertheless be convenient and economical to time-share the memory. When it is anticipated that the program will be in a constant state of change, it is advantageous to utilize a RAM, since the expense of processing special equipment for programming EPROMs can then be avoided.

Constants Constants, such as the numerical value of gravitational force in the example or the value of π, do not require a memory that has a Write capability. Most microprocessor applications require so few constants that utilizing a dedicated read-only memory for them is unwarranted.

Temporary Storage Temporary words, which are the fourth type of information stored in the memory, can be illustrated by noting that in the falling body problem the microprocessor does not perform all the operations at the same time. It may, for example, determine a value of gt^2 and store it, determine the value of $V_0 t$ and store it, and subsequently add the two terms together. The intermediate results, which are temporary words, are stored in a working area of memory called the *scratch pad area*. The scratch pad need not be very large, since the same area can be used over again during another portion of the instruction program.

The Memory Volatility Issue

After a program is loaded into a computer, a power transient may cause the program just loaded to be destroyed and require the entire program to be reloaded. The load failed because of the technology used; the memory of the computer was *volatile.* A volatile memory is one unable to retain information without continuous power: if the memory "forgets" when power is removed or when the voltage is reduced below a minimum value, it is volatile. Volatile memory devices are:

- Flip-flops
- Read-write memories

Nonvolatile memories retain the information stored in them regardless of whether power is removed. Nonvolatile memory devices are:

- ROMs, PROMs, and EPROMs
- Magnetic tape
- Floppy disks
- Core and bubble memories

Consider as an example the transistor-transistor flip-flop. This widely used device, once it has been set to a logic 1 state, should retain its state; however, should there be a loss of power (even momentarily), the flip-flop may enter the 0 state instead of the desired 1 state when power is reapplied. Since the former state of the flip-flop is unknown when power is reapplied, the contents stored therein are considered lost. RAM memories are closely related to the one-cell flip-flop which we have just described; hence they are volatile. RAMs consist of many one-cell flip-flops implemented in a variety of different technologies.

The seriousness of the loss of power to a computing system using RAMs can be realized by noting that when a power loss occurs, all volatile devices will lose data. This includes the registers within the microprocessor chip as well as the read-write RAMs. Loss of RAM data is particularly significant if the instruction portion of the computer is stored in a RAM. In this type of situation, should there be a loss of power, it would become necessary to completely reload the instructions, which is both time-consuming and costly.

To protect against losses due to power interruption, there are several workable approaches. One method is to select a technology (such as a ROM or a PROM) which does not lose information when power is interrupted or removed. Not much can be done to keep the processor from losing data except to store the important microprocessor register information in a writable nonvolatile memory. This requires that sufficient time (100 ms or so) be made available for data transfers for storage purposes and that power failure–detection circuitry be incorporated in the system design. An alternative approach is to provide a backup power system that can take over should the primary power fail. Batteries are normally used for this function, although in larger systems this may not be too practicable.

Before the emergence of microprocessors, most large computer systems utilized magnetic ferrite-core memories as the main storage element. Core memories are nonvolatile and provide the best solution in many cases where memory alterations induced by power loss cannot be tolerated. Many large computing systems containing large programs use core memories. Once the data has been processed in real time, many of these same systems transfer the data and programs to secondary mass-storage files using other forms of nonvolatile storage, such as a magnetic tape system or a floppy disk.

Memory Device Structures

Semiconductor memories such as RAMs or ROMs are described by the number of bits in the device. The total number of bits is the nearest power of 2 to the expressed value of the unit. A 1K memory, therefore, contains 2^{10}, or 1024, bits. A 4K memory has 2^{12}, or 4096, bits.

There are many different memory organizations of chips available on the market which will support microprocessors using different word lengths. The 1K-word–by–1-bit and the 256-word–by–4-bit chips were commonly used initially as memory building blocks in 8-bit microprocessing systems. With the availability of higher-density units, the 4K and 16K units are frequently used to develop systems. If a small, 256-word (by 8 bits) ROM memory system using only the 256-by-4 memory chips is required, then the number of 256 $\times$ 4 memories will be

$$\text{Devices needed} = \frac{\text{required memory system configuration}}{\text{basic memory building block size}} = \frac{256 \times 8}{256 \times 4}$$

$$= 2 \text{ chips}$$

A typical diagram of a 256 $\times$ 8 memory system is shown in Fig. 2-3. In this configuration, eight Address lines are needed to address a memory of this size ($2^8 = 256$). The lines AD0 through AD7 of both memory chips are connected in parallel. When the Chip Enables are set to logic 0, the devices will be activated. A logic 1 on the Chip Enable line deactivates the chip and causes the output to be either tri-stated or open (using open-collector transistors). The individual chip specification sheets will determine the proper output configuration.

Another configuration, a 512 $\times$ 4 memory system, is shown in Fig. 2-4. Here the Address and also the output lines from each chip are tied together. Since 512 words require nine Address lines ($2^9 = 512$) and a 256-word memory has only eight Address lines, a design technique is to use the Chip Enable for memory expansion (AD8). The ninth memory Address line, AD8, is used to enable only the upper memory chip when AD8 is at logic 0 or to enable only the lower memory chip when AD8 is at logic 1.

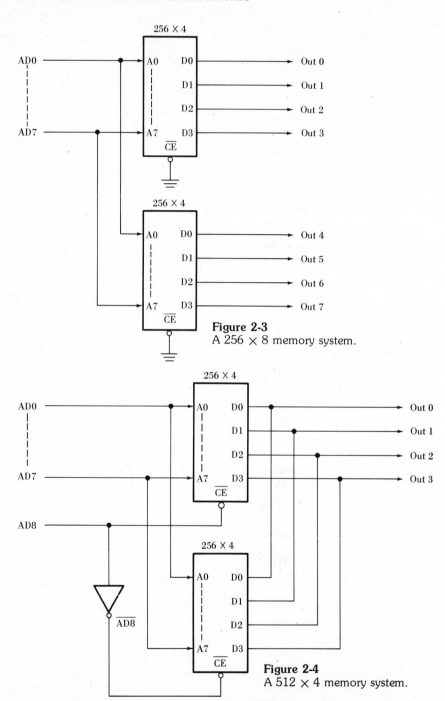

Figure 2-3
A 256 × 8 memory system.

Figure 2-4
A 512 × 4 memory system.

The utilization of 512×8 memory systems are much more common today than that of 512×4 systems, and this can be attributed to the popularity of longer word-length units. The approach of implementing the 512×8 system, shown in Fig. 2-5, is similar to that of the 512×4 unit in that the Chip Enable signal is used to provide the ninth Address signal.

For larger systems which require memory expansion, such as a $1K \times 8$ system, 10 Address lines are needed. One approach is to utilize decoders on the two most significant Address lines, AD8 and AD9. Since there are four possible states (with two inputs), each output of the decoder will be used with a 256×8 memory configuration.

Memory Word Selection

Every word in memory, regardless of its internal structure, is uniquely specified by a memory address. To select a memory location, the binary equivalent of the word's number must be transmitted to memory from the computer. This action is commonly referred to as *addressing* the memory. Word 65 of a memory system, for example, can be addressed by selecting its corresponding binary code of 0100 0001 (41H). The binary information in the form of binary bits comes from the computer to memory via a unidirectional parallel bus. This bus is called the address bus, since it enables specific address locations to be accessed for purposes of reading or writing data.

With one parallel transmission from the processor, an 8-bit address can access any one of 256 different memory locations. However, most computer systems require greater addressing capability. This is achieved by utilizing a wider address bus rather than transmitting twice over the bus. The result is a "standard," 16-bit-wide address bus which will permit 65,536 locations to be accessed (2^{16}).

There are several control signals which interface with memory, including the Read/Write signal (R/W), which is used to control the operational mode of the memory. The Chip Enable signal selects those chips in the memory system which contain the locations to be accessed. Figure 2-6 illustrates a processor-to-memory interface.

2-2 COMPUTER ORGANIZATION

The digital computer consists of only a few functional elements. These are:

- The arithmetic and control units
- The instruction memory
- The data memory
- The input-output units

The arithmetic and control unit processes data by performing arithmetic and logic operations. The arithmetic portion has built-in arithmetic capability

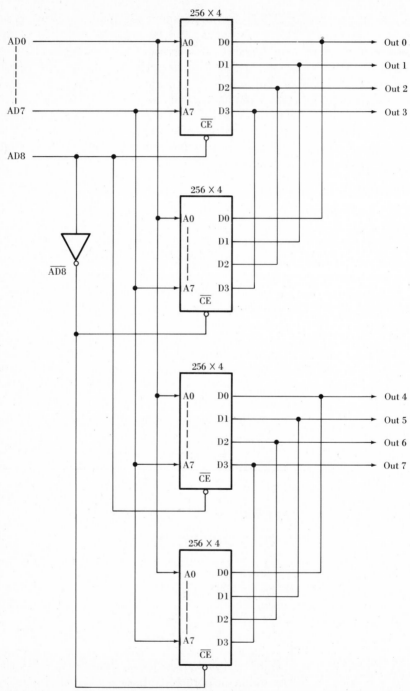

Figure 2-5 A 512 × 8 memory system.

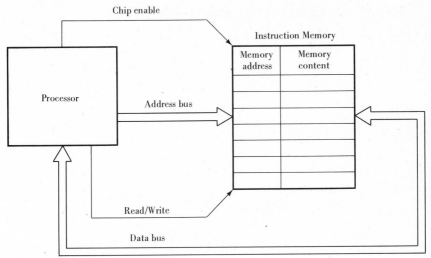

Figure 2-6 Processor to instruction memory interface.

in the form of hardware circuits which perform these functions. The control unit contains the circuits which enable rapid sequences of instructions to be processed.

The instruction and data memories can be combined or separated, as discussed in Sec. 2-1 under "Functional Use of Memories." Programs in the form of instructions have to be written and stored in memory before the computer is made operational. Data can be stored before turn-on or during the computer's operational run.

The input-output units are the computer peripherals which enable real time communication with the external environment. These devices are slow and must be formatted generally from serial to parallel so as to be compatible with the data transfer channels of the computer.

A block diagram of these major units is shown in Fig. 2-7.

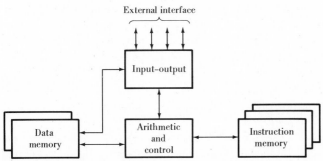

Figure 2-7 Major functional elements of a digital computer.

2-3 ARITHMETIC AND CONTROL

The combined arithmetic and control section of the computer has been traditionally referred to as the *central processing unit* (CPU). This expression dates back to the early computer days when first racks and then chassis contained all the computer circuits in one central location. The primary functions of the CPU are to:

• Retrieve or fetch instructions from memory and decode and execute their binary contents

• Transfer to and from data memory or the input-output (I/O) section information which may be required in the execution of the instructions

• Respond to external control signals, called *interrupts,* which may suspend normal operations and may cause new sequences of program procedures or instructions to be followed.

To enable these functions, there are many elements which must be identified. Some of these, such as the arithmetic logic unit (ALU) and the accumulator, reside within the arithmetic section; while other elements, such as the instruction register and decoder, are part of the control section of the CPU. A brief overview of the processing system follows here before the detailed functional description of the registers and of the controlling elements.

The Processing Overview

The primary role of the arithmetic section of a digital computer is to provide the logic and computational capability for the processor. Addition and subtraction functions are typical arithmetic operations, while logic operations include the AND, OR, and EXCLUSIVE OR functions. The control section coordinates the various elements, such as counters and registers, by directing the proper sequence for each instruction. Commands for processing data are received by the processor in the form of instructions from the instruction memory. The data used to perform an operation is called *operand data,* or simply the *operand.* It may be necessary to retrieve this data if it is external to the processor, as when it is stored in the data memory. Once the operand is retrieved, it is temporarily stored in a computer register and subsequently processed. Figure 2-8 illustrates the primary circuits which are contained in the functional elements of a computer system.

A software program consists of a group of instructions which are normally stored sequentially in memory. To command the instructions, the microprocessor must address the memory location (one location at a time) where the instruction is stored. Once the instruction is retrieved, it is decoded and executed. This may involve retrieving the operand, as earlier indicated. Upon

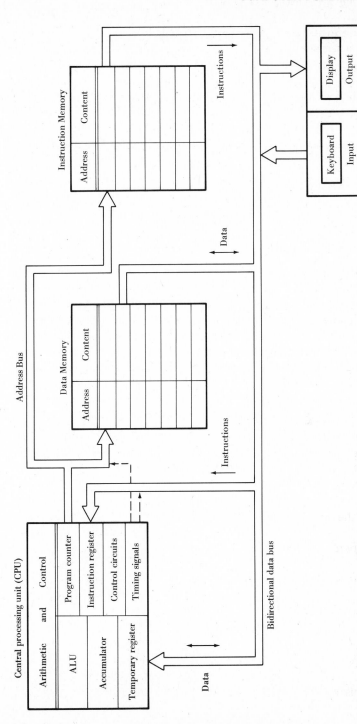

Figure 2-8 Simplified computer system.

executing the instruction, the processor initiates the next sequential instruction. The program counter is an essential register in the computing system because its function is to keep track of where the processor is in the program, i.e., what instruction is being executed. It performs this function by having the contents of the program counter equal to the memory location address of the next instruction to be executed. Once the present instruction is decoded, the program counter is incremented, so that it will always point to the next instruction. There are certain exceptions to this procedure; these will be covered in the next section.

Major Processing Registers

There are several registers which have been traditionally used in the design of a computing system; these devices include the program counter, the instruction register, and the accumulator. The program counter is the pointer of the program. By reading its contents one can quickly determine the instruction presently being executed. The present instruction is determined by merely subtracting 1 from the contents of the program counter. Thus a count of 3 infers that it is executing the instruction residing at memory location 2. The program counter will normally act as a reference by sequentially counting the address locations where the program instructions are being executed; however, there are certain instructions which when encountered will cause the sequence to change. For example, if the program contains a Branch instruction, the instruction flow will jump nonsequentially to the memory address specified by the Branch instruction; hence, if after the instruction located at address 4 is executed a Branch instruction is encountered which directs the program to memory address 26, the program's next instruction will be at memory location 26. This will be reflected by a change in the contents of the program counter to number 26.

Although the value of the program counter correlates with the program's next instruction, the contents of the program counter have an even more significant role. They actually generate the address of the next instruction. The contents of the program counter are transmitted on the address bus to memory, allowing the next instruction at the selected address location to be transferred to the microprocessor (see Fig. 2-9). The contents of the program counter will normally be a 16-bit word. The memory will access the word whose location is equivalent to the binary contents of the program counter. For example, if word 18 is accessed (12H), only 2 of the 16 address bus bits will be high. All other bits transmitted from the microprocessor to memory will be in the low state. After being decoded at the memory, the contents of memory location 18 are transferred to a data register in memory, where they are then transmitted back to the processor on the data bus. The operation of accessing the instruction and transmitting it to the processor is called *fetching*.

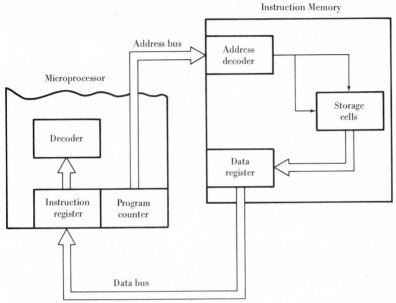

Figure 2-9 Selecting an instruction.

The instruction register is a processor register whose function is to store the contents of the accessed instruction. In the previous illustration, word 18, or 12H, was accessed. If the content of this memory location is 0FEH, then it is this value that will be transferred to the instruction register. The input to the instruction register is from an 8-bit-wide data bus, and the output of the instruction register goes to an instruction decoder within the processor which will translate its contents (0FEH) to a meaningful operation or instruction. Thus each instruction which is read from memory follows the same functional flow; it is stored in the instruction register and then decoded. This is shown in Fig. 2-9.

The accumulator is perhaps the most versatile and important register of the CPU. Most instructions involve the accumulator. The primary role of the accumulator is to temporarily store data, arithmetic, or logic. Many of the instructions are performed with one of the operands in the accumulator. The results of the operation are normally stored back in this register.

Within the arithmetic unit are flip-flops called *flags*, which are normally used to determine whether certain limits or conditions have been exceeded or met. Consider, for example, a Subtract operation whose results yield a 0 in the accumulator; the result would be that a Zero flag is set to indicate this status. Another important flag is the Carry flag, which is used to signify arithmetic operations which have developed a carry, thus setting the flag corresponding to this condition. There are types of instructions which, rather than setting a flag, will cause one or more flags to be reset. Some instructions do not affect the flag register at all. Each computer manufacturer describes the instructions by including information on the status of flags. Additional descriptions of flags will be contained in Chaps. 3 and 5.

The Control Unit

A main function of the control unit is to provide the logic gating necessary for the flow of instructions and data within the computer. The computer operates in discrete steps during each program instruction, and many elementary operations, such as enabling gates, disabling gates, and transferring data from one register to another, are performed during each step. The logic and control signals to permit this movement reside within the control section. All instructions require unique data movements through gates, which must be enabled when the instruction is active. Coordination must therefore exist between the instruction and the timing signals to propagate data correctly. Figure 2-10 shows the major sections of the control unit.

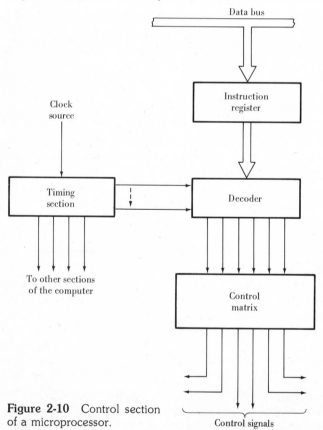

Figure 2-10 Control section of a microprocessor.

The contents of the instruction register are in the form of binary 1s and 0s. To convert these bits to a meaningful instruction, decoding networks called *matrices* are used; these extract information from the instruction word. For example, a register-to-register Add instruction enables an Add operation to take place between two internal computer registers. Upon execution, the instruction will be transferred to the Instruction register and then to the decoding matrices, where selection of the two registers to be employed in the instruction will be made. The control matrix will provide internal signals controlling the addition operation and the data movement between the registers.

Another important function provided by the control unit is the generation and distribution of all timing signals necessary for the computer to operate. Most processors utilize either an external quartz crystal or a built-in clock from which other timing signals are developed. Generally, either a two- or a four-phase clock generator is used to produce the timing signals. The clock establishes the universal time reference for events that are to occur internally. The speed of the computer is directly related to the clock speed, since most internal functions are timed by the reference signal. It must, however, be pointed out that the access time of the memory also dictates the speed of the computer and that clock speed and access time must be compatible for maximum performance.

2-4 THE INPUT-OUTPUT SECTION

The input-output (I/O) section of the computer serves as the communication channel for enabling the transfer of information to and from the processor. Data which is processed by the computer requires an external destination, such as a video display, a printer, a magnetic recorder, or another device that will translate the binary data to useful output forms. In a similar manner, communication to the computer must be entered via an input device such as a paper tape reader or a keyboard. The channel which transfers the intelligence to or from the processor is a bidirectional data bus. The I/O interface to the bus from the device is called the *port*. During normal program execution, the number of data transfers via the channel is generally small; the processor requires only a small amount of data for initialization of an operation. However, there may be occasions when an I/O device will be required to communicate with the processor after the program has been initiated. It may be necessary for the I/O device to store data, receive data, or simply notify the processing system that some condition within the I/O or external to the I/O has occurred. Since the processor functions at a much faster rate than the I/O, this results in an undesirable condition of having incompatible operational speeds. To maintain the faster operational speed of the computer, a technique is employed whereby storage buffers are used within the I/O device to temporarily store data and/or status information and reassemble it for subsequent transmission to the processor. Rather than waiting for impending data, the processor is designed to continuously execute the program and be alerted to the new conditions as they develop.

The signal which alerts the computer to an impending condition or status is called the interrupt. Interrupts are generally externally generated and require the microprocessor to take a specific action. Since there may be more than one I/O device attempting to alert the processor, the interrupts are uniquely coded so that the processor recognizes each interrupt and jumps to that portion of the program which interfaces with the specific I/O device. This reduces reaction time or latency time in handling or servicing an interrupt. Priorities are normally assigned to the I/O devices so that the most important I/O devices are serviced first. A more detailed discussion of I/O devices is presented in Chap. 9.

2-5 THE COMPUTER SYSTEM

This chapter has introduced the basic elements of a computer system and illustrated their interrelationships. Each of the units—I/O, memories, and processor—interfaces with the bus system providing a common communication path (see Fig. 2-11). In its most basic form only two buses and several

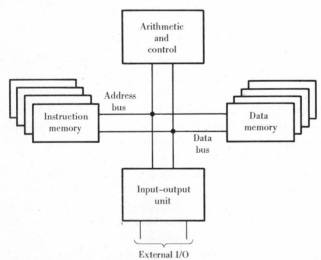

Figure 2-11 The basic computer system.

control signals are required to structure the elements into a computer system. The address bus is unidirectional, transmitting address information from the computer to the memory and I/O. The data bus is bidirectional, transferring operand data to and from memory and I/O. The instructions time-share the data bus as the program is read into the computer and the instructions are individually decoded.

The basic operations described in this chapter are applicable to microprocessors as well as to computers in general. The operation of all the functional elements will be the same, although the material in this chapter has been simplified in keeping with the introduction of fundamentals.

Technology plays an important part in the physical appearance of a computer system. Today's computer system may be built with medium-scale and large-scale integrated circuits mounted on a large variety of board layouts and employing different technologies. Most of the technologies which you will encounter will be described in Chap. 4. It is not uncommon to mix technologies, that is, to utilize a bipolar processor and an MOS memory; all that is necessary for proper operation is to have interface compatibility at the bus and the control signal level. The biggest challenge lies in the diversified manner in which the reader may find new and exciting ways of using microprocessors.

PROBLEMS

1. Explain the difference between sequential and random-access memories.

2. What are the four different forms of information stored in main memory?

3. Define volatile and nonvolatile memories. Determine which classification the following devices fall into:
   a. Latch
   b. Magnetic core
   c. JK flip-flop
   d. Floppy disk
   e. Read-write memory (RAM)
   f. Read-only memory (ROM)
   g. Magnetic tape

4. Give two alternative approaches for protecting a memory system against power interruptions.

5. Using a 2K $\times$ 8 ROM which has one Chip Enable, design a 4K $\times$ 8 memory system. Repeat for a 4K $\times$ 16 memory system.

6. Determine the memory address for the following locations:
   a. 275_{10}
   b. 600_{10}

7. What is meant by accessing memory?

8. Describe the functional elements of a digital computer.

9. What is the function of the following registers?
   a. Program counter
   b. Instruction register
   c. Instruction decoder
   d. Accumulator
   e. Flag register
10. What are the major functions of
    a. The control unit
    b. The input-output section
11. Describe the role of an interrupt.

REFERENCES

1. Burroughs Corporation: *Digital Computer Principles,* McGraw-Hill Book Company, New York, 1962.
2. Gear, C. W.: *Computer Organization and Programming,* McGraw-Hill Book Company, New York, 1974.

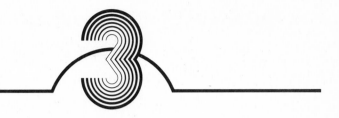

Elements of a Microprocessor

In the two previous chapters, discussion centered about the basic fundamentals of computers up to the development of the microprocessor. In this chapter microprocessing elements will be defined and functionally described as entities and as part of a chip of a microcomputing system. For a further understanding of the microprocessor, the instruction execution cycle and its relationship to the internal timing of the unit will be discussed.

3-1 PARTITIONING THE MICROPROCESSOR

The microprocessor designer has to determine how much of a computer goes on a chip. The first product developed along the lines of a microprocessor was a pocket calculator chip which contained all the functional computer parts: arithmetic, control, I/O, and memory. The first microprocessor chip, the 4004, was developed by the Intel Corporation of Santa Clara, California, in 1971, and it contained all the functional parts of the calculator except for the memory. Only 16 pins were used in this design, requiring unique timesharing of pins and the placement of some normally internal microprocessing elements outside the chip. A later Intel product, the 8080, partitioned the microprocessor to a configuration that has become somewhat standard today. Figure 3-1 shows a typical microprocessor containing dedicated data registers.

The microprocessors discussed in this chapter are those units which are not microprogrammable.* Microprogrammable units will be covered in

*Microprogrammable units allow the user to develop a personal instruction set, in contrast to the standard microprocessors, which have a fixed or predetermined intruction set.

51

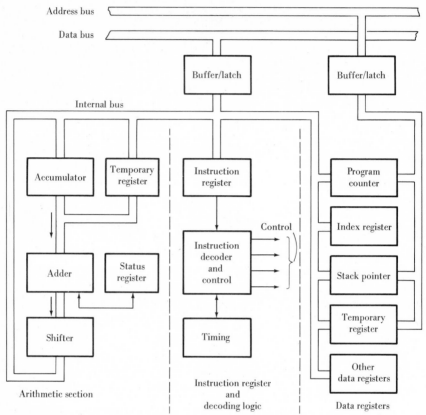

Figure 3-1 Functionally partitioned microprocessor with dedicated data registers.

Chap. 8. The present chapter will emphasize the typical or generic microprocessor chip and the functional characteristics of its elements. Stressing the operation of its functional elements will help prepare the reader to understand new chip developments that may redistribute the functions onto more than one chip.

Functional Partitioning

A typical microprocessor is grouped, or partitioned, into three functional groups structured around a bus system. The three functional groups, as shown in Fig. 3-1, are the arithmetic unit, the instruction register and decoding logic, and the data register section. The three groups communicate with one another by use of the internal bus. Each of these groups will be described separately; then the movement of address, instruction, and data through the microprocessor bus system will be described.

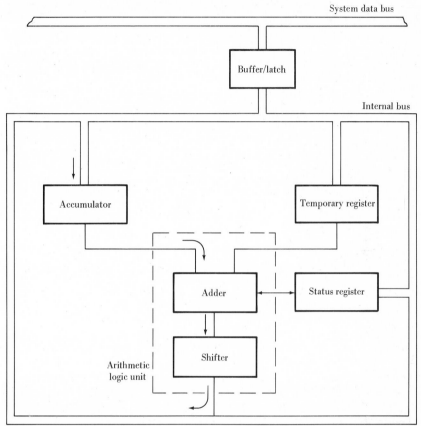

Figure 3-2 The arithmetic section of a microprocessor.

The Arithmetic Unit

The arithmetic unit consists functionally of an adder, an accumulator, a shift register (commonly called a *shifter*), a temporary register, and a status register. Some systems utilize the term *arithmetic logic unit* (ALU) to describe the adder and the shift function. A diagram of the arithmetic section is shown in Fig. 3-2. Typically an arithmetic section has 8 bits. The shifter may transfer data from the accumulator to the bus by either shifting it left, shifting it right, or transferring it directly. Functionally the shifter is used to perform logic and arithmetic operations. The temporary register is used to hold bus data to or from the ALU and the status register. Most operations in the ALU involve the accumulator. For example, in an Add operation that requires a retrieval, or fetch, from memory for the second operand, the first operand will normally reside in the accumulator. After the Add operation, the result will go back to

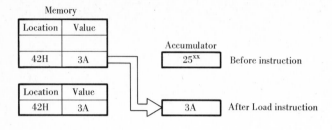

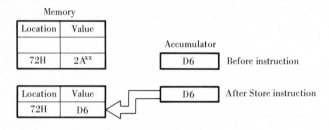

^{xx}Indicates that before execution of instruction the
accumulator or memory could contain any
value (don't care)

Figure 3-3 Example of the Load and Store instructions.

the accumulator. Data transfers, excluding direct memory accesses, are handled exclusively through the accumulator. Two of the most common operations, the Load and the Store instructions, utilize the accumulator as a temporary data register. The Load instruction permits one data word to be transferred from memory and placed in the accumulator. The Store operation transfers a data word which has temporarily been in the accumulator to a specific memory location (see Fig. 3-3).

The basic function of the ALU is to perform arithmetic operations. The unit handles binary and decimal addition and subtraction instructions. Subtraction is performed by adding the complement of the subtrahend Y to the minuend X, thus reducing the amount of arithmetic hardware. Multiplication and division instructions are generally executed by subroutines or specially developed software programs used to perform these operations. There is no "special hardware" identifiable with multiplication and division instructions as there is with the adder and the Add operation. The absence of multiplication and division hardware circuits within the ALU results in increased execution times for these operations. For example, an Add operation may be executed in 5 microseconds (μs), while a Multiply instruction executed by the use of subroutines may take 200 μs. As microprocessors advance in technology, Multiply hardware circuits will probably be included within the arithmetic unit. Present-day microprocessor manufacturers have

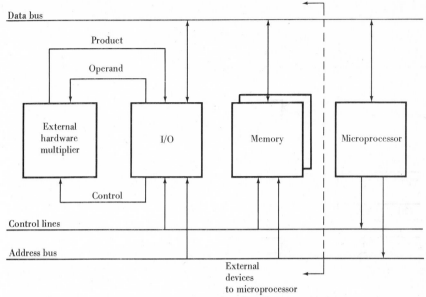

Figure 3-4 A microprocessor system with a hardware multiplier.

designed special external chips containing multiplication circuitry that can be utilized within the microcomputer system if higher-speed performance or execution is required. An example of such a system is shown in Fig. 3-4.

There are several modes in which the ALU can be utilized. In the Decimal mode, decimal numbers are represented in binary-coded decimal form and the ALU can add or subtract a two-digit decimal number, for example, with each integer or digit using 4 bits of an 8-bit ALU. When the two numbers produce a sum that is greater than decimal 99, then a carry bit in the status register is used to denote that occurrence.

Decimal operations are selected by the user with the Decimal flag of the status register raised. The addition is performed in binary with an adjustment generated to properly store the corrected sum in the accumulator.

In adding two-digit decimal numbers, the adjustment consists of adding the number 6 to the least significant digit whenever that digit assumes a value greater than 9. The BCD number 6 added to any "illegal" 4-bit digit (numbers from 1010 to 1111) adjusts the digit and propagates a carry to the most significant digit, with the result that the sum is correct in BCD form. Two examples showing the addition of decimal numbers are illustrated:

EXAMPLE A

$$+8 \quad 0000\ 1000$$
$$+2 \quad \underline{0000\ 0010}$$

```
                        0000 1010    Illegal
        Add   +6        0000 0110
              +10        0001 0000    Corrected sum
```

EXAMPLE B

```
              +45       0100 0101
              +39       0011 1001
                        0111 1110    Illegal
        Add   +6        0000 0110
              +84       1000 0100    Corrected sum
```

Binary numbers are treated in one of two manners: either the unsigned binary system or the signed 2's complement system. In the unsigned number system, the range of the 8 bits extends from 0 to 255. The Carry flag will be generated when the sum of two 8-bit numbers exceeds 255.

In the signed 2's complement system, the assignment of one bit to the sign reduces the number of usable bits to 7 but effectively maintains the same overall range, since numbers are represented as either positive or negative. Thus the range of the 7 bits is -128 to $+127$. The overflow bit in the status register is generated whenever the operation exceeds the register bit limit of the arithmetic unit. In an Add operation, to determine if an overflow is to be generated, carry bits corresponding to bits 6 and 7 are EXCLUSIVE ORed. Should the result of this operation be equal to 1, then an overflow bit is set in the status register. A 0 indicates no overflow. Four examples are shown in Fig. 3-5.

```
                        7 6 5 4 3 2 1 0

Case I        +100      0 1 1 0 0 1 0 0
              + 25      0 0 0 1 1 0 0 1
No overflow   Sum       0 1 1 1 1 1 0 1
              Carry    (0 0)0 0 0 0 0 0

Case II       +100      0 1 1 0 0 1 0 0
              + 30      0 0 0 1 1 1 1 0
Overflow      Sum       1 0 0 0 0 0 1 0
              Carry    (0 1)1 1 1 1 0 0

Case III      -100      1 0 0 1 1 1 0 0
              - 25      1 1 1 0 0 1 1 1
No overflow   Sum       1 0 0 0 0 0 1 1
              Carry    (1 1)1 1 1 1 0 0

Case IV       -100      1 0 0 1 1 1 0 0
              -30       1 1 1 0 0 0 1 0
Overflow      Sum       0 1 1 1 1 1 1 0
              Carry    (1 0)0 0 0 0 0 0
```

Figure 3-5 Overflow generation during Add operation.

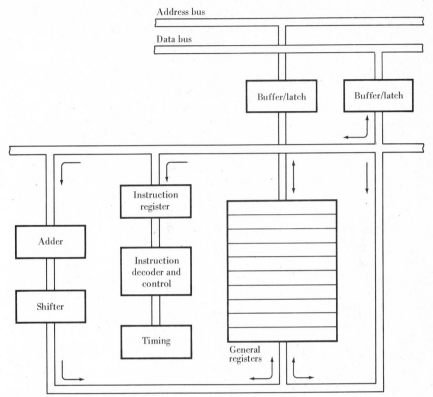

Figure 3-6 A general-register microprocessor.

A number of microprocessors have more than one accumulator. In those instances, the second accumulator is used as an extension of the first accumulator to functionally time-share those tasks scheduled for the first unit. When the architecture of the microprocessor is of the general-register form, the registers may have nonrestrictive use; hence they can be assigned as accumulators. A general-register microprocessor is shown in Fig. 3-6.

Logic Operations of the ALU   There exists in microprocessors a class of instructions which permit logic operations to be performed. The AND, OR, and EXCLUSIVE OR functions are typical instructions of this type. The logic operation to be performed is between the accumulator and an operand residing either at a designated register or in memory. The results of the operation derived on a bit-to-bit basis remain in the accumulator. For example, assume that the accumulator contains the value 5BH before an EXCLUSIVE OR operation. The result 67H remains in the accumulator at the end of the operation when the operand 3CH is used.

Accumulator before operation	5BH = 0101	1011
Operand	3CH = 0011	1100
Accumulator after operation	67H = 0110	0111

When a microprocessor performs a logic AND operation, a similar bit-by-bit comparison is performed, with the result remaining in the accumulator. Assume that the accumulator contains a value equal to 1EH; then an operand with a value of 4DH will result in a new accumulator value equal to 0CH.

Accumulator before operation	1EH = 0001	1110
Operand	4DH = 0100	1101
Accumulator after operation	0CH = 0000	1100

When the same values are chosen for a logic OR instruction, the accumulator will contain a new value equal to 5FH.

Bit manipulation instructions are logic instructions specifically used to clear, set, or complement one or more bits of the accumulator. The same three logic operations—AND, OR, and EXCLUSIVE OR—are used. In Example A of Fig. 3-7, a specific bit of the accumulator, the most significant bit (MSB), is to be cleared (reset to 0) without disturbing any of the other bits. To accomplish this, a selected pattern, or *mask,* is assigned to a register or memory location that will act as the operand. The accumulator will be compared or manipulated with the operand bit by bit by use of the logic AND instruction. Since no other bit of the accumulator is to change, the mask will contain all 1s except in the only bit position in which the accumulator is to be cleared; that one will contain a 0. The resultant operation yields a 0 in the MSB position.

If any of the accumulator bits are to be set to a 1, a similar technique is used. A mask containing a 1 is used on those bit positions which are to be set from a 0. A logic OR operation is then called for. A 0 on the mask bits will have no effect on the corresponding accumulator bits. Only bits on the mask equal to 1 will change the accumulator. In Example B of Fig. 3-7 the least significant bit (LSB) is set to a 1.

To complement bits in the accumulator, the corresponding bits in the mask are set to a 1. An EXCLUSIVE OR operation is performed. Mask bits with a 1 will force the corresponding accumulator bits to be complemented, while accumulator bits corresponding to mask bits of 0 will be unaffected. In Example C of Fig. 3-7, the MSB and LSB accumulator bits are to be complemented. The operand mask has a 1 in those bit positions.

The Status Register   The status register is also called the *auxiliary,* the *flag,* or the *condition code register* by different microprocessor manufac-

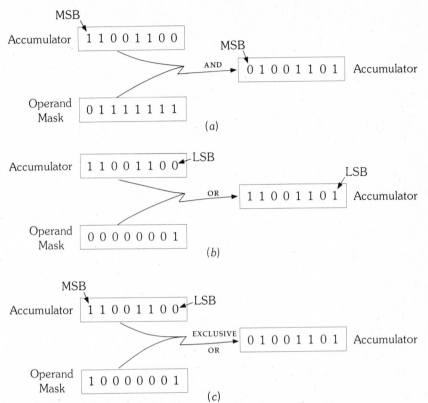

Figure 3-7 Bit manipulation instructions. (*a*) Example A: Reset MSB of the accumulator to 0. (*b*) Example B: Set LSB of the accumulator to 1. (*c*) Example C: Complement LSB and MSB of the accumulator.

turers. The register contains a group of single-status bits, or flags. For example, a bit or flag in the register may represent a negative sign while the adjacent bit assignment represents the carry from the accumulator. There is no set number of conditions which the status register must specify, and the format with regard to bit assignments is arbitrary and assigned by the manufacturer. Functions whose status is of concern include Carry, Interrupt, Decimal mode, Overflow, Zero Test, Negative Number, and Parity. The flags which make up the status register are not centrally controlled. Individually they may be set by the programmer or automatically set and reset as a result of an operation. A generic status register is shown in Fig. 3-8. Additional information on status registers as related to individual instructions will be covered in Chap. 5.

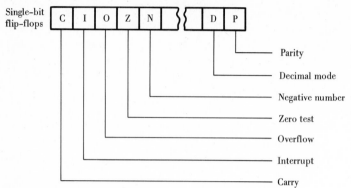

Figure 3-8   A status register.

The Instruction Register and Decoding

The instruction register is used to store the contents of the next instruction to be executed by the microprocessor. Instructions stored in the program memory, typically a ROM, are transferred to the microprocessor when a new instruction cycle is initiated (see Fig. 3-9).

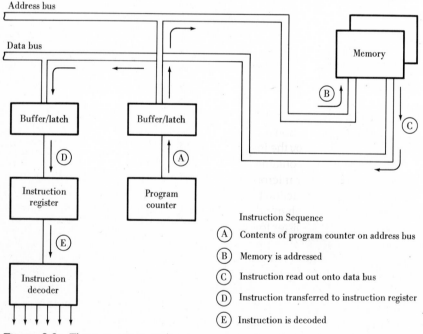

Instruction Sequence

(A) Contents of program counter on address bus

(B) Memory is addressed

(C) Instruction read out onto data bus

(D) Instruction transferred to instruction register

(E) Instruction is decoded

Figure 3-9   The instruction cycle.

The number of bits assigned to the instruction register is generally dependent on the data path of the microprocessor. Typical word lengths are in increments of 4 bits (8, 12, or 16 bits). Depending on the design, the contents of the instruction register may be partitioned into several groups, or fields. A field is a group of bits whose particular position takes on a specialized assignment. Thus, in one field, 001 could represent register 1 and 010 and 011 could represent registers 2 and 3, respectively. The description of the structure and number of the fields and their length in bits within the instruction register is called the *format*. Instruction word formats vary widely, since there is no standard which microprocessor manufacturers are required to follow.

The instruction word must contain the basic information, which includes, as a minimum, the OP code (the designation which defines the basic operation), the address mode in which the instruction is to be executed (direct, immediate, relative, etc.), and the address of the operand. When the microprocessor has a fairly large word length (12 or 16 bits), the above information can be specified with three fields in one instruction word. Smaller microprocessors, 4 and 8 bits wide, may require several bytes to describe the same information.

A comparison of 8- and 16-bit instruction word formats for several different types of instructions is shown in Fig. 3-10. Note that instructions are specified in 1, 2, or 3 bytes when 8-bit microprocessors are used. A 1-byte instruction in an 8-bit microprocessor system represents instructions which do not require any further operand reference beyond that specified by the byte format. Typical instructions in this category are register-to-register operations.

Almost all 8-bit microprocessor instructions require 2 or more bytes. The first byte of the instruction is the OP code with its address mode designation. This data is received by the instruction register. The operand data or address information which is contained in the remaining bytes of the instruction word is transferred to other microprocessor registers after the instruction register receives the first instruction byte. Multiple-byte instructions will be discussed further in Chap. 5, when address modes are explained.

The instruction register for an 8-bit microprocessor contains 8 bits, which theoretically enables 256 different OP codes/address modes to be designated. Instructions normally have more than one address mode, such as Load Direct or Load Indirect. All address modes of all instructions must be uniquely designated by the 8 bits of the instruction register. If a microprocessor has 60 instructions, 40 of which have three address modes and 20 of which have only one mode, then 140 (i.e., $40 \times 3 + 20$) different codes must be used to uniquely address each one. An example of OP code

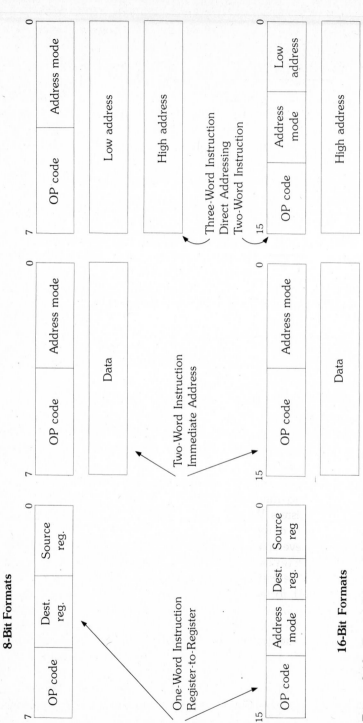

Figure 3-10 Typical 8-bit and 16-bit instruction formats.

TABLE 3-1   OP Code Assignment for an 8-bit Microprocessor

INSTRUCTION	MNEMONIC	HEX ASSIGNMENT	INSTRUCTION REGISTER	
Load Accumulator	LD	3EH	0011	1110
Store Accumulator	ST	3FH	0011	1111
Add Accumulator	ADD	3AH	0011	1010
Logic AND	AND	36H	0011	0110
EXCLUSIVE OR	XR	38H	0011	1000
Branch on Results Positive	BRP	0A4H	1010	0100
Increment	INC	12H	0001	0010

assignments for an 8-bit microprocessor is shown in Table 3-1. Note that associated with every instruction is an implicit addressing mode.

The decoder part of the instruction register receives the contents of the instruction register and develops control signals that enable or inhibit data paths necessary to execute the instruction.

Data Registers

The third functional part of the microprocessor is the data register section, which is used to manipulate data exclusive of the arithmetic section. The total number of registers contained in the microprocessor chip varies according to the manufacturer's design; typically, these are from just a few to as many as 64. These registers are part of the dedicated registers shown in Fig. 3-1 or the general register set of Fig. 3-6. Dedicated registers are specifically assigned to function as either program counters, temporary registers, or index registers. When a general-register type of microprocessor is used, the assignment of register functions is left to the discretion of those individuals who are developing the software program. For a general register to function as an index register, it must have the capability to both increment and decrement. In some designs, the general registers have limited capability. Decrementing to 0, for example, is not available in all registers, and so the programmer must have a thorough knowledge of the capability of the general register set before assignment. The use of a large number of registers in some designs permits the registers to function as a small scratch pad.

Data Buses

The total number of buses associated with the microprocessor varies, but most units are structured about two external buses and one internal bus. One of the external buses is dedicated to transmitting address information, while the second bus is time-shared between data and instructions. The internal bus is used to transmit information between registers of the microprocessor. The number of bits associated with each bus is dependent on the function for which the bus is being used. The address bus will normally contain 16 bits, to provide for an addressing capability of up to 64K of memory. The bus carrying the data is nominally compatible in bit width to the microprocessor. When the microprocessor configuration is structured differently so that address, data, and instructions are multiplexed on the same bus, then extra hardware in the form of an address latch must be added externally to the microprocessor (Fig. 3-11). The motivating factor for this approach is that additional pins become available within the chip for other functions.

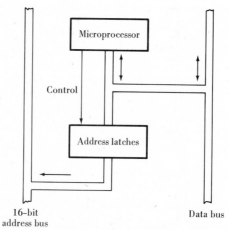

Figure 3-11   Multiplexing address and data.

3-2   THE INSTRUCTION EXECUTION CYCLE

Up to this point, we have described the basic elements separately; we will now see how they are integrated functionally in a typical sequence of operations.

The basic instruction cycle is initiated by placing the contents of the program counter on the address bus. This value represents the address of the next instruction to be executed. When placed on the bus it will permit a memory word representing the instruction to be read out onto the data bus; this operation is called a *fetch*. The contents of the instruction register will vary with each type of instruction, and is transmitted to the instruction decoder where the fields are decoded, enabling the instruction to be executed. During the cycle the program counter is incremented in preparation for the next instruction. The fetch sequence, A to E, is shown in Fig. 3-9.

When the instruction calls for an operand to be retrieved from memory, then additional fetches from memory are required. If an operation is to be performed between registers not requiring memory accesses, then the execution portion of the instruction is shorter. Thus, the execution time of instructions varies according to the number of times that the microprocessor has to interface with memory. In summary, the overall sequence of processing instructions can be thought of as a two-step operation: instruction acquisition for a constant duration and instruction execution over a variable processing time (see Fig. 3-12).

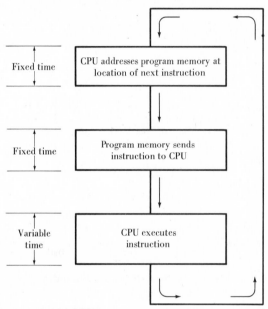

Figure 3-12 The basic steps in an instruction cycle.

Internal Timing

Within the basic instruction cycle just described, there are timing sequences which have taken place. To understand these operations, several terms must be introduced. The two most common terms used in describing the internal timing are *states* and *machine cycles*.

A state is the smallest unit of processing activity and is defined as the time interval between two successive positive-going transitions of phase 1 clock pulse. During a state, a distinct and individual function takes place within the microprocessor, such as incrementing the program counter or transferring data to a register. An instruction will execute many states, on the average 10 to 20. States are structured around machine cycles, which are groups of states that occur when the memory or the I/O is accessed. Only one address

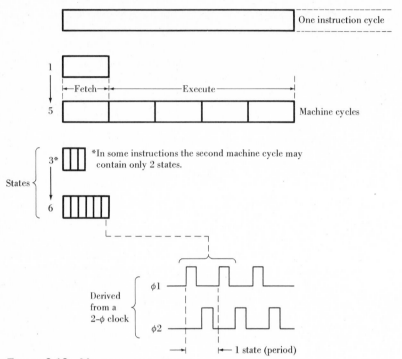

Figure 3-13 Microprocessor timing.

is generated per machine cycle. There are normally 3 to 6 states per machine cycle. As an example, an instruction which accesses memory three times will have at least 3 machine cycles. Figure 3-13 illustrates a typical microprocessor timing relationship between instruction, machine cycles, and states.

An example of two typical instructions to be executed is shown in Fig. 3-14. In each instruction an Add operation is to be performed, the first from an operand residing in a register and the second from an operand in memory. Each machine cycle fetch uses 3 state times, while the actual register-to-register Add is performed in 1 state. The total time for executing the first instruction, a register-to-register Add, is 4 states. The second instruction, Add M, is longer, since it must fetch its operand from memory. An additional machine cycle is taken, and thus 7 states are required to complete this instruction.

3-3 A MICROCOMPUTER SYSTEM

The basic microprocessor, when designed into a bus-oriented microcomputer system, will require additional elements to support it. To produce the

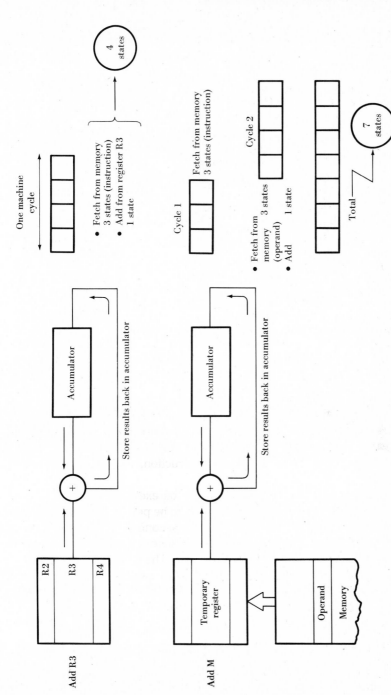

Figure 3-14 State timing examples. (*a*) Add R3 to accumulator; (*b*) add M to accumulator.

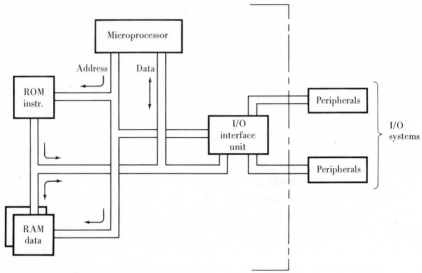

Figure 3-15 A microcomputing system.

minimum microcomputer system, memory and I/O modules must be included. A generic system is shown in Fig. 3-15. Note that the address and data buses are now internal to the system and that all external communication is handled by the I/O interface unit. As technology progresses, microprocessors will have greater capability. The integration of ROM and RAM memories and some form of I/O within the microprocessor will result in lower costs and higher performance. These units will no longer be microprocessors, but rather microcomputers on a chip.

PROBLEMS

1. What are the three functional groups of a microprocessor?
2. What are the main parts of the ALU? Describe the function of each element of the ALU.
3. Explain what causes overflow. When overflow occurs, how is it detected?
4. Determine whether there is an overflow as a result of the indicated operations.

   a. 0100 0110   b.   1001 1111
       +0011 1100   +1100 0111

5. Determine the operand mask, logical operation to be performed, and results for the following:

   a. Clear bits 2^0 to 2^3 when the accumulator is all 1s.

b.   Set bits 2^1, 2^4, and 2^6 when the accumulator is 1000 0101.

c.   Complement bits 2^0, 2^3, 2^6 when the accumulator is 0110 1100.

6.   What flags are normally included in the status register?

7.   What is the difference between a field and a format?

8.   In a 3-byte instruction, the first byte of information on the data bus is always transferred to which register? What is the function of this register?

9.   What are the functions of the data registers? Name two data registers found in microprocessors.

10.   Name the two external buses used in microprocessing systems. When the microprocessor is pin-limited, what alternative technique is used?

11.   What are the two main parts of the instruction cycle? What is the penalty for having the operand in memory?

12.   Explain the relationships between states, machine cycles, and instructions.

13.   What differentiates a microcomputer from a microprocessor?

REFERENCES

1.   Intel Corporation: *8080 Microcomputer Systems User's Manual,* September 1975.

2.   Motorola: *Microprocessor Applications Manual,* McGraw-Hill Book Company, 1975.

Technology

4-1 A TECHNOLOGY OVERVIEW

The rapid advances in LSI have led to the development of microprocessors and supporting hardware at an unprecedented rate. The intent of this chapter is to familiarize the reader with the basic technologies and provide some insight into the evolution and trends currently taking place. Technological advances have resulted in dramatic reductions in costs and more reliable microprocessing systems, all to the benefit of the present-day user.

There are several directions in which technology has advanced in microprocessing systems. For example, the microprocessor was originally developed using 4-bit PMOS technology. Since then, 8-bit NMOS units have become the most popular processors, even though larger units soon followed. Sixteen-bit devices are available, and even 32-bit units, which will compete directly with minicomputers, are emerging. It is quite an achievement to advance from a rather simple, by today's standards, 4-bit unit with 2000 transistors on a chip, to a sophisticated 16-bit microprocessor with over 20,000 transistors on a chip. The breakthrough was a result of numerous advances in technology. Some of the more significant advances include better layout procedures in producing the chip; the redesign of circuits to make them simpler, with fewer transistors and only a single power source; and the utilization of better technologies to fabricate the chip. The results have been denser units, whose operating speeds are more than one order of magnitude faster than the original microprocessors.

70

Memories are not to be overlooked in a discussion of these technological advances. The original semiconductor memory chip contained only 256 bits. Later the 1K × 1 chip received a lot of attention, since it was easily adaptable to the early microprocessor units. The growth of memories has rapidly accelerated, and today 64K-bit memories are already available, and 128K-bit memories now on the drawing board will soon become a reality. This means that the basic memory cell, which we have related to a flip-flop in function, has dimensions of less than 0.001 in on each side.

There are many other functions which have evolved to support the new processor and memory devices. Most of these are in peripheral units, such as keyboard scanners and controllers for CRT raster scan displays, floppy disks, and dot-matrix printers. These units are available in 40-pin chips, thereby simplifying the system circuit design to one of interface.

Today we are headed towards an even greater level of integration, which will impact the design philosophies of computing systems. The new generation of LSI is called VLSI, or very large-scale integration. We will examine VLSI after reviewing the growth of integrated circuits from their initial development.

The early integrated circuit chips consisted of diodes and transistors, which could be fabricated economically, along with a few low-value resistors and capacitors, which were difficult and expensive to make. As integrated circuit (IC) fabrication processes became more advanced, transistor-transistor logic (TTL or T²L) came into prominence. As shown in Fig. 4-1, a TTL two-input gate consisted of a multiple-emitter NPN transistor, three NPN transistors, four resistors, and a diode. Four of these gates could be

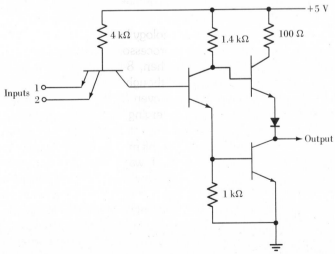

Figure 4-1 A transistor-transistor two-input NAND gate.

placed on one IC, each gate having a typical size of 0.050 in^2. Further improvements in integrated circuit technology resulted from government spending for space and military projects in the 1960s, which led to the development of small-scale integration, medium-scale integration and eventually large-scale integration.

Small-Scale Integration (SSI)

Devices which contain 12 or fewer gates on a single IC chip are defined as SSI units. There are typically four to six transistors per gate in typical SSI devices such as inverters, gates, and flip-flops.

Medium-Scale Integration (MSI)

Devices which contain more than 12 but fewer than 100 gates are considered MSI units. MSI devices include shift registers, decoders, multiplexers, and adders.

Large-Scale Integration (LSI)

The dividing line between LSI and MSI is based on the number of components contained within the device. LSI devices have a complexity of more than 100 gates. In LSI, as in other forms of ICs, the active and passive elements (transistors and resistors, respectively) are simultaneously formed on a substrate, or base, material. Thus, this process, when silicon is used, is commonly referred to as *silicon, monolithic, integrated circuit technology*. It generally places a large number of identical circuits on a single chip. Semiconductor memories, microprocessors, one-chip microcomputers, and keyboard scanners are examples of LSI devices.

Very Large-Scale Integration (VLSI)

VLSI represents an extension of LSI, providing circuits with a complexity equivalent to 10,000 to 20,000 gates on a single chip. To efficiently develop this technology, which utilizes small geometry devices, the mask-making technology, which provides the transformation of the circuit onto the wafer (see Sec. 4-2), will have to be changed. A technique in which an electron beam writes circuit patterns directly on the material is the most promising approach for achieving the microdimensions required for the projected densities.

4-2 LSI PROCESSING TECHNIQUES

The basic material, or substrate, used to construct most circuits is silicon. The following steps, as shown in Fig. 4-2, are typical of the operations required to fabricate a monolithic integrated circuit.

Steps

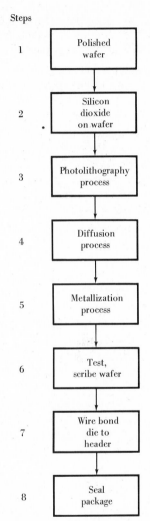

Figure 4-2 Fabrication of an integrated circuit.

1. *Polishing the wafer* A single crystal ingot of silicon material is sliced into thin wafers, and each wafer is polished to a mirror finish and inspected for flaws.

2. *Growing an oxide layer* A layer of silicon dioxide is grown on top of the wafer when a thin layer of the material is deposited on the surface and the wafer is placed in a control furnace environment.

3. *Photolithography* The photolithography process involves two major areas: photographic mask making and photoresist.

a. *Photographic mask making* The initial layout of an integrated circuit is normally done at a scale several hundred times larger than the final dimensions of the finished monolithic chip. This initial layout is then partitioned into individual mask layers, each corresponding to a masking step during the fabrication process. The individual mask layers are then reduced photographically to the final dimensions of the integrated unit. The reduced form of each of these patterns is then contact-printed on a transparent glass slide to form a photographic mask of the patterns to be etched on the silicon dioxide surface. To facilitate batch processing, a large number of these masks are contact-printed on the same glass slide to form a masking plate. The plate is sufficiently large to cover the entire surface of the silicon wafer to be masked. Thus, in a single masking operation, an array of a large number of identical masks can be applied simultaneously over the wafer surface. During the masking operation, the mask is transferred from the masking plate to the wafer surface by photolithographic techniques.

b. *Photoresist* As shown in Fig. 4-3, the wafer is then coated with photoresist, a coating which is sensitive to light. The glass mask is placed in contact with the wafer, and ultraviolet light is directed on the mask. The areas of the mask that are transparent allow the light to penetrate through and remove that portion of the photoresist which the ultraviolet rays strike. A buffered hydrofluoric acid solution placed on the wafer causes the silicon dioxide to be etched away where the photoresist has not been exposed. The remaining photoresist is then removed from the wafer, and the wafer is now ready to undergo a diffusion process.

4. *Diffusion* The wafer is again placed in a furnace, where impurities are diffused into the parts of the wafer where the silicon dioxide has been etched away, making those parts of the wafer either N-type or P-type material.

5. *Metallization* Steps 2 through 4 are repeated for the various masks or diffusions that are necessary to produce the integrated circuit. The final process requires metallization, which defines the interconnection paths on the chip. Contact windows are opened in the silicon dioxide layer. A metal, usually aluminum, is evaporated over the entire surface of the wafer and the interconnecting contacts are formed by a photolithography step in which unwanted metal is etched away.

6. *Testing and scribing the wafer* The wafer will undergo a cursory test, such as continuity or visual inspection, and then be scribed or cut into a die.

7. *Wire bonding* Each die is wire-bonded to the package or header.

8. *Sealing the package* Each die is sealed and made ready for final test.

In addition to the standard IC processes, the fabrication of LSI devices requires some unique processes, consisting primarily of multilevel interconnection and computer-aided mask design. The first-level metallization is used

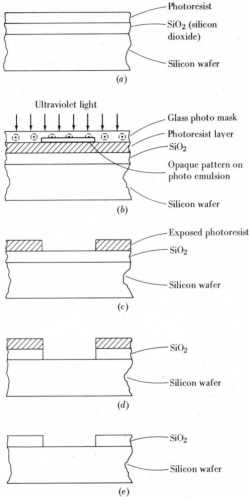

Figure 4-3 The photoresist process. (*a*) Initial coating; (*b*) contact printing; (*c*) after developing; (*d*) after oxide etch; (*e*) after strip.

to interconnect ICs on a single wafer to form an LSI circuit, additional interconnection layers, and therefore additional masks, are required. LSI masks are so complex that the use of a computer is required to lay out the mask. This computer-aided design technique, commonly known as CAD, is fairly expensive for the LSI manufacturer. The trend in LSI mask design is toward more complexity and increasing circuit densities. This means that the mask pattern will have narrower and narrower line widths. In order to achieve this level of mask complexity, LSI manufacturers will be using CAD and optical techniques, such as electron beam (or E-beam) lithography wafer printing, that can produce very narrow line widths, less than 1 micrometer (μm). Typical LSI line widths are presently 4 to 6 μm while the first ICs developed in 1961 used line widths of 1 mil (0.001 in, about 25.4 μm). The E-beam system produces maskless printing on the wafer using computer-controlled electron beams. The standard E-beam technique scans the entire wafer in a way similar to a raster scan in a television set; another E-beam method just scans the desired pattern. Both methods, however, are slow and require that each wafer be scanned separately. E-beam equipment is very expensive, and as a result the circuits initially produced using it have a high cost.

4-3 SEMICONDUCTOR TECHNOLOGIES

There are many semiconductor technologies available to the manufacturer of microprocessors, memories, and associated LSI devices. Devices using silicon as a substrate material (see Fig. 4-4) fall into two general categories,

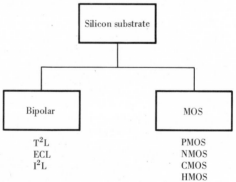

Figure 4-4 Semiconductor technologies for microprocessing systems.

bipolar and MOS. The following discussion presents an overview of the technologies, summarizing their most important features and limitations.

NMOS

NMOS (N-channel metal-oxide-semiconductor) is one of the most popular technologies because of its relatively high speed and density. Although the early microprocessors were PMOS (P-channel MOS) devices, NMOS devices soon became available and proved very popular, since this type of construction resulted in potential switching speeds two or three times faster than PMOS offered. NMOS processors have received and will continue to receive a great deal of competition from the remaining technologies; however, in the memory area they have successfully overshadowed all the others. Further advances are being achieved in some RAMs by introducing high-impedance polysilicon load resistors to assume functions previously carried out by transistors, thus reducing the number of transistors per memory cell and the power dissipation. A limitation on NMOS circuits is that they have very little drive capability and therefore require additional circuitry in the form of output drivers.

A derivative of NMOS technology is HMOS. This technology scales down the physical geometry of the devices and reduces the operating voltage proportionately. The chips' smaller dimensions result in a smaller level of impurities (doping) required in the semiconductor material. These characteristics result in a device that is four times faster than but dissipates only the same amount of power as an NMOS device. Intel was the innovator in this technology.

Complementary MOS (CMOS)

There are two forms of CMOS devices on the market: CMOS/SOS and bulk CMOS. When sapphire (Al_2O_3) is used as a substrate material instead of silicon, then the technology is called CMOS/SOS, or complementary MOS/silicon on sapphire. When silicon is used, the process is called bulk CMOS, or just CMOS. It appears that after a difficult start in achieving a satisfactory yield and reasonable production cost, the CMOS/SOS technology has matured sufficiently and is considered more advantageous than CMOS. Both devices contain PMOS and NMOS transistors in their basic gate design; however, the SOS device has lower capacitance and therefore an increased operational speed. The most redeeming feature of CMOS and CMOS/SOS is low power dissipation. Circuits displaying CMOS technology (both bulk and SOS) require much less power* than their equivalents in bipolar or NMOS technology. If a simple bipolar inverter dissipates milliwatts of power, its CMOS equivalent's power dissipation will be in microwatts. This extremely low power dissipation is a result of having only one of the two transistors, the PMOS and the NMOS that form the inverter, conducting at any one time (see Fig. 4-5a). Other CMOS and CMOS/SOS advantages include high performance (speed), the use of only one power supply voltage, high noise immunity, and a wide operating range with respect to the supply voltage at ambient temperatures. Their main disadvantage is their high cost and the fact that they do not have high density, because of their utilization of PMOS and NMOS transistors for each basic inverter, gate, or memory cell.

*When the speed of operation is 1 MHz or less.

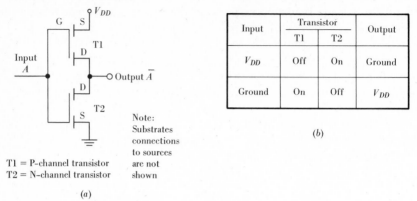

Input	Transistor		Output
	T1	T2	
V_{DD}	Off	On	Ground
Ground	On	Off	V_{DD}

(b)

T1 = P-channel transistor
T2 = N-channel transistor

Note:
Substrates
connections
to sources
are not
shown

(a)

Figure 4-5   A CMOS inverter. (a) Inverter circuit; (b) truth table.

Their production process is also more complex, since it is necessary to produce both kinds of transistor on the same chip.

Transistor-Transistor Logic (TTL)

The initial integrated circuit boom was a result of perfecting bipolar technology; TTL circuits became industry standards in SSI and MSI chips. However, the relatively high gate area per chip and the high power dissipation of TTL has prevented the development of TTL microprocessors in any form other than in "bit slices." Bit-slice designs provide the user only a portion of the total arithmetic section on a chip; it requires several of these units to build up the total arithmetic section (see Chap. 8). The use of Schottky diodes and low-power TTL has resulted in a family of low-power Schottky (LPS) devices that are extremely fast and dissipate relatively low power. LSI bipolar technology is also used in RAM memories.

Emitter-Coupled Logic (ECL)

Emitter-coupled logic has long been recognized as the form of technology to select for microprocessor circuits where operational speed is the ultimate design goal. It is still one of the fastest technologies, but it does suffer from the penalty associated with high-speed operation, namely, high power dissipation. ECL has the same disadvantage as TTL: it requires a large "real estate," or transistor area, to implement its functions. Most of the advanced arithmetic circuits, such as high-speed multipliers used in special processing applications, are implemented with ECL. It is not uncommon to have ECL circuits whose delay times are in the order of several nanoseconds (ns, or 10^{-9} seconds). Forms of ECL are being developed which should reduce the power without sacrificing the speed. ECL is difficult to interface with, because of its low voltage swing (less than a volt) and extremely high speeds of operation.

Integrated Injection Logic (I²L)

Integrated injection logic (I²L) may perhaps be the bipolar technology with the most potential. As shown in Fig. 4-6a, it utilizes NPN and PNP transistors with common areas. The base area of the PNP transistor is integrated with the emitter area of the NPN transistor, and the collector area of the PNP transistor also functions as the base area of the NPN transistor. The PNP transistor acts as the injector, providing a current source to the circuit. The NPN transistor with its multiple collectors acts as an inverter. See Fig. 4-6b

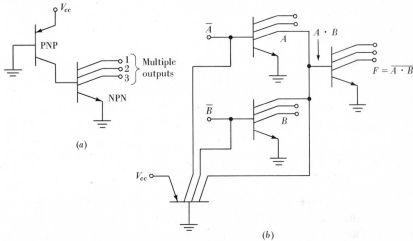

Figure 4-6 Integrated injection logic. (a) Basic circuit; (b) NAND function. Copyright © 1977 by the Institute of Electrical and Electronics Engineers, Inc. Reprinted, with permission, from *IEEE Spectrum,* June 1977, p. 31.

for the design of a NAND circuit. Note that the circuits are directly coupled to one another and that I²L eliminates the need for resistors in its gate design, saving both real estate and power. Low-voltage operation (approximately 1 V) results in favorable operating speeds.

I²L has a promising future, as manufacturers are introducing new techniques such as Schottky diodes that will enhance its performance even further. However, the newness of I²L makes it expensive compared with NMOS technology. Also, the development of I²L memories has been disappointing thus far, in that no devices with sufficient speed or density have been produced to render the technology competitive for the fabrication of memories.

The application of these technologies to the microprocessor and the I/O devices will be presented in Chaps. 8 through 10. The remaining sections in this chapter will discuss the development of technology as applied to main storage systems.

4-4 MAIN STORAGE MEMORIES

RAMs can be implemented with any of the technologies previously discussed (TTL, ECL, I²L, NMOS, and CMOS). The NMOS RAMs are generally more attractive because of their performance, high density, reasonable power, and low cost. The following descriptions of the RAM will therefore be limited to NMOS technology.

There are two basic forms of NMOS RAMs: static and dynamic. Internally, each cell of a dynamic RAM consists of a single transistor and a capacitor, while the static RAM has four transistors per cell. Thus, dynamic RAMs are denser than their static counterparts. Dynamic RAMs must be *refreshed* by the use of regenerated timing signals to prevent data from being lost by leakage from the diffused capacitors of the cells. In a static RAM, once the cell is set or reset, it will maintain that logic state indefinitely as long as power is maintained. Although refreshing dynamic units adds an overhead to the system, the technology still offers lower cost and remains sufficiently attractive to outsell the static units by a ratio of approximately 5 to 1.

Most of the demands for the dynamic units come from designers of large systems, who readily take advantage of 16K- and 64K-bit density chips in their designs. The small-memory user continues to employ the static units because their simplicity requires no refresh timing or clock signals. Smaller systems can readily utilize the many low-density chips which are on the market. Some of these are the 1K × 1, 256 × 4 and 4K × 1 chips.

Both static and dynamic RAMs will be described further in this chapter after some memory-related terms are defined. Figure 4-7 is a representation of static RAM (read and write) timing relationships; it will illustrate some of these terms.

Some Basic Memory Terms

Address lines (A0 to A15) The Address lines are input lines to memory from the microprocessor that are used to select the memory word that is being written or read. The cross-hatch section of the Address lines in Fig. 4-7 indicates that the signals on the line are not to be considered valid at the time. Address lines are shown going from logic 1 to logic 0 and vice versa. Note that either state is valid depending upon the memory location that is being selected. For example, when memory location 17_{10} is selected, Address lines A4 and A0 will go to logic 1, while all other lines will remain at logic 0.

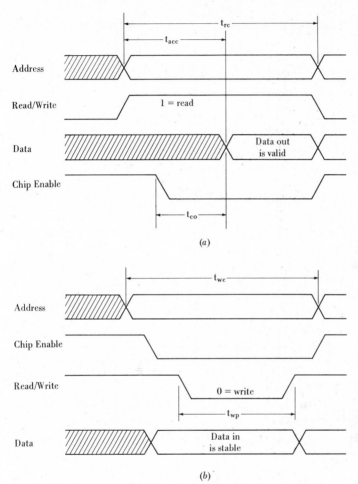

Figure 4-7 Static RAM timing relationships. (*a*) Read cycle;
(*b*) write cycle.

Read cycle (t_{rc}) The time required for the Read operation as specified in
terms of the minimum address signal accepted by the chip.

Write cycle (t_{wc}) The time required for the write operation as specified in
terms of the minimum address signal accepted by the chip.

Access time (t_{acc}) To read out information, the processor must address the
word in memory from which it needs data. The access time is defined as
the time elapsed from when the address signals are stable to when valid
data is present on the bus. The access time is related to the speed of the
device. A fast microprocessor that can update a memory address in 50 ns,
for example, does not operate efficiently unless the memory access time is

less than 50 ns. If the memory access time is greater than 50 ns, the microprocessor must wait for the memory to be ready.

Read/Write (R/W) The Read/Write signal is a microprocessor signal to the memory which selects the mode in which the memory is to function. Typically, logic 1 is used to read and logic 0 to write. The Write pulse width (t_{wp}) is defined as the minimum time that the write signal must remain at logic 0 to guarantee writing data successfully.

Chip Enable (CE) The Chip Enable signal selects those memory devices which must be active to perform the operation at the desired address location. If the chip is not enabled, the output line is either open or tri-stated.

Chip Enable to Output (t_{co}) During the Read mode, t_{co} defines the maximum time it takes for data to be valid from the time the Chip Enable signal is active.

At one time, the number of address pins used for memory addressing was directly proportional to the bit density of the memory. Thus a 1K static memory chip had 10 pins, one for each required Address line (A0 to A9). When the more highly populated dynamic memory chips were developed, the Address lines were decreased by multiplexing the Address lines but requiring two transmissions per Read or Write cycle. Thus, a 4K memory chip has only six pins available for the addresses; without multiplexing, 12 bits would be required. The 16-pin package for a 4K chip was standardized, therefore, reducing costs of the extra pins while maintaining the relatively high board-packaging density of the fewer-pin ICs.

Internal Organization

Static RAMs Static RAMs can be partitioned into five separate areas, as shown in Fig. 4-8. They are:

- Address decoders
- Memory array
- Clock generation circuitry
- Sense amplifier(s)
- Data input-output section

A 1K $\times$ 1 RAM (see Fig. 4-9) has a memory array consisting of 1024 cells. The organization is such that there are 32 rows and 32 columns of memory cells, each being 1 bit. For any cell to be selected there must be coincidence between any one out of 32 rows and any one out of 32 columns. The address decoder of Fig. 4-8 selects the proper row and column based on the address location of the cell. (A 4K $\times$ 1 memory requires selection of one out of 64 rows and one out of 64 columns in order to address a particular cell.) The bit density and organization of the memory array dictates the number of address

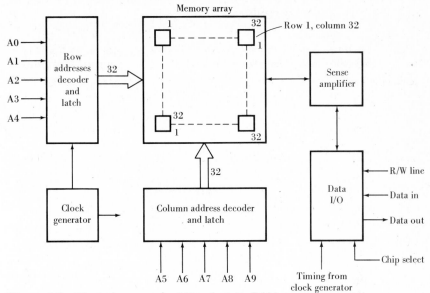

Figure 4-8 Block diagram of a 1K × 1 static RAM.

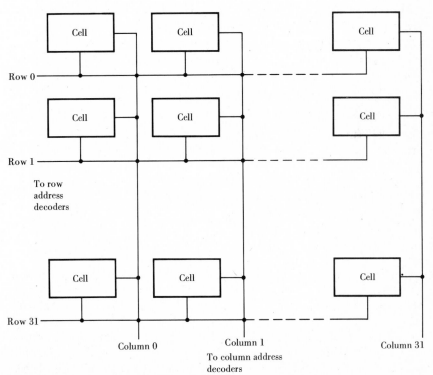

Figure 4-9 Cell matrix of a 1K × 1 RAM.

decoders required for columns and rows. The two address decoders, one for row and the other for column, contain latches used to capture address data on the bus. The clock generator circuitry provides the internal timing signals for decoding and "strobing" the gate logic of the memory. During the Read mode, the state of the memory cell (1 or 0) is sampled by the sense amplifier(s) and then transferred to the I/O section. The number of sense amplifiers in a memory chip corresponds to the number of output bits of the memory. If the organization of a 1K memory is 256 words by 4 bits, the chip contains four sense amplifiers to accommodate the four output bits. The data input-output section is available with either common or separate input and output lines. The Chip Enable and Read/Write signals interface with the data I/O section.

Dynamic RAMs Functionally, dynamic RAMs are very similar to static RAMs, since the dynamic RAM contains all five functional areas of the static RAM. However, the organization is structured differently. A typical 4K × 1 dynamic RAM block diagram is shown in Fig. 4-10. Note that the number of sense amplifiers in a dynamic RAM increases to the number of columns contained in the memory array.

It is not uncommon to find multiplex addressing on higher-density static and dynamic chips. This greatly reduces the total pin count required for

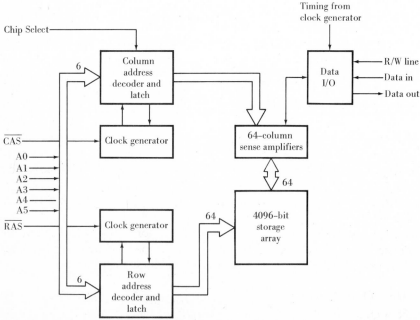

Figure 4-10 A 4K × 1 dynamic RAM.

addresses. However, two additional signals are required to designate whether the multiplexed addresses from the microprocessor represent row or column information. These input signals are called $\overline{RAS}$ (row address strobe) and $\overline{CAS}$ (column address strobe). Thus, the $\overline{RAS}$ and $\overline{CAS}$ signals coincide with the addresses and are related to the row and column of the memory, respectively. A timing diagram for a dynamic multiplexed RAM is shown in Fig. 4-11.

Dynamic memories must be sensed and restored by a procedure called *refreshing;* otherwise the cell data stored in the capacitor would leak off. Refreshing is performed by rows, one row at a time, and the number of cycles that the memory must be refreshed is equal to the number of rows in the cell matrix. The basic period for refreshing dynamic memories is typically 2 ms. As an example, a 4K chip, which contains 64 rows and 64 columns, will have 64 refresh cycles every 2 ms. A 16K device, containing 128 rows and 128 columns, will have 128 refresh cycles that must be updated every 2 ms. Comparing the requirements of these two memories, it is apparent that the 16K device, which requires more refresh cycles, constitutes a greater burden on the system. The more cycles required to refresh the memory, the less time is available to the microprocessor system, since the memory cannot service the microprocessor and be refreshed simultaneously. The time in percent that the memory requires to be refreshed is:

$$\text{Time required to refresh} = \frac{\text{no. of refresh cycles} \times \text{Write cycle time}}{\text{refresh update}} \times 100\%$$

A 4K $\times$ 1 memory, which uses 64 refresh cycles every 2 ms and has a write cycle time of 500 ns, will be in a refresh state 1.6 percent of the time.

There are two basic approaches to refreshing: *burst mode* and *cycle stealing.* In the burst mode a 4K device that requires 64 refresh cycles will execute all 64 refresh cycles consecutively every 2 ms. During this refresh time, the processor cannot utilize the memory. For example, a 500-ns memory would require 32 consecutive microseconds to be refreshed. Such an approach, although straightforward, is not recommended, since it uses up too much processing time all at once. As an alternative, cycle stealing can be used. Every 31 μs (2 ms/64) a memory cycle of 500 ns is stolen from the processor and dedicated to refreshing. The term *cycle stealing* in this context refers to the time the processor does not have full use of the memory, such as when it is time-shared with the I/O or used for refreshing. The term as applied to newer microprocessors also defines a period when a cycle can be taken from the processor without impacting processing speed.

Other Memories

Although the static and dynamic RAMs provide an attractive form of main storage devices, they are volatile. Their use may require auxiliary power or a

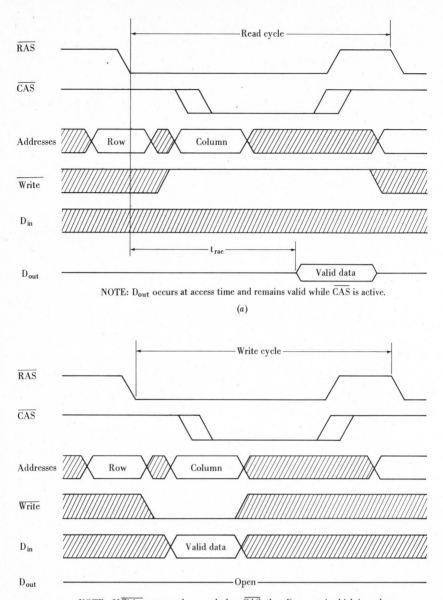

NOTE: D_{out} occurs at access time and remains valid while $\overline{CAS}$ is active.

(a)

NOTE: If $\overline{Write}$ command occurs before $\overline{CAS}$, then D_{out} remains high impedance.

Figure 4-11 Dynamic RAM timing relationships. (a) Read cycle; (b) write cycle.

backup secondary memory, such as a floppy disk, which can be used to reload the main programs. As an alternative, there are several attractive nonvolatile technologies which are commonly used. They include the following:

- Read-only memories
- Programmable read-only memories
- Erasable programmable read-only memories

Read-Only Memory (ROM) The storage content of a read-only memory is fixed so that only the read operations are permitted. The memory content is written in the memory cells during a manufacturing process in which the program mask unique to the chip is produced. This custom chip design for a specific ROM contains a program that is considered "firmware." * Before any ROM design is released to the semiconductor houses developing the units, the user must be completely satisfied with the software program. Such a program, of course, must be developed and tested in some other, less permanent memory technology. Once the ROM has been produced, any programming errors which it may contain will require correction, a costly process involving redesign, since ROMs cannot be patched up or fixed. The ROM design is a custom technology; it is expensive. However, if enough units are manufactured, the cost can be reduced, making the technology competitive with other memories.

ROMs are available in both bipolar and MOS technologies. Bipolar ROMs are extremely fast, some having access times of less than 50 ns.

The ROM user usually provides the vendor with program information via punched cards or paper tape, which allows the vendor to develop custom masks. An example of how a ROM may be programmed by the vendor is shown in Fig. 4-12. The 16-bit segment of a ROM consisting of 16 MOS

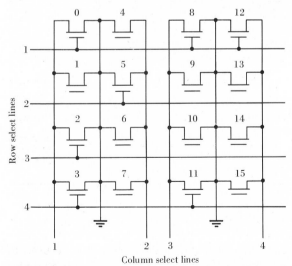

Figure 4-12 A segment of a programmed MOS RAM.

*Firmware refers to software instructions permanently contained in a ROM.

transistors is programmed to logic 1 or 0 by either connecting or floating the gate of each transistor. A gate which is not connected (is floating) represents a logic 0 when interrogated by the proper row and column Select lines. The output is sensed in the column Select line. For example, when row 2, column 1 is selected, MOS transistor 1 *cannot* be turned on, since its gate is floating, and therefore the column select line is open. This represents logic 0. Conversely, if row 1, column 3 is selected, MOS transistor 3 will turn on and column select 3 will be at logic 1. Standard output logic levels are then developed within the ROM.

Programmable Read-Only Memory (PROM) A PROM is a form of ROM that permits the program of the memory to be written at some later time than when the chip is being manufactured. For example, an unprogrammed memory available in all 0 or all 1 states is delivered to the user, who, after designing the program, electrically programs the PROM. Early PROM designs were based on a fusible-link principle (see Fig. 4-13), in which, at a

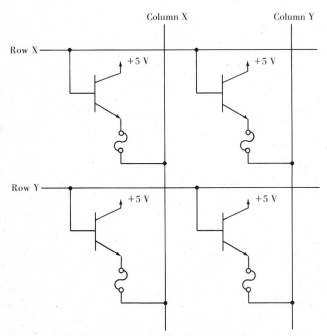

Figure 4-13 A segment of a fusible-link PROM.

cell being programmed to a 0, sizable current causes the corresponding metal connection between the row and column lines to "blow." This stores the logic 0 at the cell. To program a logic 1, the fuse is left intact. PROMs, like ROMs, cannot be reprogrammed and can be used for only one program.

If an error is made in programming, the device must be discarded unless the programming error did not blow the fusible link. When purchased in small quantities, PROMs are less expensive than ROMs; however, for large quantity purchases, ROMs are less expensive than PROMs.

Erasable Programmable Read-Only Memory (EPROM)   Erasable PROMs are extremely popular, since these devices feature all the desired characteristics necessary for system development. The unit is nonvolatile, programmable on the user's premises, and erasable. Thus EPROMs can be used over and over again, giving them a distinct advantage over the PROM. Each EPROM cell contains two gates, a select gate and a floating gate (see Fig. 4-14). The select gate is connected to the row decoder, while the floating

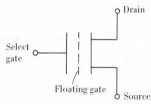

Figure 4-14   An EPROM storage cell.

gate is used for charge storage. The bits are programmed into the memory by subjecting each single-bit memory cell to a very high voltage, which causes the charge to be trapped on the floating gate. All memory cells must be programmed sequentially. EPROMs can be erased by exposing the entire chip to a high-intensity ultraviolet light source for a duration of approximately 30 minutes. This neutralizes the stored charge on the floating silicon gates of all the cells. The simplicity in erasing the total memory easily permits program modifications.

PROBLEMS

1. Define SSI, MSI, LSI, and VLSI.
2. *a.* What are the present methods of making very narrow line widths?
   b. What is the overall effect of reducing line widths?
3. Describe the important features of the following technologies:

   · NMOS
   · CMOS
   · TTL
   · ECL
   · I²L

4. Explain the difference between CMOS and CMOS/SOS.

5. Name three technologies in:
   a. The MOS family
   b. The bipolar family
6. Describe the major differences between dynamic and static RAMs.
7. Describe the function of:
   a. The Read/Write signal
   b. Chip Enables
   c. Address lines
8. What are the functions of the five areas of a static RAM?
9. What is meant by $\overline{CAS}$ and $\overline{RAS}$?
10. What are the major features of ROMs, PROMs, and EPROMs?
11. A dynamic RAM is designed with a 256-cycle, 4-ms refresh requirement. If the Write cycle time of the memory is 400 ns, determine the percent of the time that the memory is in a refresh state.

REFERENCES

1. Coker, Derrell: "16K—The New-Generation Dynamic RAM," Mostek, *Memory Book and Designers Guide,* Technical Brief.
2. Hnatek, Eugene R.: *A User's Handbook of Semiconductor Memories,* John Wiley and Sons, Inc., New York, 1977.
3. Johnston: "The 64K RAM: Which Way to Refresh?" *Electronics,* vol. 52, no. 1, January 4, 1979, p. 145.
4. Khambata, A. J.: *Introduction to Large Scale Integration,* John Wiley and Sons, Inc., New York, 1969.
5. Millman, J. M., and C. C. Halkias: *Integrated Electronics,* McGraw-Hill Book Company, New York, 1972.
6. Monrad-Krohn, L.: "The Micro and the Minicomputer," *Mini-Micro Systems,* vol. 10, February 1977, p. 28.
7. Sippl, Kidd: *Microcomputer Dictionary and Guide,* Matrix Publishers, Champagne, Ill., 1976.

Programming
Fundamentals

The availability of low-cost microcomputing systems has resulted in a merger between the hardware and software disciplines. Previously these areas (see Fig. 5-1) were well defined: the programmers wrote the software programs and the hardware engineers specified, tested, and integrated the components. Part of the reason for this structure was the low level of integration that was available. With today's technological advances, it is practical, because of much large-scale integration on the chip, to give both responsibilities to individuals who can handle the hardware and software problems alike. Microprocessors have thus created a challenging problem to hardware-oriented personnel, who must now learn software, and to the software people, who invariably become involved with hardware problems. It is the former whom we address in this chapter, because they generally have some familiarity with the hardware and only a limited knowledge of programming. Chapter 5 will concentrate on the structure of instructions and their addressing modes. A microprocessing feature, the stack, which has evolved from advances in LSI technology and is used as a form of storage, will also be discussed.

5-1 DEFINING THE INSTRUCTION SET

Instructions are program commands written to enable the hardware to function in a microcomputing environment. Without an intimate knowledge of the instruction set of a microprocessor, it is extremely doubtful that one

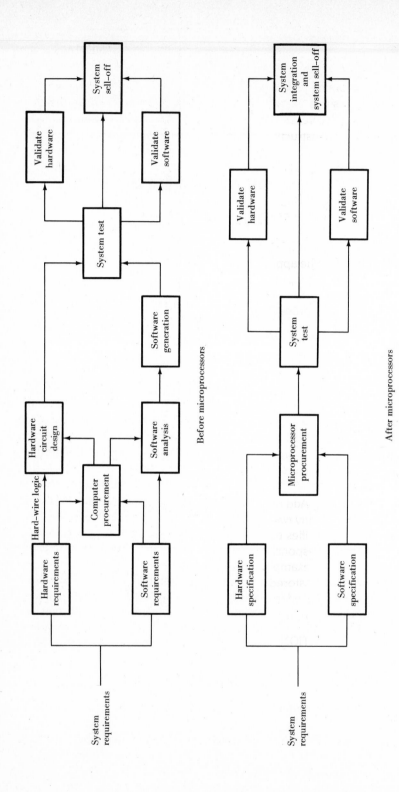

Figure 5-1 Implications of task reductions by use of microprocessors.

can develop a working program without painfully revising the program over and over again, since certain instructions may not function as the user expects. It is for this reason that microprocessing manuals have detailed descriptions of each instruction, which should be thoroughly understood by someone attempting to write any programs. There are many different types of instructions, ranging from simple instructions that perform only a single operation to advanced instructions that perform multiple operations, such as Branch and Decrement Register (see Fig. 5-2). The total number of instructions found in microprocessors varies, most systems having at least 50 instructions in their repertoire. Not all microprocessors utilize the same set of instructions, resulting in many different instruction formats among microprocessing units. The approach of this chapter is to present a generic set of 30 basic instructions representative of the most popular microprocessors and to define their operations and their effects on the various functional elements of the microprocessor.

Operands and Instructions

Instructions are generally executed on data or operands, which are stored either in memory or in registers internal to the microprocessor. Operations such as EXCLUSIVE OR and Subtract must be fully described by specifying not only the command or instruction but also the operand. Expressed colloquially, the instruction must show "who does what to whom." That is, based on microprocessor architecture, the registers and memory locations involved in storing the operand have to be specified. Assignment of registers as related to Instruction register decoding was covered in Chap. 3.

If, for example, a microprocessor has four accessible registers and it is possible to perform an Add operation not only between the accumulator and memory but between any two registers, then the person writing the software program not only specifies the operation but also selects the registers to be used. It is the user's responsibility to keep track of where the operands are stored. The following example demonstrates operand movement.

A data word initially stored in memory is added to the accumulator, and the sum is then transferred to register 3. A two-step instruction program can implement this function as follows:

STEP	INSTRUCTION	COMMENT
1	Add M to accumulator	The instruction takes the operand (data) stored in memory and adds it to a quantity that is stored in the accumulator.
2	Move A to register 3	The instruction transfers the result of the sum which had been in the accumulator to register 3.

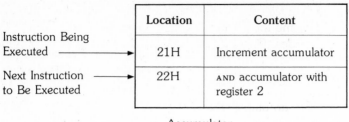

Instruction Memory

Location	Content
21H	Increment accumulator
22H	AND accumulator with register 2

Instruction Being Executed → 21H

Next Instruction to Be Executed → 22H

Accumulator

34H		35H

Before Instruction   **After Instruction**

(*a*)

Instruction Memory

Location	Content
53H	Branch and decrement register 2
54H	Compare accumulator with register 2
74H	Load register 1 with 15H

Instruction Being Executed → 53H

Next Instruction to Be Executed → 74H

Register 2

3H		2H

Before Instruction   **After Instruction**

(*b*)

Figure 5-2 Comparison of single and multiple-action instructions. (*a*) Increment Accumulator instruction; (*b*) Branch and Decrement instruction. (Note: This instruction is not part of the generic instruction set, but it is typically found in 16-bit microprocessors.)

Addressing Modes

There are many different ways of specifying an instruction and the data or operand that it must process. Since the data may be stored in memory, in the

I/O, or in other registers outside of those which will operate on the data, the data must first be retrieved. Most instructions contain several alternative approaches which define the retrieval method of the operand; these are called *addressing modes*. One of the simplest addressing modes is the inherent, or register, mode, whose operation is between the internal registers of the microprocessor. A Subtract Register 2 from Register 1 is an example. The inherent mode requires no retrieval of operands from memory. Addressing modes which do utilize the memory are the direct, indirect, and indexed modes. These are but a few of the many other modes that exist, all of which will be covered thoroughly later in this chapter. The material which follows will not initially stress addressing modes, but rather will concentrate on developing an understanding of what instructions are and how they function.

5-2 THE GENERIC INSTRUCTION SET

Instruction sets, no matter how large, can be partitioned into groups of functionally similar instructions. Table 5-1 shows six different categories of instructions, with several instructions within each category. For example, an

TABLE 5-1   Generic Instructions Partitioned into Functional Groups

ARITHMETIC (9)		TRANSFER, CONTROL, AND SKIP (6)	
Add	Increment	Jump	Conditional Call
Subtract	Decrement	Conditional Branch	Return
Multiply	Rotate Right	Call	Conditional Return
Complement	Rotate Left		
Compare			

LOGIC (3)	INPUT-OUTPUT (2)	
AND	Input	
OR	Output	
EXCLUSIVE OR		

DATA TRANSFER (4)		INTERRUPT AND MISCELLANEOUS (6)	
Load	Move	Enable Interrupt	Pop
Store	Exchange	Disable Interrupt	Halt
		Push	No Operation (NOP)

instruction called Add to Memory can be put into the same functional group as Multiply Accumulator Register by Memory. Operationally, the Add and Multiply instructions are quite different, but because of common *arithmetic* command structure and elements, the instructions are similarly categorized. The EXCLUSIVE OR instruction and the AND instruction are operations which fit into the *logic* class of instructions. Other functional categories include *data transfer instructions,* which move data between memory, accumulator, and registers. The *transfer, control,* and *skip* instructions alter the sequential flow of the program. A Skip or Jump instruction is also commonly referred to as a Branch, and it can be either unconditional or conditional, depending on the results of a previous operation. I/O instructions are a fairly well-isolated group of instructions used to transfer data between a specific I/O channel and the microprocessor or memory. In the *interrupt and miscellaneous* category all interrupt-related instructions, such as Enable Interrupt, and the Push and Pop instructions are included. Throughout the chapter each of the 30 listed instructions will be explained in detail. These instructions are only a sample of the overall microprocessing instructions found in most systems.

5-3 INTERPRETING THE INSTRUCTION

There are two symbols, the parentheses ( ) and the arrow →, which are commonly used as shorthand notations in describing the instruction set. The instruction itself describes the operation of the microprocessor, while the symbols provide information about the instruction. The arrow → is used to specify the direction of the instruction to be executed. If the accumulator is to be reset or cleared to 0, the instruction Clear A will be specified with a notation next to it of $0 \rightarrow A$ to indicate that the value 0 goes into the accumulator. Parentheses are used to denote "the contents of," so that (register 3) signifies "the contents of register 3" and (loc 20) represents the data stored at memory location 20. Both symbols are typically combined in specifying many instructions. A simple data-transfer instruction that moves the contents of register 1 to register 2 can be described as

$$\text{Move} \quad (R1) \longrightarrow (R2)$$

A double set of parentheses is commonly used to signify the address of the memory location involved in the operation. As an example, a Store instruction which transfers information from the accumulator to memory is represented as

$$\text{Store} \quad (A) \longrightarrow ((\text{Byte 2})(\text{Byte 3}))$$

The instruction is interpreted as follows: The contents of the accumulator are moved to the memory location whose address is specified in bytes 2 and 3 of the instruction. This operation is illustrated in Fig. 5-3, where the

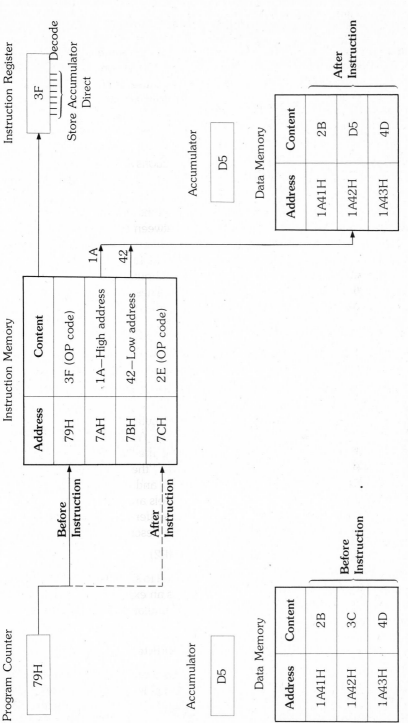

Figure 5-3 Example of a Store Accumulator Direct instruction.

instruction and the address of where the data is to be stored are contained in the instruction memory. Assume the Store instruction is in location 79H while the address of where the data is to be stored (the operand address) is at locations 7AH and 7BH. Before the instruction is executed the program counter has a value of 79H. This represents the location of the first byte of the instruction, or the storage of the OP code.

Every instruction has an address mode associated with it; in this case the direct mode is used. Addressing modes will be discussed in Sec. 5-6. The execution of the instruction consists of:

1. Addressing the instruction memory with the contents of the program counter

2. Reading out the three bytes of the instruction, that is, the OP code and operand address, onto the data bus

3. Decoding the OP code at the instruction decoder

4. Addressing the data memory with the operand address

5. Transmitting the contents of the accumulator through the data bus for storage in the data memory

6. Incrementing the program counter during the instruction, which results in an updated value of 7CH, which signifies the next instruction to be performed

Sequencing

All instructions are normally stored and executed sequentially. The number of bytes per instruction can vary from 1 to 3, depending on the type of instruction and the location of the operand. The first byte always contains a description of the operation, while the second and sometimes third bytes contain data related to the instruction or operand address information. A program may contain instructions of various byte sizes; such a program is shown in Fig. 5-4. The program counter has been incremented so that it will point to the first instruction of this program, which resides at location 81H. The program counter will be incremented one count at a time during the processing of each byte and will always be pointing to the next sequential byte to be executed. After the three-instruction program is executed, the program counter will read 87H.

Transfer instructions are the most notable instructions that allow the sequential flow of instruction commands to be "skipped." There are two basic forms of transfer instructions, conditional and unconditional instructions. When an unconditional instruction such as a Jump is reached, the program counter will change out of sequence to a value specified by the transfer instruction. A more "cautious" type of instruction is the Conditional Branch instruction, which permits the program counter to be changed out of

One-Word Instruction

1A (Add Register instruction)

"Add contents of register 2 to register 3"

Two-Word Instruction

2E (Load instruction)
18H

"Load accumulator with the value 18H"

Three-Word Instruction

3F (Store instruction)
High address = 02H
Low address = 00H

"Store accumulator at memory location 0200H"
$0200H = (512)_{10}$

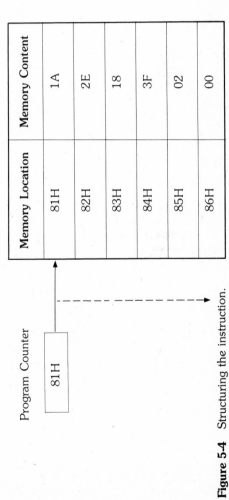

Instruction Memory

Memory Location	Memory Content
81H	1A
82H	2E
83H	18
84H	3F
85H	02
86H	00

Program Counter

81H

Figure 5-4 Structuring the instruction.

sequence only when a condition is met and a bit in the status register is set. If the condition is not met and the status register bit is reset, the program then continues in sequence. A variation of this instruction is to permit a Branch if the specified condition is *not* met and to continue sequentially if the specified condition has been met. In the example shown in Fig. 5-5, after executing Instruction 3 there are two alternatives for the program to follow:

1. If the accumulator is positive, not meeting the condition established, the program will execute the instruction at 6H.

2. If the accumulator is negative, the program will jump to the instruction at 0AH.

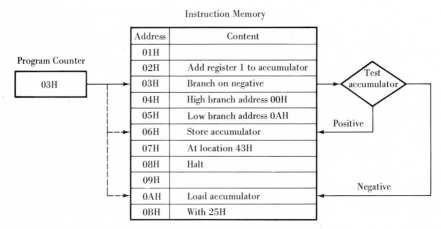

Figure 5-5 Utilization of the Conditional Branch instruction.

5-4 DETAILED DESCRIPTION OF THE GENERIC INSTRUCTION SET

A generic instruction set is described in this section by diagrammatically representing the function in terms of the major elements affected during program execution. A small group of instructions related to stack processing will not be covered in this section; however, they will be discussed after the concept is introduced in Sec. 5-7.

The complete generic set with its related addressing modes is shown in Tables 5-2 and 5-3. The first column of Table 5-2 is the *mnemonic,* or abbreviated code, for the listed operation. As an example, LD represents Load and XCH is the mnemonic for the Exchange instruction. The mnemonics assigned to the instructions are unique to the generic instruction set of this book. Most popular microprocessors have mnemonics which are

TABLE 5-2 Generic Instruction Set with Assigned Address Modes and Mnemonics

OPERATION	MNEMONIC	IMPLIED OR INHERENT	IMMEDIATE	DIRECT	EXTENDED	INDIRECT REGISTER	INDIRECT MEMORY	PROGRAM RELATIVE	PROGRAM BASE	INDEX
Add	ADD	1A	2C	3A	4A	5A	6A	7A	8A	9A
Subtract	SUB	1B	2B	3B	4B	5B	6B	7B	8B	9B
Multiply	MPY	1C		3C	4C					9C
Complement	CM	11			4D			7D	8D	9D
Compare	CMP		2D	31	41	5C	6C	7C	8C	99
Increment	INC	12			42	5D	6D			92
Decrement	DEC	13			43	5E	63			93
Rotate Right	RR	14		34	44					94
Rotate Left	RL	15		35	45					95
AND	AND	16	22	36	46	5F				96
OR	OR	17	21	37	47	50		70	80	97
EXCLUSIVE OR	XR			38	48	51				98
Load	LD		2E	3E	4E	52	6E	7E	8E	9E
Store	ST			3F	4F	59	64	7F	8F	9F
Move	MOV	1E	81			58	68			90
Exchange	XCH	18				53				91
Jump	JMP		2F							
Conditional Branch	*									
Call	CALL					54	6F			
Conditional Call	*									
Return	RET					55	60			
Conditional Return	*									
Input	IN			32	40					
Output	OUT			33	30					
Push	PUSH	19				56	61			
Pop	POP	1D				57	62			

*Assignments listed in Table 5-4.

TABLE 5-3   Miscellaneous Instructions

OPERATION	MNEMONIC	ASSIGNMENT
Input	IN	*
Output	OUT	*
Enable Interrupt	ENI	1F
Disable Interrupt	DII	1D
Halt	HLT	10
No Operation	NOP	00

*Assignments listed in Table 5-2.

similar, but there is a strong possibility that between leading competitors, in particular those units which are not software-compatible, the same functional instruction may not have identical mnemonics.

There are many options in describing instructions, since there are many resources such as memory, accumulators, and registers to implement them. An Add instruction, for example, can be performed between:

1. Registers within the microprocessor
2. Memory and a register
3. Accumulator and memory

In describing the instructions, only one method was selected, in most cases a typical form of the instruction. Although all instructions contain addressing modes, for learning purposes the retrieval of the operand can be separated from the internal actions of the processing unit. In a later section of this chapter, the various addressing modes for all instructions will be given. Note also that, unless otherwise stated, the values contained within registers, accumulator, and memory are operands and not the assigned OP code of the instruction.

When the XX notation is found in the accumulators, registers, or I/O ports of the following instructions, it signifies that the contents of these units before the execution of the instruction have no significance ("don't care").

Arithmetic Instructions

Add (ADD)

The memory operand is added to the contents of the accumulator. The sum is retained in the accumulator. The memory retains the original operand.

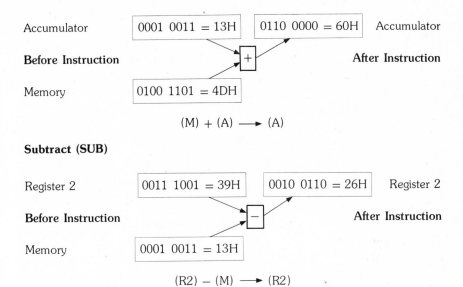

Accumulator   0001 0011 = 13H   0110 0000 = 60H   Accumulator

Before Instruction   +   After Instruction

Memory   0100 1101 = 4DH

$$(M) + (A) \longrightarrow (A)$$

Subtract (SUB)

Register 2   0011 1001 = 39H   0010 0110 = 26H   Register 2

Before Instruction   −   After Instruction

Memory   0001 0011 = 13H

$$(R2) - (M) \longrightarrow (R2)$$

The memory operand is subtracted from the contents of register 2. The difference is retained in register 2. The memory retains the original operand.

Multiply (MPY)

Accumulator   0001 0001 = 11H   0101 0101 = 55H   Accumulator

Before Instruction   •   After Instruction

Memory   0000 0101 = 05H

$$(M) \times (A) \longrightarrow (A)$$

The memory operand is multiplied by the contents of the accumulator. The result is retained in the accumulator. The memory retains the original operand.

Complement (CM)

Accumulator   0100 0010 = 42H   1011 1101 = 0BDH   Accumulator

Before Instruction   After Instruction

$$(\overline{A}) \longrightarrow (A)$$

The contents of the accumulator are inverted or 1's-complemented.

Compare (CMP)

Accumulator | 0101 1010 = 5AH   0101 1010 = 5AH | Accumulator

Before Instruction   **After Instruction**

Register 3 | 0101 1011 = 5BH   0101 1011 = 5BH | Register 3

| Carry   0 | Zero   0 | | Carry   1 | Zero   0 |

$$(A) - (R3)$$

If (R3) = (A) then Z = 1; otherwise Z = 0

(R3) > (A) then Cy = 1; otherwise Cy = 0

The contents of the accumulator are compared with the contents of register 3. If the contents of the accumulator are less than those of register 3, then the Carry flag, Cy, is set. If the contents of the accumulator equal those of register 3, the Zero flag is set. If the contents of the accumulator are greater than those of register 3, the flags remain reset. Note that both the accumulator and register 3 are unaffected by the Compare instruction.

Increment (INC)

Register 2 | 1001 0111 = 97H   1001 1000 = 98H | Register 2

Before Instruction   **After Instruction**

$$(R2) + 1 \longrightarrow (R2)$$

The contents of register 2 are incremented by 1. The instruction may also be used to increment the contents of a memory location.

Decrement (DEC)

Register 3 | 0110 1111 = 6FH   0110 1110 = 6EH | Register 3

Before Instruction   **After Instruction**

$$(R3) - 1 \longrightarrow (R3)$$

The contents of register 3 are decremented by 1. The instruction may also be used to decrement the contents of a memory location.

Rotate Right (RR)

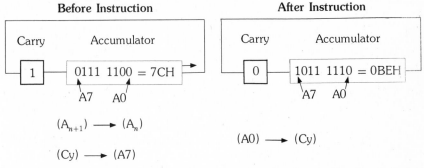

$(A_{n+1}) \longrightarrow (A_n)$

$(Cy) \longrightarrow (A7)$

$(A0) \longrightarrow (Cy)$

The contents of the accumulator are rotated right one bit through the Carry flag. If the accumulator LSB equals 1 before the instruction, then the carry will be 1 after the instruction. The contents of the Carry flag before the instruction are transferred to the MSB of the accumulator after the instruction.

Rotate Left (RL)

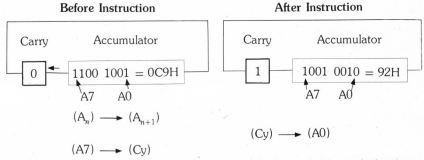

$(A_n) \longrightarrow (A_{n+1})$

$(A7) \longrightarrow (Cy)$

$(Cy) \longrightarrow (A0)$

The contents of the accumulator are rotated left one bit through the Carry flag. If the accumulator MSB equals 1 before the instruction, then the carry will be 1 after the instruction. The contents of the Carry flag before the instruction are transferred to the LSB of the accumulator after the instruction.

Logic Instructions

AND (AND)

The contents of register 2 are logically ANDed with the contents of the accumulator. The result is placed in the accumulator.

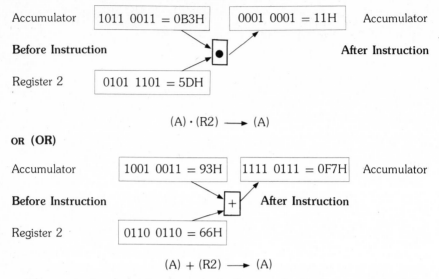

$$(A) \cdot (R2) \longrightarrow (A)$$

OR (OR)

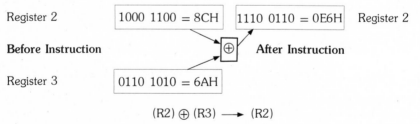

$$(A) + (R2) \longrightarrow (A)$$

The contents of register 2 are logically ANDed with the contents of the accumulator. The result is placed in the accumulator.

EXCLUSIVE OR (XR)

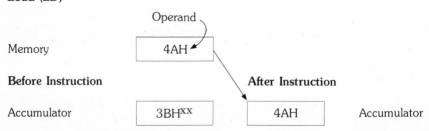

$$(R2) \oplus (R3) \longrightarrow (R2)$$

The contents of register 2 are EXCLUSIVELY ORed with the contents of register 3. The result is placed in register 2.

Data Transfer Instructions

Load (LD)

Operand

Memory   4AH

Before Instruction   **After Instruction**

Accumulator   3BH^{XX} 4AH   Accumulator

The memory operand is loaded into the accumulator. The memory address of the operand is specified by the addressing mode.

Store (ST)

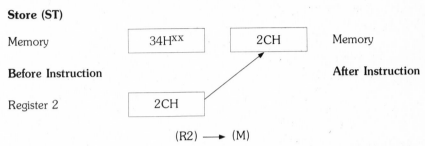

$$(R2) \longrightarrow (M)$$

The contents of register 2 are stored in memory. Register 2 retains its original contents. The memory address where data is stored is specified by the addressing mode.

Move (MOV)

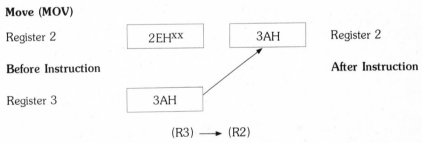

$$(R3) \longrightarrow (R2)$$

The contents of register 3 are moved to register 2. Register 3 retains its original data.

Exchange (XCH)

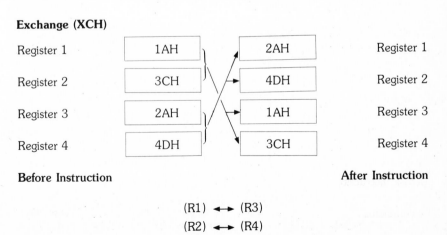

$$(R1) \longleftrightarrow (R3)$$
$$(R2) \longleftrightarrow (R4)$$

The contents of registers 1 and 2 are exchanged with the contents of registers 3 and 4, respectively.

Transfer, Control, and Skip Instructions

Jump (JMP)

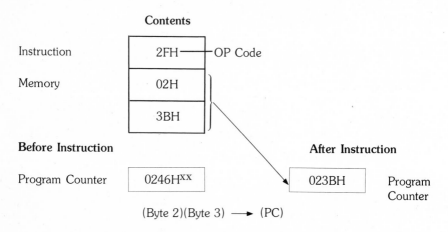

An unconditional Branch instruction. Bytes 2 and 3 determine the contents of the program counter.

Conditional Branch

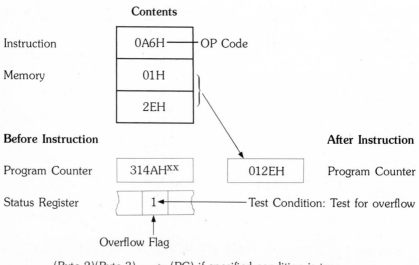

Conditional Branch is a group of control instructions. The sequence branches to bytes 2 and 3 of the instruction when the results by a previous instruction indicate that a specific test condition is true. When the test condition is not true, the program continues sequentially. The test condition can be a condition that was met, such as Branch When There Is Carry, or a condition that was not met, such as Branch When There Is No Carry. Table 5-4 lists all the Conditional Branch instructions with their mnemonics and assignments. The tests on all indicated conditions are performed as a result of having the branch instructions examine the status flags.

TABLE 5-4   Conditional Branch Instructions

	MNEMONIC			ASSIGNMENT		
OPERATION*	COND. BRCH	COND. CALL	COND. RET	COND. BRCH	COND. CALL	COND. RET
Branch on Results Zero	BRZ	CRZ	RRZ	0A1	0B1	0C1
Branch on Results Negative	BRN	CRN	RRN	0A2	0B2	0C2
Branch on Results Not Zero	BRNZ	CRNZ	RRNZ	0A3	0B3	0C3
Branch on Results Positive	BRP	CRP	RRP	0A4	0B4	0C4
Branch on No Overflow	BNO	CNO	RNO	0A5	0B5	0C5
Branch on Overflow	BO	CO	RO	0A6	0B6	0C6
Branch When There Is No Carry	BNC	CNC	RNC	0A7	0B7	0C7
Branch When There Is Carry	BC	CC	RC	0A8	0B8	0C8
Branch on Odd Parity	BPO	CPO	RPO	0A9	0B9	0C9
Branch on Even Parity	BPE	CPE	RPE	0AA	0BA	0CA

*Operation will take place based on result of the flag (Condition Code register bit) associated with each Branch instruction.

Miscellaneous Instructions

Input (IN)

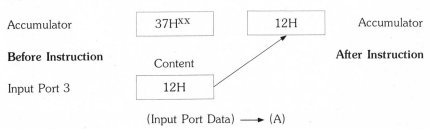

Accumulator	37H^{XX}	12H	Accumulator
Before Instruction	Content		**After Instruction**
Input Port 3	12H		

(Input Port Data) ⟶ (A)

The data placed on the data bus by the port, specified by the second byte of the instruction, is moved to the accumulator.

Output (OUT)

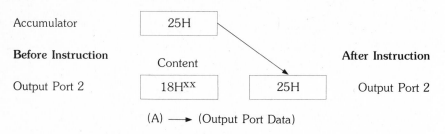

Accumulator | 25H

Before Instruction | Content | After Instruction

Output Port 2 | 18H^{xx} | 25H | Output Port 2

(A) ⟶ (Output Port Data)

The contents of the accumulator are placed on the data bus for transmission to the port, specified by the second byte of the instruction.

Halt (HLT)

Program Counter | 0245H | 0246H | Program Counter

Before Instruction | | After Instruction

(PC + 1) ⟶ (PC)

The Halt instruction causes the program counter to increment, as does any instruction; however, all processing is stopped so that the next instruction will not be fetched. The microprocessor can exit from a Halt state by
• Activating the reset input line, which forces the program counter to a known value as determined by the microprocessor manufacturer
• An interrupt, which forces the program counter to a known value determined by the microprocessing interrupt structure

No Operation (NOP)

Program Counter | 2221H | 2222H | Program Counter

Before Instruction | | After Instruction

(PC + 1) ⟶ (PC)

The NOP instruction causes no change in the microprocessor except the normal increment of the program counter.

The NOP instruction is commonly used during program development. Typically groups of NOP instructions are scattered throughout a program that is likely to change. The NOP instructions provide memory spaces in which the user can enter instructions which were overlooked. This prevents the complete program from having to be rewritten.

Enable Interrupt (ENI)

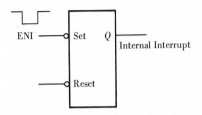

$$(PC + 1) \longrightarrow (PC)$$
$$1 \longrightarrow \text{Set the Internal Interrupt Flip-Flop}$$

The interrupt system is enabled following the execution of the next instruction. Enabling the interrupt system is delayed one instruction to allow interrupt subroutines to return to the main program before a subsequent interrupt is acknowledged.

Disable Interrupt (DII)

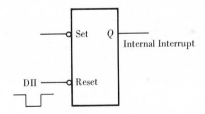

$$(PC + 1) \longrightarrow PC$$
$$0 \longrightarrow \text{RESET the Internal Interrupt Flip-Flop}$$

The interrupt system is disabled following the execution of this instruction. The status of the internal interrupt flip-flop is available via an Interrupt Enable control line.

5-5 STATUS FLAGS

The execution of some of the instructions listed in the previous section set one or more Status flags to logic 1. The following criteria for setting a flag are given for the respective bits of the generic status register shown in Fig. 3-8.

Carry A Carry flag is set if the result of an Add operation produces a carry from the most significant bit. The Subtract and Multiply instructions can also set the carry bit as a result of the operation.

Interrupt An Interrupt flag is set when the microprocessor recognizes an interrupt.

Overflow An Overflow flag is used when performing signed arithmetic operations to designate that the result of the operation has a greater value than the number contained in the 7 bits and has overflowed into the sign position. Figure 3-5 established some conditions for overflow. Some microprocessors, such as the 8080, do not contain an Overflow bit flag.

Zero The Zero flag is set when the result of the instruction has a value of 0.

Negative This flag is set when the most significant bit of the result of the operation has a value of 1.

Decimal Mode The Decimal Mode flag is set to 1 when decimal addition is performed. Each 8-bit word used in the operation contains two 4-bit BCD numbers, which are added to two other numbers.

Parity The Parity flag is set to generate an odd parity. Thus if the sum of the bits is 0, the Parity flag is set to 1.

Table 5-5 represents generic instructions which can affect the listed flags. When an operation results in a flag setting, the next instruction which also affects a flag will result in one of the following two conditions:

1. The flag will reset or clear when the operation does not cause the flag to set. For example, the execution of an instruction such as Subtract will cause the zero flag to reset should the operation not result in setting the flag.

2. The flag will remain set if an operation which can cause the flag to set does so.

TABLE 5-5   Generic Instructions Affected by Flags

INSTRUCTION	SET FLAG						RESET FLAG	
	CARRY	ZERO	OVER-FLOW	NEGA-TIVE	DECIMAL	PARITY	CARRY	OVER-FLOW
Add	X	X	X	X	X	X		
Subtract	X	X	X	X	X	X		
Multiply	X	X	X	X		X		
Compare	X		X	X		X		
Increment			X	X		X		
Decrement			X	X		X		
Rotate right	X		X	X				
Rotate left	X		X	X				
AND			X	X		X	X	X
OR			X	X		X	X	X
EXCLUSIVE OR			X	X		X	X	X

5-6 ADDRESSING MODES

Implications of Addressing Modes

In this section we will concern ourselves with the retrieval approach of the operand or data rather than with the internal movement of data and execution. Thoroughly understanding the instruction format enables the user to determine how and where the operand can be stored and retrieved.

With the exception of the inherent, or register mode, which is a 1-byte instruction, the first byte of the instruction contains the classification of the instruction, or the OP code. With 8 bits, 2^8, or 256, different combinations can be specified. This large number provides sufficient unique combinations not only for different instructions but also for the address mode designation for each individual instruction. Thus 3BH may represent a Subtract instruction in the direct mode while 6BH corresponds to the same instruction in the indirect mode (see Fig. 5-6).

The second byte of the instruction may contain data or address information which defines where the data is located (operand address). It is sometimes convenient and practical to store the data in the memory location adjacent to the instruction. The mode called the immediate mode operates in

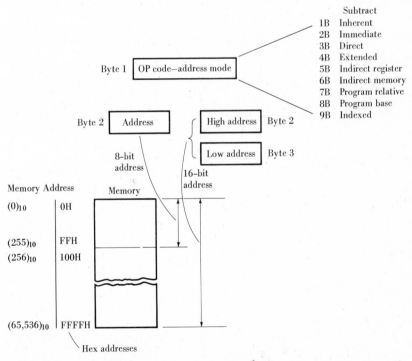

Figure 5-6 Memory address allocation and address mode structure.

this manner and will be described in the next section. When the second byte contains address information, then 2^8 combinations represent address locations available for the user to store the operand.

To expand beyond this range for larger program utilization, a third byte can be added to the instruction word, thus resulting in a total of 2^{16} bits, or 64K words which can be designated. However, the fewer the bytes used for addressing, the more efficient the program structure becomes, since fewer bytes require less memory space and shorter execution times. Thus 2-byte instructions are preferable to 3-byte instructions, and 1-byte instructions are preferable to 2-byte instructions. It should be noted that although it would be advantageous to use 1-byte instructions whenever possible, it is not always feasible, since these instructions have limited capability and address range. One-byte instructions provide for simple operations within the internal structure of the microprocessor.

The final memory address which is used to retrieve the operand is called the effective address. The effective address may be formed in several ways, depending upon the address mode selected. The effective address can be developed from the instruction word, from the contents of a register, from the contents of memory, or from combinations thereof. The following section presents the most widely used address mode techniques for 8-bit microprocessors and illustrates different techniques in generating the effective address.

Immediate Addressing

An immediate address mode is a 2- or 3-byte instruction in which the first byte is the OP code and the remaining bytes represent data or the operand. A typical operation for an immediate address mode entails the presetting or the initialization of a particular register where the second byte of the instruction is the value of data which the user desires the register to contain. In some microprocessors where the registers can operate in pairs as well as individually, a 3-byte instruction format is used. The second and third byte contain data for the register pair.

In Fig. 5-7, the Load Accumulator instruction is used in the immediate mode. The accumulator contains a value of 55H from a previous operation. It is desired to load the accumulator with a value of 5. The instruction Load Accumulator Immediate is fetched and decoded by the instruction register. The program counter, which has contained a value of 85H, advances and points to memory location 86H. Data from this location will be loaded in the accumulator, completing the instruction, and the program counter will then be incremented to 87H.

An advantage of utilizing immediate addressing on a register or memory location is that it requires less processing time, since it alleviates the necessity of retrieving the operand beyond the second byte.

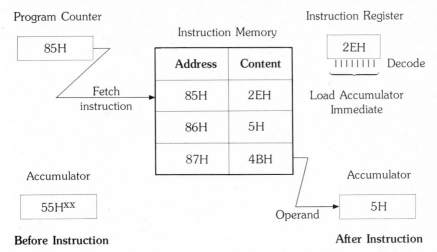

Figure 5-7 Immediate address mode—Load Accumulator instruction.

The Implied Address Mode

The implied address mode, sometimes called the inherent, or register, address mode, is a single-byte instruction. Contained within the 1-byte format is information which specifies the instruction type and the source and destination of the data. One-byte instructions provide fast execution, since memory access is not required. Their limited range decrees that the operands be available at the register level for the operation to take place. An example of the Implied address mode is shown in Fig. 5-8. Data from register 3 is to be added to register 2, with the result remaining in register 2. The instruction register decodes the source and destination registers and the type of operation to be performed.

Direct and Extended Address Modes

Direct and extended address mode instructions are used to determine the effective address of the operand in one of the simplest address modes available. If the instruction contains 2 bytes, the first byte is the OP code and the second byte contains the effective address of the operand. There is little difference between the direct and the extended address mode instructions in microprocessors that contain both modes. Direct address mode instructions utilize 2 bytes, while extended address mode instructions utilize 3 bytes.

A direct address mode instruction utilizes the second byte in making available the first 256 locations in memory where the operand can be stored. When a greater range is required, the extended address mode is used. An example of a direct address mode operation is shown in Fig. 5-9. To load the accumulator with the contents of memory location 8FH, a 2-byte instruction

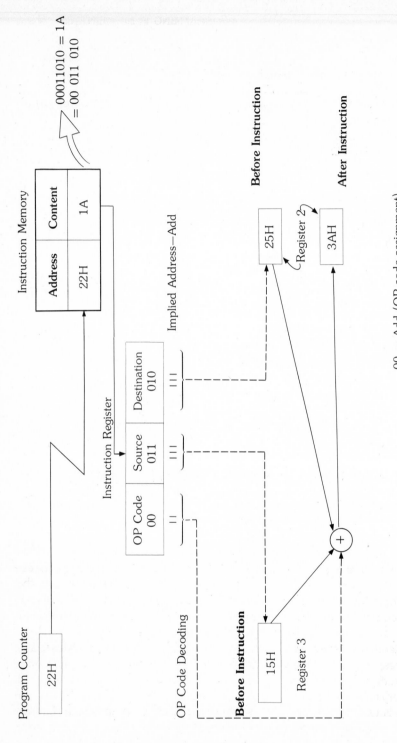

Figure 5-8 Implied address mode—Add instruction.

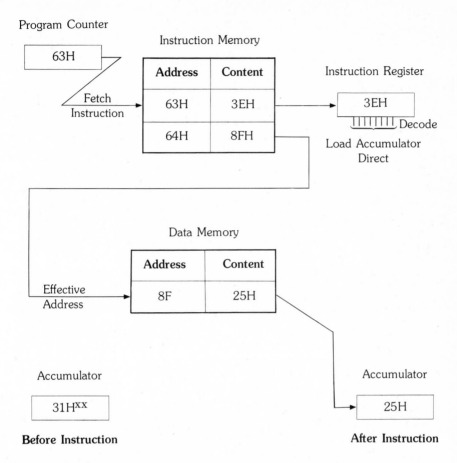

Figure 5-9 Direct address mode—Load Accumulator instruction.

is used. The first byte, residing at memory location 63H, contains the value 3EH, which when decoded represents the Load Accumulator direct address mode instruction. The second byte at memory location 64H, contains the value 8FH, which is the effective address of the operand in the data memory. The retrieval of data for this location allows the accumulator to be loaded with a new value, in this case number 25H.

Extended address mode instructions are 3-byte instructions. Bytes 2 and 3 correspond to the higher and lower effective address. In some microprocessors, these bytes are reversed. The 16-bit address enables 64K locations of memory to be accessible to the mode. Whenever possible, the direct address mode is used rather than the extended, since less memory space requires

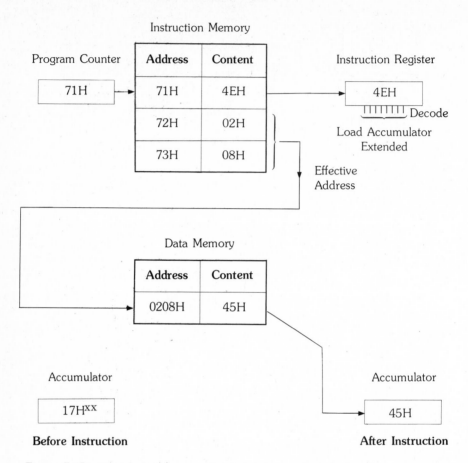

Figure 5-10 Extended address mode—Load Accumulator instruction.

less processing time. An example of an extended address mode instruction is shown in Fig. 5-10.

Indirect Addressing

Indirect addressing differs from direct addressing in several ways. In direct addressing the effective address was derived directly from the second byte of the instruction. In indirect addressing the instruction points to a memory location or a register that contains the effective address that is specified by the instruction. When the pointer is a register, the technique is called *register indirect addressing* (see Fig. 5-11).

In Fig. 5-12 the pointer is a memory location, and thus the technique is called *memory indirect addressing*. The contents of memory location 42H are used to point to the data memory where the effective address is stored.

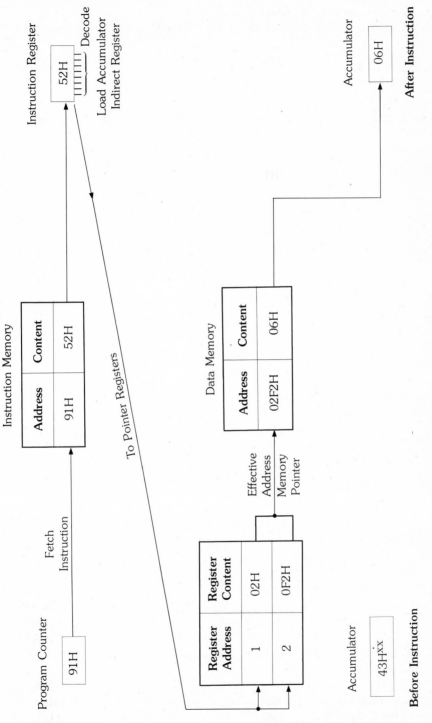

Figure 5-11 Indirect register address mode—Load Accumulator instruction.

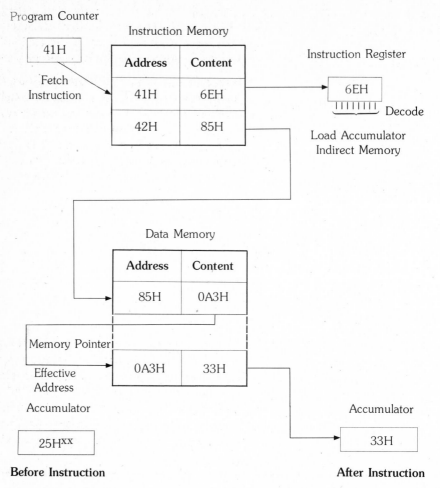

Figure 5-12 Indirect memory address mode—Load Accumulator instruction.

The contents of the effective address in data memory are used to perform the operation.

Register indirect addressing is more commonly employed, since it is faster to execute and requires fewer memory cycles than memory indirect addressing. When full addressing capability is required, the contents of a register pair instead of a single register are used as effective address designators.

The advantage of indirect addressing is that the operand may be relocated without extensive programming changes, since only changes to the pointer are necessary.

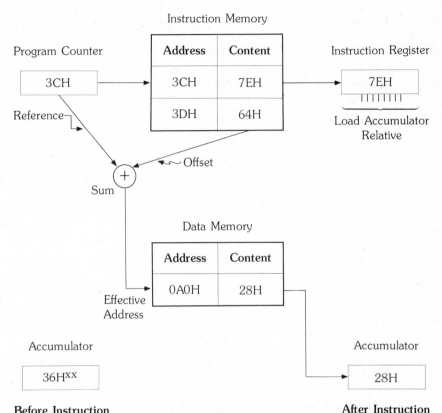

Figure 5-13 Program relative address mode—Load Accumulator instruction.

Relative Addressing

The use of the Relative address mode requires that a calculation be performed to derive the effective address of the operand. There are three addressing techniques that utilize relative addressing:

1. Program relative
2. Base relative
3. Index addressing

All three modes have the same objective: to keep the instruction address short and to relocate programs or modify them as simply as possible. Program relative addressing utilizes the program counter as a reference and the contents of the second byte of the instruction as an offset. These two values are added together to develop the effective address. An example of this mode is shown in Fig. 5-13. The mode can be used to move instruction programs into unoccupied areas of memory. The offset is expressed in 2's complement so that memory storage in either direction of the program counter can be accessed.

Base relative addressing may utilize either a memory location or a register called a *base* as the reference. Its operation is similar to program relative addressing in that the offset is added to the reference to arrive at the effective address. The base relative address mode provides more flexibility in instruction execution than the program relative address mode, since the base register can be set to any number. An example of the base relative instruction is shown in Fig. 5-14.

Index addressing is one of the most important addressing modes found in microprocessors. It utilizes one or more registers, called *index registers,* in its execution of instructions. Generally the more index registers available to the programmer, the greater the flexibility and manipulation available in developing the software programs. There are a variety of instructions which can

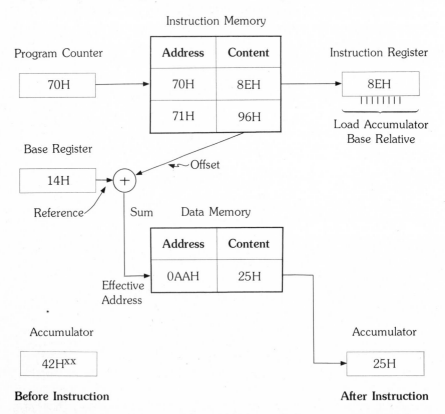

Figure 5-14 Base relative address mode—Load Accumulator instruction.

store, modify, or test the contents of the Index register, making it a powerful architectural feature in microprocessors.

The formation of the indexing instruction is shown in Fig. 5-15, where the effective address is a result of adding the index register to the address field of the instruction, byte 2. Notice the similarity between its implementation and that of the base relative address mode of Fig. 5-14. In the index address mode, the index register can be made to increment and decrement and generate the new effective address. In the base relative mode, the base register, which is the reference, is held constant and the offset is changed, producing the new effective address.

There are many uses for the index address mode. For example, the mode can be used when the same series of calculations, implemented by a program, is to be made on a group of operands. The program can be structured so that the first of the group of operands is used in sequencing through the program. To perform the same computations on the next operand, the index register merely needs to be incremented one count to allow the next operand, which has been stored in the next sequential data memory position, to

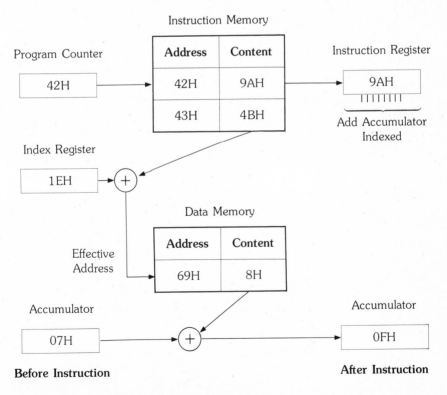

Figure 5-15   Index address mode—Add instruction.

be used. An important feature of the indexing mode is its ability to increment or decrement the index register in a manner similar to a programmable counter, thus permitting the index addressing mode to be used in controlling the number of times that a sequence of operations can take place.

5-7   STACKS

Some of the remaining instructions involve the use of the *stack* element. It is therefore appropriate to discuss stacks before describing these instructions.

A stack is a group of storage devices used to temporarily store data. The stack can be implemented in several ways. In some microprocessors, it is a series of hardware storage registers with data movement similar to a shift register. Other microprocessors reserve a portion of their read/write storage area as the "stack area." Both forms have become quite popular in recent years; however, it is the characteristics of the latter approach which will be described.

There are several uses for stacks in microprocessing systems; one of the most common is to store the return address for *subroutines.* Subroutines are specialized programs stored once but used many times throughout the instruction sequence. Typical subroutines are programs which have been developed for a special purpose, such as evaluating the sine or cosine of a number (trigonometric functions) or the square root of another number. When a subroutine is used, the program will branch to where the subroutine is stored. To get back to the branch point, the stack will store the return address.

The stack is also used to hold temporary data from registers during interrupt processing. When an interrupt occurs, the program will branch to service it. The status of the registers, however, must be saved so that the program can return to this point upon completing the interrupt. The stack will temporarily store the contents of the program counter, accumulator, index register, status register, and other pertinent data needed to resume its operation.

The stack keeps track of information somewhat differently from a conventional random-access memory. Associated with the stack is a counter-register called the *stack pointer,* whose function is quite similar to that of the program counter. The program counter will point to or show the next sequential instruction to be executed. The stack pointer will point to the last location that has been written into; that is, the stack pointer holds the address of the last item inserted into the stack. In some microprocessors, the stack pointer will point to the next available location where data can be written into. We are interested here only in the pointer's ability to show the location of our last entry.

The number of words that can be inserted into the stack in a single operation is highly dependent on the specific microprocessor used. In one microprocessing system, 2 words at a time, corresponding to a register pair or two 8-bit registers concatenated into a 16-bit register, are written into or read from the stack. The description which follows assumes that in a single operation only 1 word can be transferred from or to the stack.

An example of stack movement is shown in Fig. 5-16, where 3 words are already stored in a stack and 5 more words are to be stored. The stack

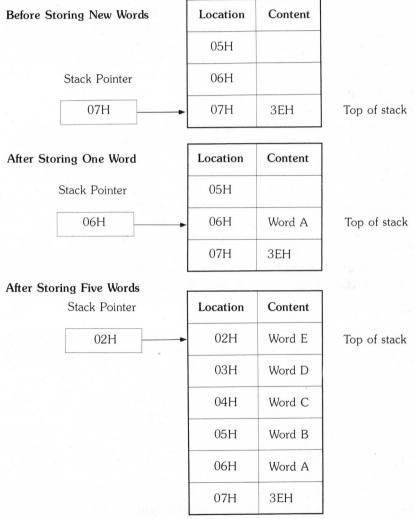

Before Storing New Words

Location	Content
05H	
06H	
07H	3EH

Stack Pointer: 07H → 07H Top of stack

After Storing One Word

Location	Content
05H	
06H	Word A
07H	3EH

Stack Pointer: 06H → 06H Top of stack

After Storing Five Words

Stack Pointer: 02H →

Location	Content
02H	Word E
03H	Word D
04H	Word C
05H	Word B
06H	Word A
07H	3EH

02H Top of stack

Figure 5-16 Storing data in the stack.

pointer has a value of 7H, which corresponds to the last item in the stack. The storage sequence begins by first decrementing the stack pointer and then storing word A. The stack pointer is decremented again and word B is stored. The same sequence continues until all 5 words are stored and the stack pointer reads 2H. The last word written is located in what is commonly called the *top* of the stack. This writing operation is referred to as "pushing the stack," since word A of new words A to E is initially written at the top of the stack and then appears to be "pushed down" as words B to E are written above word A and the stack pointer continues to be decremented. That is, as a result of the storing of words B to E, word A is no longer at the top of the stack but is ultimately pushed down to the fifth position from the top.

The retrieval of data from the stack requires that the last word entered be the first word read out; thus in order to read out word C, it is first necessary to read out words E and D. This last word in, first word out data structure is commonly referred to as a LIFO (last in, first out). Note that although this organization is sequential, its actual implementation is with read-write main storage, which is random access. The sequential approach to stack architecture provides an orderly method of storing data. The retrieval of data is performed by reading out or accessing from the top of the stack only. This is followed by incrementing the stack pointer. Extracting data (reading) is called "popping the stack," while storing data (writing) is called "pushing the stack" (see Fig. 5-17). It is important to keep track of the number of available data locations in the stack so as to prevent rewriting over previously stored information or causing a stack overflow and a loss of data. A program can be utilized to provide status data on the stack. Note that when the Pop

Push
Writing into the stack: Words 4 to 7 are to be stored

Location	Content
15H	
16H	
17H	
18H	
19H	Word 3

Stack Pointer

19H ⟶ 19H

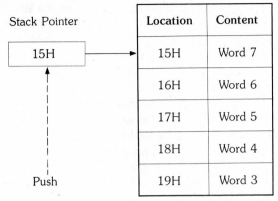

Pop
Reading from the stack: Words 10 to 12 are to be retrieved

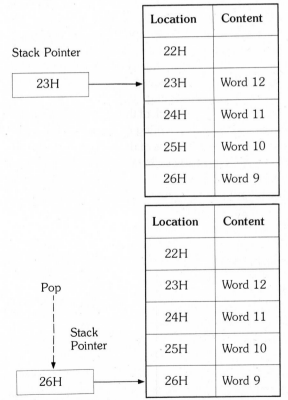

Figure 5-17 Pushing and popping the stack. (*a*) Push instruction—writing into the stack; (*b*) Pop instruction—reading from the stack.

instruction is executed, information which is read out from the stack still remains in the stack for future use. This action is similar to reading data out of a RAM.

To change information in the stack, the data content of the information to be changed is popped to other registers in the processor in which the data is alterable. After their contents are modified they are pushed back into the stack.

Subroutine Sequencing with the Call and Return Instructions

The stack is often used as temporary storage when subroutines are serviced. The Call and Return instructions permit the instruction sequence to branch to the subroutine and subsequently to return to the main program after completing the subroutine.

Figure 5-18 illustrates a typical sequence flow when a subroutine is executed. The Call instruction is a 3-byte instruction containing the OP code and the starting address of the subroutine. When the instruction is executed, it causes the existing value of the program counter, which is the high and low addresses of the next instruction location (6AH in this example) to be stored in the stack. The starting address of the subroutine is then transferred to the program counter. The first two instructions of the subroutine are Push instructions permitting the accumulator and status register data to be stored in the stack; thus data will be saved for later restoring the registers. Other registers which are used may also require storage in the stack. The next instruction is the first actual instruction of the subroutine and corresponds to memory location 85H. Memory location 96H is the last active instruction of the subroutine. Two overhead instructions, both Pops, are used to revert the status register and accumulator back to their original value by popping the data from the stack. The execution of the Return instruction completes the program. The Return instruction restores the original contents of the program counter, bringing the program back to where it was before servicing the subroutine. The instruction at memory location 6AH is then processed.

Stack-Associated Instructions

The final six instructions, Push, Pop, Call, Conditional Call, Return, and Conditional Return, which are associated with stacks and subroutines, will now be discussed. Conditional instructions are performed when the result of a test condition is true depending on the status of the Condition Code flag register. When the condition is not true, the main program continues to be executed sequentially. Note that in some microprocessors it may be unnecessary to fetch all three instruction bytes of the conditional instruction if the condition is not met. In these cases, the microprocessor evaluates the condition during the second instruction byte and jumps to fetch the next instruction if the specified condition is not satisfied. This allows for faster

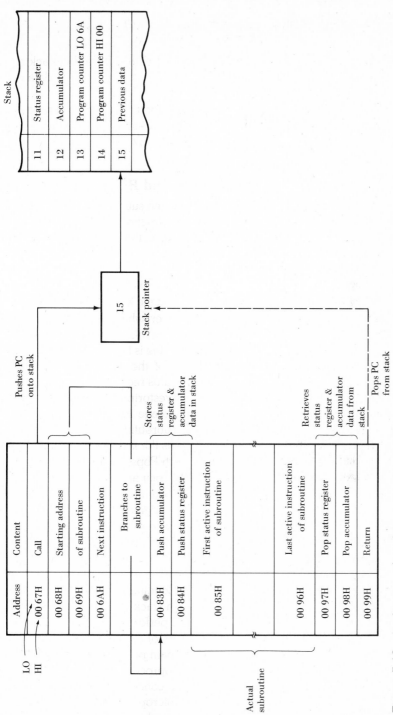

Figure 5-18 Application of stack-associated instructions to subroutines.

TABLE 5-6   Tests on Conditional Call, Return,
and Branch Instructions

Branch on Results	Zero
Branch on Results	Not Zero
Branch on Results	Negative
Branch on Results	Positive
Branch on	No Overflow
Branch on	Overflow
Branch When There is	No Carry
Branch When There is	Carry
Branch on Parity	Odd
Branch on Parity	Even

execution times. Table 5-6 gives conditional tests applicable to Call, Return, and the previously described Conditional Branch instruction.

Push (PUSH)

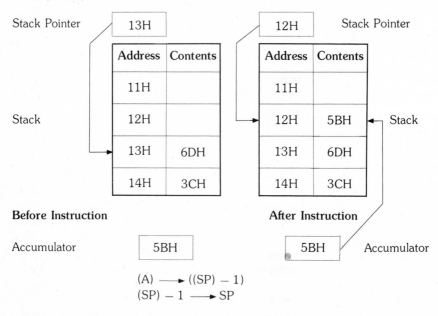

$$(A) \longrightarrow ((SP) - 1)$$
$$(SP) - 1 \longrightarrow SP$$

The content of the accumulator is moved to the memory location whose address is 1 less than the content of the stack pointer. The content of the stack pointer is decremented by 1.

Pop (POP)

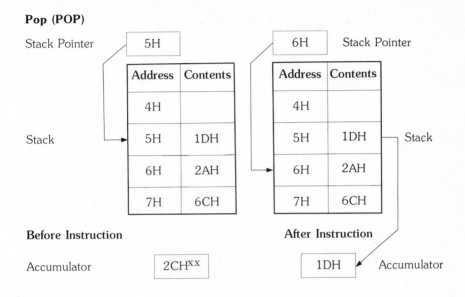

Before Instruction

After Instruction

$$((SP)) \longrightarrow (A)$$
$$(SP) + 1 \longrightarrow (SP)$$

The content of the memory location whose address is specified by the content of the stack pointer is moved to the accumulator. The content of the stack pointer is incremented by 1.

Call (CALL)

The address of the instruction following the Call instruction (as specified by the program counter) is transferred into the stack. High address is stored in the memory location of the content of the stack pointer minus 1, and low address is stored in the memory location of the content of the stack pointer minus 2. The contents of the stack pointer are decremented by 2. (See diagram on page 132.) The contents of the address specified by the Call instruction are then transferred to the program counter for execution.

Conditional Call (See Table 5-4 for mnemonics)

If the specified condition on the instruction is true, the operation of the instruction will be identical to the Call instruction and all actions specified by the Call instruction will be performed. When the condition is not true, the program continues sequentially.

Call

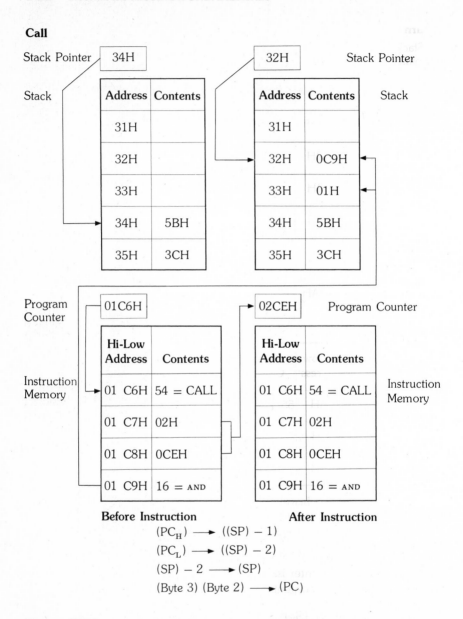

Stack Pointer | 34H

32H | Stack Pointer

Stack

Address	Contents
31H	
32H	
33H	
34H	5BH
35H	3CH

Address	Contents
31H	
32H	0C9H
33H	01H
34H	5BH
35H	3CH

Stack

Program Counter | 01C6H

02CEH | Program Counter

Instruction Memory

Hi-Low Address	Contents
01 C6H	54 = CALL
01 C7H	02H
01 C8H	0CEH
01 C9H	16 = AND

Hi-Low Address	Contents
01 C6H	54 = CALL
01 C7H	02H
01 C8H	0CEH
01 C9H	16 = AND

Instruction Memory

Before Instruction   **After Instruction**

$$(PC_H) \longrightarrow ((SP) - 1)$$
$$(PC_L) \longrightarrow ((SP) - 2)$$
$$(SP) - 2 \longrightarrow (SP)$$
$$(Byte\ 3)\ (Byte\ 2) \longrightarrow (PC)$$

Return (RET)

The content of the memory location whose address is specified in the stack pointer is moved to the low-order bit positions of the program counter. The content of the memory location whose address is 1 more than the

Return

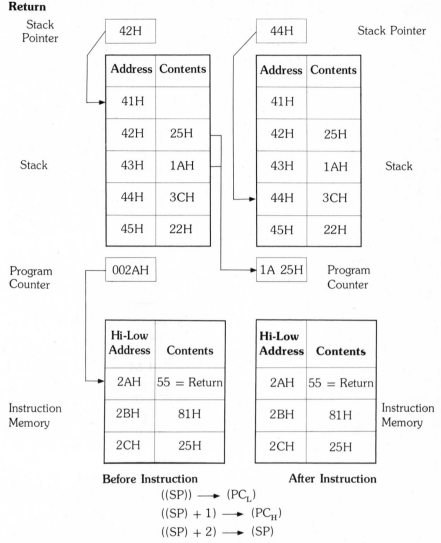

Before Instruction   **After Instruction**

$$((SP)) \longrightarrow (PC_L)$$
$$((SP) + 1) \longrightarrow (PC_H)$$
$$((SP) + 2) \longrightarrow (SP)$$

content of the stack pointer is moved to the high-order bit positions of the program counter. The contents of the stack pointer are incremented by 2.

Conditional Return (See Table 5-4 for mnemonics)

If the specified condition of the instruction is true, the operation of the instruction will be identical to the Return instruction and all actions specified by the Return instruction will be performed. When the condition is not true, the program continues sequentially.

5-8 APPLICATION OF ADDRESSING MODES

In the previous sections, nine different address modes have been presented. Their utilization is highly dependent on the program application and the capabilities of the individual instructions designed with these address modes. Every microprocessor instruction has one or more address modes. The complete generic instruction set with its related address modes was shown in Tables 5-2, 5-3, and 5-4. Note that most of the instructions were specified to contain a variety of address modes providing flexibility in structuring programs.

Use of the Comma

A convenient symbol frequently used when writing instructions is the comma (,). It is frequently used in the implied and immediate address mode instructions. The comma signifies that the listed second operand will be transferred to the location of the first operand. Thus, an instruction which transfers the contents of register 1 to register 2 can be described simply as MOV R_2, R_1. Recall that this operation can also be functionally specified as MOVE $(R_1) \rightarrow (R_2)$. In the Immediate address mode, the instruction LD (Immediate) R_1, 35H signifies that the data 35H will be loaded into register 1. Other address modes also utilize the comma notation. MOV M, A and MOV A, M are two additional examples of the use of the comma. In the first example, the contents of the accumulator will be transferred to memory, while the second instruction has the accumulator receiving data from memory. In both of the examples, the memory locations will be derived by use of the register indirect address mode which was previously discussed.

The Generic Instruction Set Compared with
Actual Instruction Formats

The instructions described in this chapter provide the reader with basic fundamentals. No attempt will be made to further define the characteristics of the processor in terms of the number of registers which utilize the generic instruction set. Note that all microprocessors on the market have specific OP code assignments which permit the programmer to select the desired registers. As an example, the 8080 has seven registers (see Fig. 5-19a) which the user can select in executing a MOV implied instruction. Each register is coded by a 3-bit field. This results in separate OP code assignments, as shown in Fig. 5-19b, to correspond to the source and destination registers of the 8080. By contrast, the generic instruction set assigned one OP code to the MOV implied instruction.

To further familiarize the reader with how to apply the various address modes, several illustrative examples are given. In Example One, shown in

Register	Assignment
B	0 0 0
C	0 0 1
D	0 1 0
E	0 1 1
H	1 0 0
L	1 0 1
A (accumulator)	1 1 1

(a)

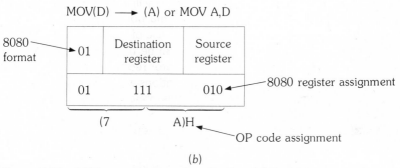

MOV(D) ⟶ (A) or MOV A,D

(b)

Figure 5-19   8080 assignments and application. (a) Register assignments in the 8080; (b) example—move contents of D register to the accumulator.

Fig. 5-20, two numbers are added and stored in memory. The accumulator is loaded with the contents of location 73H by use of an indirect address mode. Register 2 is preset with a Load immediate address mode instruction. Since both operands are microprocessor registers, an Add inherent instruction was selected. In this example it was decided to store the results of the Add operation in a distant memory location, thus requiring the use of a Store extended address mode instruction.

In Example Two, shown in Fig. 5-21, the program unconditionally jumps to the location specified in bytes 2 and 3, in this case 0210H. The instruction

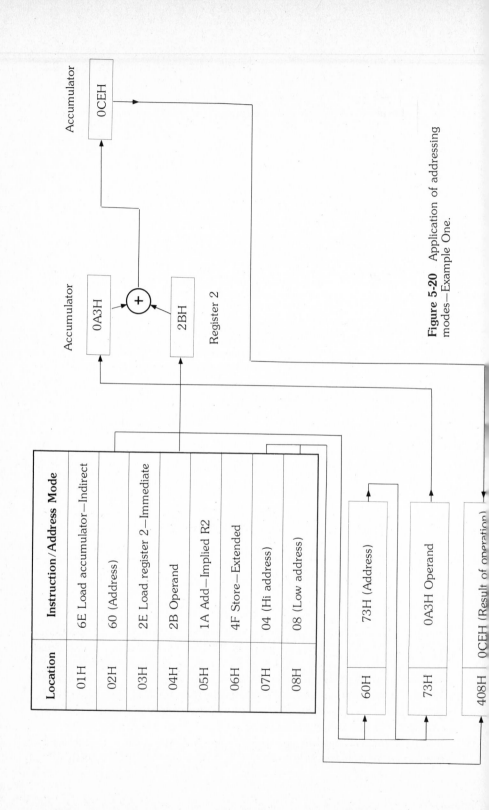

Figure 5-20 Application of addressing modes—Example One.

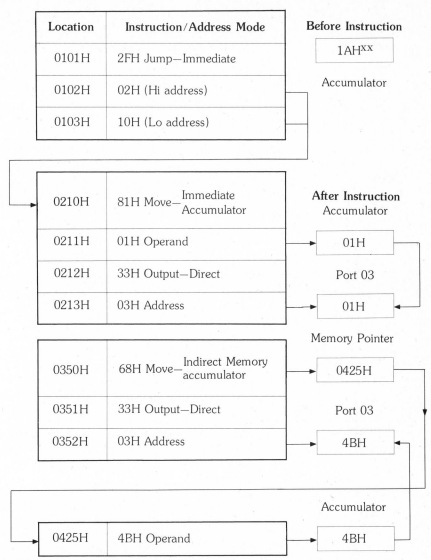

Location	Instruction/Address Mode
0101H	2FH Jump—Immediate
0102H	02H (Hi address)
0103H	10H (Lo address)

Before Instruction

1AH^{xx}

Accumulator

0210H	81H Move—Immediate / Accumulator
0211H	01H Operand
0212H	33H Output—Direct
0213H	03H Address

After Instruction
Accumulator

01H

Port 03

01H

Memory Pointer

0350H	68H Move—Indirect Memory / accumulator
0351H	33H Output—Direct
0352H	03H Address

0425H

Port 03

4BH

Accumulator

0425H	4BH Operand

4BH

Figure 5-21 Application of addressing modes—Example Two.

at this location places the second byte into the accumulator. The next instruction transfers the contents of the accumulator to the port specified by the second byte of the Output instruction, Port 03. Further along in the program the accumulator is changed by an indirect Move instruction. Although this instruction is only 1 byte, it causes the microprocessor to use the memory pointer registers, whose content is 0425H. 0425H is the address of a memory location whose content, 4BH, is an operand which is moved to the accumulator. The next instruction outputs the accumulator to Port 03.

Examples Three through Six are found at the end of Sec. 5-9 of this chapter.

5-9 REVIEW OF THE INSTRUCTION EXECUTION SEQUENCE

Instructions are usually specified as having 1-, 2-, or 3-byte lengths. The microprocessor has specific sequences which it performs as it fetches, interprets, and executes varying-length instructions. These sequences are described step by step and illustrated by several programming examples.

The Instruction Sequence

1. The contents of the program counter (PC) are latched onto the address bus (memory fetch).

2. The memory responds with the instruction via the data bus.

3. The microprocessor latches the data and transfers it to a temporary register.

4. The PC is incremented after each fetch.

5. Since the first byte from memory is an instruction, the contents of the temporary register are transferred to the instruction register.

6. The instruction is decoded.

7. Depending on the instruction, the instruction can be 1, 2, or 3 bytes long.

    a. If the instruction is 1 byte, no further fetches are necessary and the instruction is executed.

    b. If the instruction is 2 bytes, then the second byte can be either the data or the operand address. The byte is fetched via the data bus and stored in a temporary register.

    c. If the instruction is 3 bytes,

        (1) The first 2 bytes are identical to the 2-byte instruction.

        (2) If the third byte is an address, it must correspond to the low address (the second byte is the high address) of the operand. The fetching and transfer of the third byte are identical to those of the 2-byte instruction. A second temporary register is used to hold the low address.

        (a) The two temporary registers form a register pair, which now contains the 16-bit address of the operand.

        (b) The 16-bit address from the register pair latches the address bus.

(c) Operand data (via the data bus) is either stored in memory via the 16-bit address or transmitted to the microprocessor from a location as specified by the 16-bit address.

(3) If the third byte is data, then it is fetched. Bytes 2 and 3 correspond to a 16-bit data word which is loaded into a register pair.

Initialization

When power is applied to a microprocessor, the program counter will come up in a random state. Usually a microcomputing system will have a power on reset circuit, which will cause the program counter to come up in a known state; otherwise it is up to the user to manually reset the microprocessor. The instruction in this fixed location will now be executed by the microprocessor. If the PC is initialized incorrectly so that the first byte is not an instruction but data or an address, then that data or address will be decoded and treated as an instruction. This type of error usually causes malfunctions and must be avoided!

EXAMPLE THREE

MOV B,A (1 byte)

1. PC is latched onto address bus.
2. Operation code (OP Code) is fetched.
3. PC is incremented.
4. Contents of register A are transferred to register B.

EXAMPLE FOUR

MOV Immediate A, 06H (2 bytes)

1. PC is latched onto address bus.
2. OP code is fetched.
3. PC is incremented.
4. PC is latched onto address bus.
5. Data byte 06H is fetched and stored in a temporary register.
6. PC is incremented.
7. Temporary register (with 06H) is transferred to register A.

EXAMPLE FIVE

ST Accumulator, 0104H (3 bytes)

1. PC is latched onto address bus.
2. OP code is fetched.
3. PC is incremented.

4. PC is latched onto address bus.
5. Address byte 01H is fetched and stored in temporary register 1.
6. PC is incremented.
7. PC is latched onto address bus.
8. Address byte 04H is fetched and stored in temporary register 2.
9. Temporary register pair 1,2 is latched onto address bus.
10. The contents of Register A are latched onto data bus and stored in memory.

EXAMPLE SIX

PC	Data
0000	MOV B,A
0001	LD Immediate accumulator
0002	32H (Data)
0003	ST Accumulator
0004	04H (high address)
0005	01H (low address)
0006	(Next instruction)

After execution of this program, the PC is at 0006H, register B contains the old contents of register A, register A contains 32H, and memory location 0401H also contains 32H.

PROBLEMS

1. The generic instruction set has six different categories of instructions. What are they?
2. Explain the difference between the following notations:
    a. $(A) \leftarrow (byte\ 2)$
    b. $(A) \leftarrow ((byte\ 2))$
3. After the Compare instruction is executed, the Carry flag is set. If register B is compared to the accumulator,
    a. Which register is larger?
    b. Has register B or the accumulator changed?
4. Determine the instructions which perform the following functions:
    a. Transfer the contents of a register to another register
    b. Cause the program counter to contain the value of the second and third bytes of the instruction
    c. Result in no change except the normal increment of the program counter

5. Determine the addressing mode in each of the following statements:
   a. A 3-byte instruction where the second and third bytes are address
   b. A 1-byte instruction where the instruction specifies a register whose content is the effective address
   c. A 1-byte instruction where the instruction specifies a source and destination register
   d. An instruction where the PC is added to the second byte to obtain the effective address
   e. An instruction where the second byte is added to a register to obtain the effective address
   f. An instruction where the second byte is data

6. If a program has just executed a Halt instruction, determine the approaches required to resume execution.

7. Explain the difference between:
   a. Direct and extended address modes
   b. Program relative and base relative address mode instructions

8. Define a stack. Discuss two forms of stacks.

9. What is the difference between pushing and popping the stack?

10. Explain the difference between a Call and a Jump instruction.

11. What is the purpose of a Return instruction?

12. Why is it important to initialize the program counter with a value corresponding to an instruction rather than to data or an address location?

13. The following program was run in an attempt to modify stack words 3EH and 4CH, located at locations SP and SP + 1, respectively.

POP	Register 1
POP	Register 2
INC	Register 1
DEC	Register 2
DEC	Register 2
PUSH	Register 1
PUSH	Register 2

    If the stack pointer is at location SP, determine the contents of locations SP and SP + 1 after the program is run. What is wrong with the program?

14. Register B = 0101 0101
    Register A = 0000 0000
    The following program is run:

```
MOV A,B
ADD B
AND B
HLT
```

a. After this program is executed, what are the contents of register B and register A?
b. Which flags are set or reset? Which instructions cause the flags to change?
c. Register B = 1111 1111
   Register A = 0000 0001
   If registers A and B are changed as shown, what are the new contents of registers A and B?
d. What flags are now affected?

15. The program in Prob. 14 is modified as follows:

```
MOV A,B
ADD B
OR B
RL
OUT, 05
HLT
```

Register B = 0110 0000
Register A = 0000 0000

a. Determine the value of the data received by port 05.
b. Determine which flag registers are affected.

16. List all generic instructions which will affect the flag bits of the status registers.

REFERENCES

1. Intel Corporation: *8080 Microcomputer Systems User's Manual*, September 1975.
2. Motorola: *Microprocessor Applications Manual*, McGraw-Hill Book Company, New York, 1975.

Software

The wide utilization of microprocessors in existing systems has resulted in a high level of integration of hardware. The associated procurement costs of these LSI devices is decreasing as less and less is spent on hardware. Software has now taken a major role in the cost of developing microprocessing systems. The significant responsibilities of designing, integrating, and testing a system are now software-oriented. This chapter will describe the basic approaches, techniques, and tools which are available to produce the necessary software for a microprocessing system.

6-1   DEFINING SOFTWARE

Software can be defined as all the concepts, activities, and procedures which result in the generation of programs for a computing system. The objective of "good software" is to improve the likelihood of getting the software written on time and having it more cost-effective because of more efficient utilization of personnel and resources. Software can be partitioned into three different forms:

- Operating
- Program development
- Diagnostic

The operating software can also be partitioned into two further categories: application programs and operating systems. The application programs are written to accomplish specific tasks or requirements. The executive programs which supervise the sequencing and processing of application programs by the microprocessing system make up the operating software.

Program development software consists of programs that translate application programs written in a language such as Basic or Fortran to a language acceptable to the microprocessor. Statements such as GO TO, READ, IF, etc., which are typically found in these languages, are converted to microprocessing instructions whose formats must contain only binary 1s and 0s. Fortran and Basic are two of the most popular "high-level languages," and they will be discussed in Sec. 6-6.

All the instructions described in Chap. 5 have symbolic names in the form of mnemonics; these were shown in Tables 5-2 and 5-3. Thus the typical mnemonics INC, SUB, MOV, and MPY represent instructions describing the Increment, Subtract, Move, and Multiply operations. A program written with these mnemonics is commonly called an *assembly language program*. Note that every executable command contained within the assembly language structure can be represented by a single instruction in mnemonic form. By contrast, the higher-level language (HLL) statements, sometimes referred to as *high-order language* (HOL), describe broader actions or commands of the program. For instance, a HLL statement expressed as an equation, $a = b + c$, may be equivalent to five instructions. It is this basic difference which distinguishes the assembly language from the high-level language. A more detailed description of the language differences will be given in Secs. 6-4 to 6-6.

Program development software translates higher-level language or assembly programs to programs whose format is compatible with the microprocessor. Since only binary 1s and 0s are used within any digital processor, the language that specifies the various instructions by OP code format and addresses in binary form is called *machine-code language*. The early digital computers were initially programmed in machine language. Program development software enables programs to be written in a more effective language and then translated into machine language.

Diagnostic software consists of programs specifically written to detect, discover, and further isolate a malfunction within the hardware or software of the computer system. Diagnostic software can be a permanent part of executive software, providing under program control a continuous testing and validation of the system. Another technique is to have diagnostic programs reside in an external mass memory and transfer the programs to the resident memory as they are required.

6-2 APPROACH TO SOFTWARE

The basic procedure of developing software can be partitioned into several steps. They include:

1. Defining the problem. The scope of the problem should be known and the usefulness of the microprocessor determined.

2. Determining the solution. Generally speaking, there will be several approaches that can be utilized; however, the one that is most cost-effective should be selected.

3. Identifying the solution steps and arranging them in a logical order. The equivalent of a schematic in the software world is a *flowchart,* and flow-charting (described in Chap. 7) should be performed. The sequence of developing software is presented in flowchart form; see Fig. 6-1.

4. Coding the program. Thus far we have learned that there are several approaches that can be used to prepare the application programs. These programs must be written or coded in a particular language, and that language must be subsequently translated to the language of the microproc-essor, namely, the machine language.

5. Running the program. There are several choices of approaches in program operational verification. These will be described later. The user, independent of the approach selected, must debug the program, modify it, and recode portions of the program as necessary or the whole program if changes are extensive.

6. Writing into memory. If the program works, the user is ready to "burn" (program) a PROM or write the final program into memory.

7. Validation. The program is then integrated, tested, and validated in its final configuration. The programmer outputs and documents the software.

8. Program revision. Program maintenance is performed in the last step: revising for errors and modifying to adjust to changes in external interfaces and system upgrades. Depending on the scope of the changes, it may be necessary to repeat one or many of the previous steps.

6-3 LANGUAGE TRANSLATION

To function, a microprocessor must receive inputs that it can interpret and act upon. In order to be interpreted, these inputs must be in a language understood by the machine. As previously stated, the only language that can be interpreted by the microprocessor is machine language. The machine code or language consists of instructions and data represented only as binary information in the form of 1s and 0s. Although the hex or octal notation can be used instead of binary to represent instructions and data, the microprocessing system will act only upon data in binary format. The programs which contain the binary notation are said to be in *object code,* since this is the final

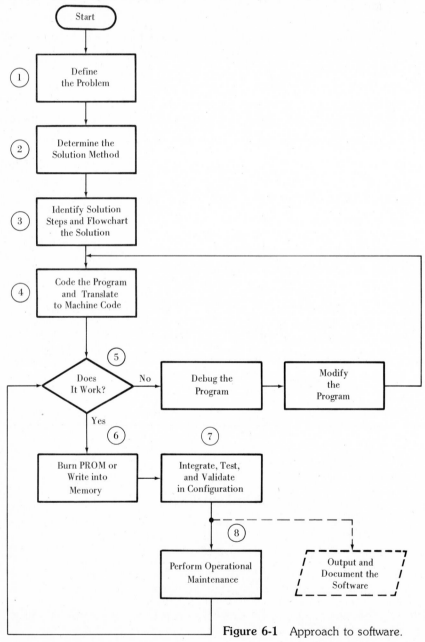

Figure 6-1 Approach to software.

code acceptable by the processor which will run the program. The machine code is sometimes referred to as the *target language* and the microprocessor as the *target machine*.

In Fig. 6-2a, the instruction segment of a small three-step program is shown. A Move, Store, and Load operation are involved. Note that each new step or instruction is given in both binary and hex, the latter only as a convenience to the programmer, since it is not recognized by the processor. When writing larger programs, as in Fig. 6-2b, it is easy to see why the binary format (or its object code) is conducive to errors. A mistake of only a single digit can generate an improper instruction. Machine language coding therefore has very limited applications in large programs.

A different approach to language can be used in developing programs. As was indicated earlier, programs can be written utilizing the mnemonics of the instruction. The same three instructions are easily written as MOV, ST, and LD; see Fig. 6-2c. This technique, which forms programs by utilizing symbolic language notations in the form of mnemonics, is referred to as *assembly language programming*. Even the longer program of Fig. 6-2b, now shown in mnemonic notation in Fig. 6-2d, is more manageable to read or write when assembly language is used. But since the microprocessor does not accept

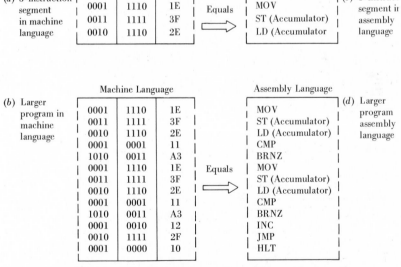

Figure 6-2 Comparison of machine and assembly language programming. (a) Three-instruction segment in machine language; (b) larger program in machine language; (c) three-instruction segment in assembly language; (d) larger program in assembly language.

information in assembly language, it must be translated or converted to object code. A software program called the *assembler* performs this function. The statements in the form of instructions written in symbolic language are called *source statements.* The assembler, therefore, translates the source statements written in assembly language into object statements written in machine language.

When programs are written in high-level language rather than in assembly language, they also require translation into machine language. The translator program in this case is called the *compiler,* but it essentially performs the same functions as the assembler. Source statements written in high-level language are translated into a machine-code object program that can be stored for later execution or run soon after translation. Figure 6-3 illustrates the various translation procedures available in producing machine instructions and addresses. The *interpreter* is a program which transforms to machine language and immediately executes each source language expression as it is read. Interpreters are written in high-level language.

In Sec. 6-6 we will discuss the many forms of high-level languages, of which some have been designed for specific types of functions while others are designed specifically for microprocessors. Fortran (*Formula tran*slation) and Cobol (*Common Business-Oriented Language*) are examples of prob-

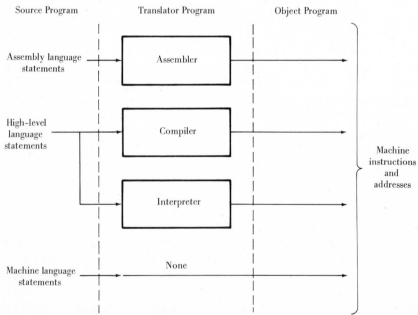

Figure 6-3 Translation procedures.

lem-oriented languages, whereas PL/M, a derivative of PL/1, was developed by Intel to support its microprocessing software.

It has been shown that assemblers and compilers are used for translating source programs to object program; however, they perform many other functions, including the "printout" of a program listing which displays side by side the source and object parts of the program and lists error messages and other forms of diagnostic information which are obtained when assembling or compiling the program.

Machine-Code Generation

A closer look at machine-code language generation technique indicates that this unsophisticated approach of manually producing code is quite efficient only when small programs of the order of 100 to 200 bytes are used. Generating code in this manner is a form of "do-it-yourself" solution to programming, since not only do every instruction and all data have to be specified and coded in binary but the programmer also has to keep track of allocating addresses of operands. This results in a slow, tedious process with a high likelihood of generating errors as the program gets longer. Persons who write programs in machine language are usually uncomfortable developing programs in this manner. To reduce the possible errors, programs are generally developed using the mnemonics associated with assembly language programs. Thus a Subtract operation is written as SUB rather than 0001 1011. Symbols are easier to read and write and easier to change. After the program has been completely written in mnemonics, all instructions are hand-converted to their respective OP code assignments. The program is now totally in binary (machine code) and is ready to be loaded into the target machine. A paper tape system or a console is normally used when loading machine-code language programs.

There are several shortcomings associated with using machine language statements. One problem is that the user is required to keep track of program addresses. In other approaches, as will be discussed later, this is done automatically by the program. Another problem with developing hand machine-code language programs is that the technique is not easily maintainable. If portions of the program are to be deleted or changed, even just a single instruction, it may mean moving and reassigning the addresses of the instructions that follow the impacted area. Again, errors are quite prevalent in the reassigning of addresses of instructions and subroutines. The longer the program, the more complicated reallocation becomes. We have mentioned earlier that assemblers and compilers provide the ability to list error conditions which result during program development. This feature is especially important when working with lengthy programs.

The disadvantages of utilizing machine-code programming do not preclude its wide utilization. It is a simple, direct manner of generating programs and is directly applicable to many utilizations by the hobbyist, the student, and industry in small systems. There is no equipment or scheduling cost associated with producing machine code, and the overall cost is minimal when compared with the costs incurred by utilizing an assembler or a compiler.

Assemblers

One of the most frequently used forms of translating source-code programs to binary machine-code language is an assembler. Assemblers perform this function on a one-to-one basis—one machine language statement in object code for each source statement. However, assemblers do more than symbolic (mnemonics) translations of predefined OP codes; they also allow the user to introduce original symbols for operands. Thus a register or a memory location may be given a name by which instructions address it. If for example, a data byte is stored at location 50 and is used several times in performing calculations, the user need only give it a name, such as "Code B," and specify its location in memory. Once the name is assigned, the programmer is not required to keep track of where the data is stored; merely specifying its name will suffice. This helps reduce the bookkeeping normally associated with machine-code language. If a name location has a different address because of a change, the assembler will automatically use the new assignment without the user's having to calculate and update the assignment list. Data in an assembler program can be specified in other forms more common to the programmer than binary and is, therefore, easier to use.

Assemblers were developed for convenience. A typical assembler listing, shown in Table 6-1, demonstrates that almost all statements are in English form, making programs easier to write and read. Each assembly line statement contains only one instruction, and the line is partitioned into groups or fields. There are up to four fields per line. The fields are:

1. The label
2. The operation (OP) code or mnemonic field
3. The operand field
4. The comment field

The label field is used as a reference to other items in the program. It can be used to indicate the beginning of the instruction address, a subroutine, or a start of a repetitive block of instructions. Hence not every statement contains a label. The operation code contains the instruction in mnemonic form, while the operand field contains the address symbol specified by the

TABLE 6-1   Assembler Format

LABEL	OP CODE	OPERAND FIELD	COMMENT FIELD
Begin	MOV	A, D	Move D Reg. to Accumulator
	ST Accumulator	B	Store Accum. in B Address
	LD Accumulator	B	Load Accumulator from B Address
	CMP	D	Compare D with Accumulator
	BRNZ	Error	Error if not Zero
Test 2	MOV	A, E	Move E Reg. to Accumulator
	ST Accumulator	B	Store Accum. in B Address
	LD Accumulator	B	Load Accumulator from B Address
	CMP	E	Compare E with Accumulator
	BRNZ	Error	Error if not Zero
	INC	B	Add 1 to Memory Address
	JMP	Begin	
Error	HLT		Halt Processor

instruction. A good programming practice is to note at key steps in the program what is taking place. These comments, such as "Initialize Port 1, Exchange Data," etc., are valuable pièces of information for documentation. Machine-coding makes no provision for this self-explanatory field. Each assembler has its own limitations as to the size of the field and number of characters that can be used to describe a symbol; in fact, there may be certain characters that cannot be used at all.

Assemblers provide error-checking capability. All statements are scanned for errors. A common type of error is the syntax form whereby previously defined OP code mnemonics or symbolic operands appearing in later statements are improperly spelled. When such an error is detected, the assembler notes the error and attempts to continue assembling the program. After reading the last statement, the assembler produces an error listing which shows all such occurrences with a message code to the user denoting each type of error encountered and its location. After the programmer corrects the errors, the programs are reentered and the process repeated until an assembled error-free object code is generated.

The assembler provides the capability of handling programs whose size far exceeds the effective range of hand-assembly machine code. Assemblers, however, are not stand-alone items and consequently require companion software elements, such as a text editor, a link loader, and a debugger program. These items will be explained more fully in Secs. 6-7 and 6-8. The assembler requires a terminal or a development hardware system to develop the programs; these represent a large investment, in comparison with hand assembly.

Assemblers provide a significant contribution to the development of efficient software and are considered a competitive approach for many applications for the compiler and the use of high-level language. Tradeoff criteria on both approaches will be included subsequent to the discussion on compilers.

Compilers and High-Level Languages

A compiler translates source statements in high-level language to object statements in binary form for later execution. While assemblers are designed for specific processors, compiler programs written in high-level language are processor-independent. This means that a language such as Fortran can be used on any processor that has a compiler for the Fortran language. A person who has studied a high-level language can therefore write programs for those machines which have compiler translators without being totally familiar with the instruction set of the processor.

Compilers are different from assemblers in that each statement written in high-level language generally represents a group of instructions. Compilers can generate several lines of object code for each line of source code. In assembly language there is a one-to-one correspondence between source and object statements. The high-level language provides a shorthand notation. High-level languages allow the user to specify mathematical operations in algebraic form without having to relate to the instruction; the compiler then translates the statements to machine-code statements, thus allowing for faster mechanization of the solution but adding to the complexity of the compiler program. In some instances, it has been demonstrated that programs utilizing compilers were written in approximately 10 percent of the time required for programs written in assembly language.

Programs compiled with high-level languages will require more memory than those with assembly language, since the programmer no longer controls what machine language the compiler produces. The internal bookkeeping, such as the detailed allocation of all registers, done by the user in assembly language, is now handled by the compiler program. This added overhead for compilers produces greater inefficiencies in comparison with assemblers. Operand assignment used in the assembler is routinely handled by the compiler. A program that uses a Fortran compiler can take from 10 to 100 percent more memory than a program implemented with assembly language. This inefficiency also manifests itself in longer execution times, since it is necessary to perform more instructions when the program is expressed with more object statements.

High-level languages are commonly used when programs are large (1000 bytes or more), since they provide greater error-detecting capabilities in compiling programs. They have excellent documentation features, facilitating the debugging phase and producing reliable software. Three of the popular high-level languages are Basic, Fortran, and PL/M. Many of the important languages will be briefly discussed in Sec. 6-6. Because of their complexity, compilers are not stand-alone items but require a hardware development system, which can be relatively expensive. The resultant object code associated with compiler usage necessitates the allocation of larger memory storage than that required by assemblers.

6-4 COMPARING THE THREE APPROACHES

The equation for a straight line can be expressed as:

$$y = mx + b$$

where m = the slope and b = the intersection of the line with the y axis. Figures 6-4, 6-5, and 6-6 represent implementations of the equation using Basic high-level language, assembly language, and machine code, respectively. The 8080 microprocessor was used to develop the programs in assembly and machine-code languages. In the illustrations it is shown that in Basic only five statements are needed to describe the equation, while assembly language and machine-code hand assembly each require 31 instructions.

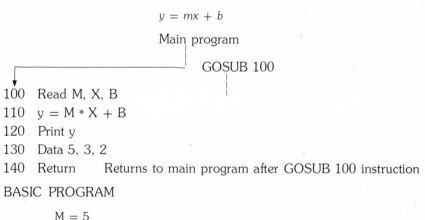

$$y = mx + b$$

Main program

GOSUB 100

```
100   Read M, X, B
110   y = M * X + B
120   Print y
130   Data 5, 3, 2
140   Return      Returns to main program after GOSUB 100 instruction
```

BASIC PROGRAM

M = 5
X = 3
B = 2

and prints y = 17

Figure 6-4 The equation of a straight line in Basic.

MAIN PROGRAM

CALL, STRTLIN

STRTLIN	PUSH	PSW	Saves registers
	PUSH	B	in stack
	PUSH	D	
	PUSH	H	
	IN	00	Input M, save in D
	MOV	D,A	
	IN	01	Input X, save in C
	MOV	C,A	
	IN	02	Input B, save in E
	MOV	E,A	
MULT.	MVI	B,00	Multiplies M and X
	MVI	H,09	(MX); result
MULT 0	MOV	A,C	stored in register A
	RAR		
	MOV	C,A	
	DCR	H	
	JZ	DONE	
	MOV	A,B	
	JNC	MULT 1	
	ADD	D	
MULT 1	RAR		
	MOV	B,A	
	JMP	MULT 0	
	MOV	A,B	
	ADD	E	Adds B to (MX)
	OUT	00	Outputs Y to port 00
DONE	POP	H	Restores registers
	POP	D	
	POP	B	
	POP	PSW	
	RET		Returns to main program

Figure 6-5 The equation of a straight line in 8080 assembly language.

STRTLIN	EQU	0400
MULT	EQU	040D
MULT 0	EQU	0411
MULT 1	EQU	041D
DONE	EQU	0426

0400	0F5		041E	47
1	0C5		1F	0C3, 1104
2	0D5		22	78
3	0E5		23	83
4	0DB, 00		24	0D3, 00
6	57		26	0E1
7	0DB, 01		27	0D1
9	4F		28	0C1
A	0DB, 02		29	0F1
C	5F		2A	0C9
D	06, 00			
F	26, 09			
11	79			
12	1F			
13	4F			
14	25			
15	0CA, 2504			
18	78			
19	0D2, 1D04			
1C	82			
1D	1F			

Figure 6-6 The equation of a straight line in machine code using the 8080 microprocessor.

Assembly vs. High-Level Language

The main reason for using high-level language rather than assembly language is that HLL programs can be written and debugged in a shorter time than programs using assembly language. The penalty of HLL is that the code which it generates occupies much more memory and hence takes longer to run in real time. Stated differently, it is simpler to write programs using HLL, but because the language is inefficient in translation, the programs will be lengthier, with the result that computer time is increased based on the running of the lengthier programs.

A look at the language issues reveals that all costs of implementing and debugging the program must be considered. This includes the rate of pay for the programmer, the amount of code the programmer can generate on a daily basis, and the costs of debugging a program. Memory costs are very important, since they reflect the size of the program and the number of memory modules used to implement the program. The present philosophy is that for high-volume production, assemblers are much more cost-effective than compilers, particularly if programs "spill over" into memory modules required only if the compiler program is implemented. When this occurs, consideration must also be given to power consumption, cooling requirements, and reliability of the hardware system being utilized. The time element must be carefully scrutinized; for example, knowing that the execution time is longer in HLL, one must determine whether sufficient time is available for other functions as well as for growth. A basic question which must be answered is, Are the programs suitable for high-level language? In many instances, programs that rely heavily on I/O routines are better suited for assembly language implementation. Compiler's and high-level languages require fairly extensive hardware support of a development system, and while assemblers are not stand-alone units, they do require less costly support. Many users of microprocessors will never find it necessary to utilize an assembler or a compiler, but the basic issues involved in their possible selection should not be overlooked.

6-5 ASSEMBLERS

Assembler Instructions

Assembler instructions, which comprise statements of assembly language programming, fall into two categories:

1. Executable assembly language instructions
2. Assembly directives, or pseudo-instructions

The executable assembly language instructions are the symbolic equivalent of machine language instructions. Each assembly language instruction input to the assembler will cause the assembler to form the corresponding machine language binary instruction in object code.

Assembler directives, or pseudo-instructions, consist of operations that are instructions to the assembler itself rather than object program instructions. Assembly directives do not generate object code but do control the assembly process. Since the assembly directives are not translatable, they do not have equivalent machine-code instructions. Commonly used expressions include ORG, EQU, and END. The first two expressions are mnemonics for Origin and Equals. ORG is used to indicate the starting location of the executable instruction which follows the ORG statement. An "ORG 0" statement located in the appropriate operand code and operand field defines

Label	OP Code	Operand	Comment
	ORG	32	Program begins at location 32
TEST 5	MOV	A, B	Move contents of B to accumulator
	ADD	C	Add contents of C to contents of accumulator (result left in accumulator)
	MOV	D, A	Move accumulator to D
	CMP	B	Compare B to D
	BRZ	X	Branch to X if result is zero
X	EQU	200	Address of operand X is at location 200
	ST	Temp 1	Store accumulator in location Temp 1
	SUB	Temp 2	Subtract contents of temporary 2 from accumulator
	BRNZ	Error 3	Branch if result of previous operation is not zero to location Error 3
	END		

Assembly directive ⟶ (ORG 32)

Assembly directive ⟶ (X EQU 200)

Assembly directive ⟶ (END)

Figure 6-7 Assembly language programming showing assembly directives.

the start of the program as location 0. An "ORG 32" would set memory location 32 as the starting point of the program that follows. EQU is used to define a symbol. "X EQU 200" signifies that the address of operand X is at memory location 200H. The END statement denotes the end of the source program. A list of other pseudo-operations or directives can be found in the software documentation for the processing unit.

A small program which utilizes the directives is shown in Fig. 6-7. Note that the directive and the executable instructions are intermixed, but only the executable instructions will produce object code.

Assembling a Program

The translation function of an assembler involves not only determining the equivalent object binary code of source statements but also replacing each symbolic operand address with its numerical equivalent. To produce the translation function, most assemblers require two sequences, or passes, of reading in the source statements before producing the final object code. These assemblers are commonly referred to as *two-pass assemblers*. The first portion of the translation is done quite easily by the assembler during the first pass, since all mnemonics for the processor are known ahead of time and the process involves determining the equivalent code for each instruction. The same basic approach is used to generate the symbolic operand address (also during the first pass), but the relation between the symbols used and the addresses of the memory cannot be known until after the program has been read in and partially processed. A symbol table is therefore formed in memory with corresponding machine addresses during the first pass. A representative symbol table is shown in Table 6-2. At a later time, during the reading of the source statements, the addresses are substituted for the symbols and the assembly listing is generated. The format for a typical assembly listing, which contains source and object statements, is shown in Table 6-3.

TABLE 6-2   Symbol Table

SYMBOL	MEMORY LOCATION IN HEX
X	200H
Temp 1	4A
Temp 2	4B
Error 3	5D

Forms of Assemblers

There are many forms of assemblers, some of which will be discussed in this section.

The Macroassembler   A macroassembler is an assembler that enables the user to replace repeated sequences of instructions with a name created for that sequence by the user. Having once defined a macro name for a group of instructions, the programmer will use the name as many times as required in developing the source statements. The macroassembler in turn will generate a series of machine language instructions (macroinstructions) that correspond to the macro. Macros are a powerful programming tool, since they save programming time by eliminating the necessity for the programmer to

TABLE 6-3 An Assembly Listing Format

OBJECT STATEMENTS IN MACHINE CODE				SOURCE STATEMENTS IN ASSEMBLY LANGUAGE			
STATEMENT LINE NO.	ADDRESS OF OBJECT PROGRAM		OBJECT INSTRUCTION IN HEX	LABEL FIELD	OP CODE	OPERAND FIELD	COMMENT FIELD
	IN BINARY	IN HEX					
1				TEST 5	ORG	32	Program begins at location 32
2	0011 0010	32	1E		MOV	A, B	Move contents of B to accumulator
3	0011 0011	33	1A		ADD	C	Add contents of C to contents of accumulator (result left in accumulator)
4	0011 0100	34	*		MOV	D, A	Move accumulator to D
5	0011 0101	35	11		CMP	B	Compare B to D
6	0011 0110	36 to 38	A1		BRZ	X	Branch to X if result is 0
7	0011 1000			X	EQU	200	Address of operand X is at location 200
8	0011 1001 0011 1011	39 to 3B	3F		ST Accum	Temp 1	Store accumulator in location Temp 1
9	0011 1100	3C	1B		SUB	Temp 2	Subtract contents of Temp 2 from accumulator
10	0011 1101	3D	A3		BRNZ	Error 3	Branch if result of previous operation is not 0 to location Error 3
11					END		

*Unassigned.

rewrite the exact instruction sequence many times. The probability of error in writing source statements is also reduced because of the use of only a single statement. Macros can be used anywhere in programs, even in the I/O. Macros are not subroutine replacements, since they are normally used to replace a small group of instructions not worthy in programming length of being a subroutine. A subroutine statement is used many times in a program and yet is stored only once. Since it is stored only once and used many times, there is an effective memory saving. There is no saving of memory space when macros are used. The normal memory allocation is used every time a macro is used.

A macroassembler can efficiently translate the user's grouped instructions while allowing the user to maintain control of specifying the object code. An example of a macro statement ("Test") is shown in Fig. 6-8. There are two

- Macro's name → TEST
- Test format is as follows:

Label	Mnemonic Field
TEST	MDEF
	MOV REG 2, REG 1
	LD Accumulator, REG 1
	MEND

- Subsequent use

Label	Mnemonic Field
	TEST

Figure 6-8 Defining a macro.

assembler directives that are used to help define the macro: the Macro Define (MDEF) instruction and the Macro End (MEND) instruction. Between the instructions are the macroinstructions. The macro is called by using the OP or mnemonic code TEST. Note that TEST must first be defined and placed in the Label field before it can be used in subsequent steps.

Absolute and Relocatable Assemblers An absolute assembler is an assembler that produces its programs in object code whose assignments have been specified by the programmer before assembly. The programs which are fixed to these assignments are absolute, in that they cannot be transferred to other addresses. A relocatable assembler generates relocatable object code, which means that the address of the programs can be moved to other portions of memory. The relocatable assembler is used in conjunction with the linkage editor or the loader, which performs the actual relocation. By use of this software feature, programs can be developed separately and linked together into a module at some later time.

6-6 HIGH-LEVEL LANGUAGES

In the preceding sections, the functions and advantages of using a high-level language were discussed. In this section an overview of the high-level languages which have compilers for microprocessors will be presented.

PL/M The first high-level language, specifically for microprocessors, developed by Intel; derived from PL/1, a problem-solving language, used for business and science calculations. There are many versions of PL/M designed by other microcomputing manufacturers. The language, however, is not machine-independent; that is, Company X's PL/M will not necessarily operate on Company Y's system.

Fortran Acronym for *for*mula *tran*slator; a very popular language suitable for engineering applications, since problems can be stated in mathematical notation.

Basic A simplified programming language extremely popular in schools and with the hobbyist. Basic contains only a limited number of statements, whose grammar and syntax are similar to Fortran. Since it is an unsophisticated language, it can require many more statements than Fortran and therefore is a less efficient language.

Algol Acronym for *algo*rithmic-oriented *l*anguage. A scientific language not suitable for programming in control of real time systems.

Cobol Acronym for *co*mmon *b*usiness-*o*riented *l*anguage. Used, as the name implies, commercially. Not popular with most microprocessing systems.

Pascal One of the most popular high-level languages, named after a French mathematician and philosopher of the seventeenth century. Its main features are simplicity, portability, good subroutine capability, and flexibility in structure. Many programmers find the Pascal language preferable to Basic, Fortran, and PL/1 languages, since it enhances the concept of structured programming.* Some major manufacturers have developed Pascal compilers to be used with their microprocessors.

Proliferation Not a language but the result of having an overabundance of unique high-level languages developed by the computer industry in an attempt to capture a share of the market.

*Structured programming is a technique of developing software which is easy to produce, test, and modify.

Large software development costs are reflected in the costs of the support software associated with a microprocessing system. The Department of Defense, for government applications, is attempting to standardize a high-level language that can be used by all the services.

6-7 SOFTWARE DEVELOPMENT APPROACHES

The implementation of the source program in ultimate machine language requires additional software development tools other than the translator. These tools, or aids, as they are commonly called, are software programs used to develop in an iterative fashion the final machine language programming. Complementing these programs is other software, including an *editor,* which permits changes to be made easily in source code; a *link loader,* which merges independent object modules in memory; and a *debugger,* which allows the user to examine and modify the programs. These aids, in conjunction with the translator, exist in two forms of software system: cross and resident systems.

A cross system will produce the object code for a processor on a computing system other than its own. The computer in the cross system is commonly referred to as a *host computer.* Programs are written in the host computer language with the outputs in the target computer object code. Assume, for example, that the language of the host is Fortran. A program would be written in Fortran and subsequently translated by the host to binary object code compatible with microprocessor "X."

Cross systems exist in two forms: timesharing and larger computer systems. Examples of larger computers are the PDP-11–type minicomputers and the computers used in data processing support, such as the IBM 370. A timesharing system is structured around a large, centrally located computer with many remote terminal users. A cross system normally contains a cross-compiler or cross-assembler, a text editor, and a simulator. A *simulator* is a program used in a host computer to test the correctness of the machine code.

A resident system has no host computer associated with it. The object programs which are to be developed are developed in their own environment, the resident system. There are two forms of resident software systems, the manual and the microcomputing development system. The manual approach is the marketed evaluation board or kit, which normally contains a modest amount of memory. These systems are hand-assembled with machine language code. Entries to the system are made by means of a hexadecimal keyboard, with a digital readout usually provided right on the board. The kit manufacturer may supply a debugger program, which allows for keyboard scan, output display, and register readouts.

Microcomputing development systems (MDS) are commonly developed by the chip manufacturer. An MDS is an elaborate system which contains the following software programs: an editor, a debugger, an assembler and/or a compiler, and a loader. Peripheral equipment associated with the MDS is generally disks for storage, a CRT and keyboard (video terminal) for inter-active display entry, a line printer, and occasionally a paper tape system consisting of a paper tape punch and reader. A diagram showing the structure of the cross and resident systems is shown in Fig. 6-9.

The early software development systems were hand-assembled by the user. Cross systems, which ran on larger systems, were developed later. Resident systems represent the latest development and are not only being uniquely developed by the semiconductor manufacturers but are also being developed by "software houses," which are competing with the products of chip manufacturers. To warrant consideration of an MDS, the size of the system programs must be extensive. There must also be a large production base of software to justify the development system. When only a limited number of programs have to be developed, the timesharing approach is a good method to pursue. The initial investment of timesharing is low, but the costs escalate as the number of programs to be developed increases; therefore, for large volume other methods are more suitable.

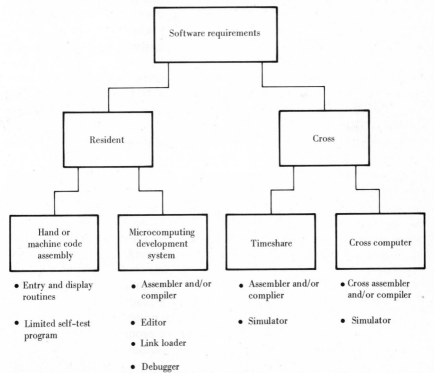

Figure 6-9   Software development approaches.

A cross-computer software development approach is quite popular, since many companies have in-house computers available so that the microcomputer object code can be developed. The user in a cross-computer system environment generally has faster computers and better peripherals, with lower initial costs in developing software.

When a heavy software utilization, one that cannot be supported by the cross-computer, is projected on a continuing basis, an MDS should probably be used. Although these systems are designed around a microcomputing system or a family of microcomputers, there is a trend toward development of more universal development systems. Such a system could support, for example, two different competing microprocessor chips which employ different technologies or characteristics. Many systems do not provide portability, and so independent systems have to be purchased when different manufacturers' parts are used. The ability to support several target codes is the advantage of these universal systems.

6-8 PROGRAM DEVELOPMENT

Our attention will now focus on other design aids which are used with the translator. Included in this group are the text editor, the debugger, the binary loader, the interpreter, and the simulator. These are all software tools. The in-circuit emulator (ICE) is a hardware development aid used to reduce software complexity; it will also be discussed in this section.

Text Editor

A text editor is a program used to develop and modify source programs. The user writes source statements in assembly or HLL, and portions of the symbolic characters must be deleted, replaced, or added before the program is translated to object code. The source program is entered via a video terminal or a teletype device into a file or buffer area in an auxiliary memory, disk, or tape. By storing the data in a buffer area or scratch pad, the user now has the flexibility to find, replace, add, or delete characters or lines. This is accomplished by using a group of commands which are made available to the user for performing the editing function. When corrections are completed, the text editor generates a source code listing, either a tape or a disk file, which will then be ready to use by the assembler or compiler in the translation.

Debugger

A debugger is a program used to facilitate testing a microprocessor system. It is sometimes called a *monitor program*. The program allows the user to:

1. Examine by displaying or printing out all the memory locations and registers of the microprocessor. When this action is performed sequentially on an instruction-by-instruction basis, it is called *tracing*.

2. Modify any memory location in RAM or in any register. A Store command to the debugger allows the user to modify, or "patch," the program directly in machine language without the necessity of returning to the editor or assembler.

3. Initiate program execution or resume program execution from any point.

4. Load memory from paper tape.

5. Stop the program when it reaches a specified point. This feature is called *breakpoint*. Setting an address at the breakpoint causes the program to stop after executing the instruction at the breakpoint address. The contents of the internal registers and stack information are available for printout. A breakpoint can also be set when a condition is met.

6. Execute the program manually on a step-by-step basis. This is called *single-stepping* through the program.

The features just outlined are important in program development, since the debugging phase can account for up to 50 percent of the software development time. Hardware debuggers, such as ICEs, have recently grown in popularity.

The debugger can exist in one of two forms, resident and nonresident. If it is resident, then enough memory must be available for both application programs and the debugger to coexist. This implies that some portion or all of the user's application programs have been translated and the user is at a point in the program that requires debugging. The user initiates the application program until a breakpoint condition is met. The debug function then accepts commands from the user that will provide assistance in determining the status of the program.

When the debugger is nonresident, the application programs not being tested are moved out of main memory into an auxiliary memory under the control of the operating system. This action is a result of a debug command initiated by the user.

Breakpoints should have the flexibility of providing execution of the program until a preset condition on the bus or an external event is encountered. Programs requiring debugging require a sufficient number of breakpoints to help determine the program's operational status. Upon reaching a breakpoint, the user can examine the registers and memory and/or execute the program in single-step fashion as an aid toward analyzing the program.

The single-step feature enables the execution of the program to be performed manually at such a speed that all the registers, including the program counter and the accumulator, can be observed as they change with each new instruction.

Trace mode involves displaying certain registers or memory locations at the end of an instruction execution. A program segment in a trace mode will indicate the contents of each specified register after each instruction is executed. A trace program may be initiated to store the microprocessor buses and control lines for a specified number of cycles. The movement can be initiated by a form of instruction, an address being specified, a data pattern, or an external event.

Binary Loader

A binary loader is a program that transfers object code, which is stored on a disk or tape, to the memory associated with the microprocessor. If a PROM is being utilized in the system, then the data will be transferred to the PROM programmer. When a RAM is utilized, a minimal-size loader program, called the *bootstrap loader,* is generally used to read in the loader program. A *link editor* (also called a *link loader*) is sometimes used to enable the loader to perform linking operations on compiler or assembler programs. Absolute and/or relocatable object programs are combined into a single program module. The link editor finalizes the addresses of the relocatable assembler so that the modules can be loaded anywhere in memory.

Simulators

A simulator is a software development tool in the form of a program which is used to debug the software. This program, which resides in a host computer, will run application programs which have been translated to object code for a different type of unit. The execution of the program creates a software model for the hardware microcomputer, so that comprehensive testing of the programs can be performed. The simulator program will normally run 10 to 100 times slower than in real time.

Among the features of simulators are trace functions, breakpoint, and control and display of the registers. The input to the simulator contains the assembled program and the simulator execution commands, which have been stored in a disk file or timesharing terminal. The commands allow for the manipulation of the simulated system memory and CPU registers. An important use of simulators is in determining the real time it takes to run program segments. Simulators are generally used in a "cross" environment where a cross-assembler or cross-compiler exists. Many simulator programs are written in Fortran. Simulators are normally used when the hardware necessary to permit software development is unavailable. After the software is debugged with the simulator, the application programs are retested in their final environment.

In addition to their being slow, simulators have several other drawbacks. Programs that contain numerous I/O operations are difficult to simulate, and random real time events are not easily duplicated. Simulators are good debugging tools but tend to be large and expensive to operate.

Interpreter

An interpreter is a software program that permits source statements to be executed on a line-to-line basis. There is no machine code saved for later execution, and the processor performs the operations by means of subroutines as each statement is translated and executed individually. Interpreters commonly use Basic as a program language and provide a convenient method for debugging and verification of source statements, thus avoiding the time-consuming process of compiling. The source code and the interpreter program must reside within the computer's memory at the same time for the technique to be operational.

In-Circuit Emulation

The in-circuit emulator (ICE), one of the newer tools in the development of software, is an optional hardware debugging unit of the microcomputing development system. An ICE is plugged directly into the microprocessing socket of the prototype or production user's equipment extending into this hardware the debugging capability of the ICE equipment. An ICE is very powerful, since it provides the capability for hardware and software debugging in the final environment of the system.

ICE hardware contains a microprocessor that replaces the prototype unit and permits the execution of the user's program during *emulation*. Emulation is a technique whereby one processor is made to behave exactly like another processor. During this mode, the ICE processor is controlling the user's hardware and executing programs in real time. An ICE provides strong debugging capabilities with its breakpoint, single-step, and trace features. An ICE allows access to the internal registers, memory, I/O, and bus data, and breakpoints can be addressed by location, event, or symbolic label. The access of memory and I/O by an ICE, and its availability to the user facilitates the isolation of hardware and software problems. A nonoperational program in a prototype system can be tested quite easily by first replacing the prototype memory with the memory of the development system and determining its operational status. If the program appears fully functional, then it proves that the software is valid and that the prototype memory is questionable. If the program does not appear fully functional with the development memory, then the program or the prototype processor or I/O is suspect. This does not necessarily imply that the prototype memory is functional. Having I/O, memory, and processor available with the ICE development configuration allows a gradual buildup of hardware to be tested in conjunction with the software. The initial programs can reside in the developmental memory and gradually be transferred to the user's memory. The same approach can be followed with the I/O and finally with the processor. See Fig. 6-10.

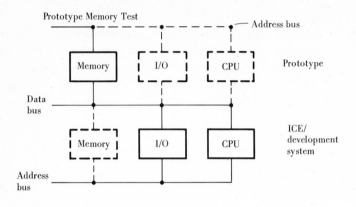

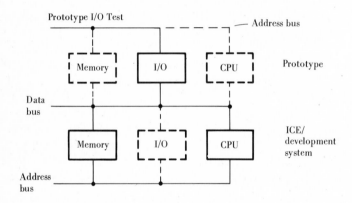

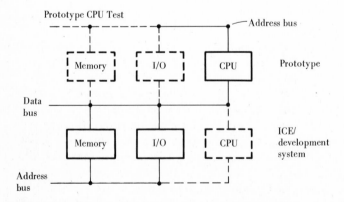

Figure 6-10 Prototype testing by use of the in-circuit emulator (ICE)/Development system.

6-9 THE ITERATIVE PROCESS

The software tools described in this chapter may be called upon to edit, translate, link, and debug many cycles before the programs take final form. The sequence of the development cycle utilizing a microcomputing development system is shown in Fig. 6-11. It may require many cycles or iterations before error-free programs are developed.

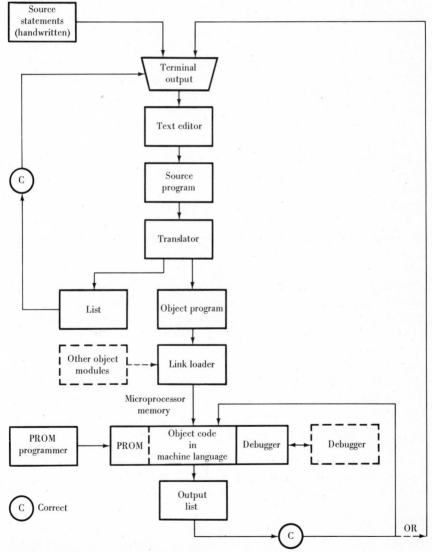

Figure 6-11 Iterative software development of a microprocessing development system.

The process begins when a handwritten source-code program is developed in assembly or high-level language and then entered into the system's buffer area. The text editor permits modification of any portion of the program. The editor will convert the source program into an output format for a disk file or punched tape. The program is then translated by use of an assembler or compiler. The translator will output an object program in machine language and an assembly listing of the program. If errors exist, the translator will detect some of them, particularly if they are in syntax. The translator will generate an error message list which the programmer can review. Corrections are made via the text editor, and the program is again translated and a new listing is generated. This iterative process will continue until an error-free program is assembled. This does not imply that the program is ready to be used in the application. There are probably still bugs that must be detected by the use of the debugger.

The binary loader is then used to load the assembled program into RAM memory. If other programs have been previously developed, a link loader will combine all the modules and relocate them to their intended areas. Implied is the fact that the assembler is relocatable. When the program resides in PROM, a PROM programmer is used to write data into the PROM. The PROM programmer verifies the PROM content.

Once the program is in memory, it is the purpose of the debugger to get the program functioning. The debugger may not permanently exist in resident memory, but to perform its troubleshooting functions it must coexist with the application programs being tested. The debugger, with all its features of tracing, single-step, and breakpoint, will generate sufficient data for the user to search out and correct programming errors. If the errors are small, they can be patched directly in object code into the memory by the debugger. However, if the errors are either numerous or major and are not easily corrected by patches, then the text editor should be used to develop a corrected source-code list on file. From this point the process of translation, correction, loading, and debugging will follow. It is iterative until no problems exist in the application programs. The debug program is then normally transferred out of the resident system.

6-10   OTHER SOFTWARE

Earlier in this chapter we were able to partition software into three groups: program development, operating, and diagnostic. We will now turn our attention to the last two.

Operating Systems

An operating system is a group of integrated programs that manage or supervise the sequencing and processing of the application programs by the microprocessor. The operating system, sometimes known as the *executive program,* also controls the utilization of the peripherals and the data transfers between the peripherals and the computer. The operating system is the link between the user and the application programs, on one side, and the computer hardware and its resources, such as disks and I/O devices, on the other side.

Diagnostic Programs

Diagnostic programs are utilized for exercising the microprocessor to detect any faults that may exist. The diagnostic programs provide fault detection and isolation procedures for the memory, arithmetic and control, and I/O portions of the system. The basic approach in the development of programs involves a building-block technique for checkout, whereby the most basic functions are first proven to be operational before more complex functions are exercised. Diagnostic programs are normally partitioned into functional areas, each of which is tested completely before proceeding with the next area of test. The tests continue until a failure occurs. The user at this point can extract the contents of the program counter and of other registers as an attempt is made to execute each instruction. In the memory area, test patterns are used to exercise the Write and Read capability by writing a test pattern into memory and then reading it back and comparing it with its known "good" test pattern.

Four of the most popular patterns used are:
1. An all-0s data word
2. The inverse, an all-1s data word
3. An alternating 1 and 0 data word
4. The inverse, an alternating 0 and 1 data word

Diagnostic tests provide a comprehensive approach for validating the microprocessing system by the use of software.

Self-tests are an abbreviated form of diagnostic tests which are part of the operational software and reside in memory within the application modules. These tests are abbreviated, since they run in the environment of the system and therefore should not take up either too much memory or too much processing time. Self-tests consist of instruction tests, I/O tests, and Read-Write tests in RAM. When PROMs or ROMs are used, the memory is validated with a memory-check sum test. This involves adding the numerical value of the contents of fixed memory and comparing the results with a previously stored value.

PROBLEMS

1. Describe the difference between operating, program development, and diagnostic software.

2. If all programs will eventually be translated into machine-code language, why aren't all programs written in this language initially?

3. What is the function of:
   a. An assembler
   b. A compiler
   c. An interpreter

4. Describe two advantages of using an assembler instead of writing directly in machine code.

5. What are pseudo-instructions? How do they differ from conventional instructions?

6. What are the advantages of having a macroassembler?

7. What is the function of a relocatable assembler?

8. From the following statements determine which type of development software is specified.
   a. Requires a host computer to generate object code
   b. Allows the program to be executed slowly, so that the internal changes per instruction can be observed
   c. Enables the user to modify the source programs before translation to object code
   d. Permits loading memory from paper tape and allows for breakpoints
   e. Resides in the host computer and allows for debugging and software modeling

9. Describe two features of an ICE.

10. What is the difference between self-test and diagnostic programs?

REFERENCES

1. Gear, C. W.: *Computer Organization and Programming,* McGraw-Hill Book Company, New York, 1974.
2. Stone, H. S.: *Introduction to Computer Organization and Data Structures,* McGraw-Hill Book Company, New York, 1972.

Programming Applications

The last two chapters have introduced the concepts of instructions, addressing modes, and software. The application of these principles is covered in this chapter with the introduction of flowcharting and the technique of converting the flowcharts into practical programs which contain specific operations of the generic instruction set.

7-1   THE FLOWCHART

A *flowchart* is a graphical representation expressing the solution to a given problem. It is an important tool to the programmer, as all major steps are logically represented on the flowchart, or diagram. Flowcharting is also a "road map," showing what alternatives are available to the user based on conditions and results of previous steps or operations. Flowcharts need not be technical; most of the sequential day-to-day functions one does can be flowcharted. Figure 7-1 represents a typical flowchart that Mr. Jones goes through on his way to work when he has limited money in his pocket and a 60-mile round-trip car drive. Similarly, the equation of a falling body, $S = V_0t + \frac{1}{2}gt^2$, originally discussed in Chap. 2, is shown flowcharted in Fig. 7-2. As in Chap. 2, the equation will be solved for a 3-second fall in increments of 1 second.

In summary, the major uses of flowcharts are:

· To aid in the development of a program
· To show graphically the logical sequence of a program

173

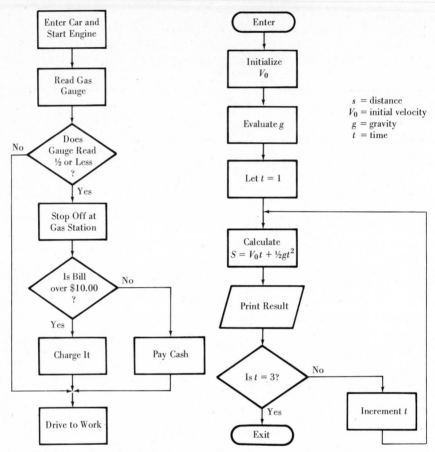

Figure 7-1 Flowchart for driving to work.

Figure 7-2 Flowchart for the equation of a falling body.

s = distance
V_0 = initial velocity
g = gravity
t = time

- To provide program documentation
- To use as a reference work sheet while writing a program

In developing a design solution to a problem, the logic designer uses the system block diagram to lay out an overall approach. The direct counterpart for a programmer is the flowchart.

Flow Symbols

To flowchart properly, the user must be acquainted with the basic techniques and be familiar with selected symbols, each of which represents a specific action. The standard flowcharting symbols were developed by ANSI.* A few of the most frequently used symbols are:

*American National Standards Institute.

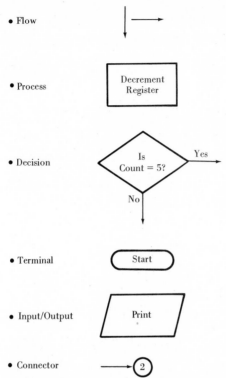

- Flow

- Process

  Decrement
  Register

- Decision

  Is
  Count = 5?   Yes

  No

- Terminal

  Start

- Input/Output

  Print

- Connector

  2

Lines with arrowheads indicate the sequence in which the various actions described in the flowchart are to be performed. Flowcharts should be drawn from top to bottom and read from left to right; however, variations are sometimes needed for symmetry and to emphasize certain flow paths.

The Process Symbol The process symbol is a rectangular figure; it can be any convenient size. Inside the box the programmer will write the description of some operation or process to be performed. For example, Clear Accumulator, Add Register B to A, Wait 10 ms, and Initialize Memory Pointer are four examples of processing statements found on flowcharts. The process symbol has only one entry and one exit arrowhead.

The Decision Symbol The decision symbol is diamond-shaped and is used to indicate a flow path direction to be taken as a result of a condition which is questioned by the symbol notation. There are one entry and two exit points (Yes and No) within the symbol. Is Carry Flag Set? and Is Register B = 0? are two examples of conditional tests performed by the symbol notation.

The Connector Symbol The connector symbol is a circular figure of any convenient size. It denotes an exit to or an entry from another part of the flowchart or another flowchart that links to the first one. Without the con-

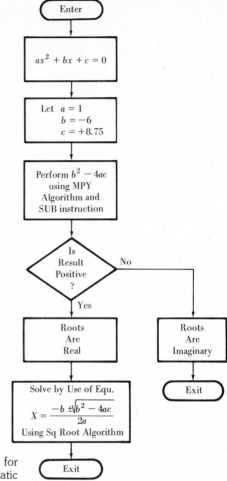

Figure 7-3 Concept-level flowchart for determining the real roots of a quadratic equation.

nector symbol, the flowchart could be a maze of symbols and arrowheads. There is only one arrowhead on a connector symbol, and it can be either an entry or an exit.

The Terminal Symbol The terminal symbol is an oblong figure, and it represents any terminal point in the flowchart. Enter, Start, Halt, Exit, and Return are expressions normally written inside this symbol. The terminal symbol has either an entry or an exit arrowhead.

The Input-Output Symbol The input-output symbol is a parallelogram. It represents I/O functions (generally in data processing systems) either as input data to be processed (Read a Card), or as output processed information (Print). In microprocessing applications which deal with I/O ports or peripherals, the process symbol (i.e., a rectangle) is equally acceptable.

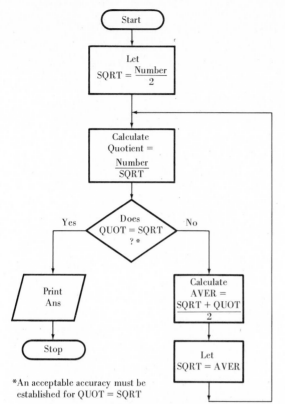

Start

Let
$SQRT = \dfrac{Number}{2}$

Calculate
Quotient =
$\dfrac{Number}{SQRT}$

Does
QUOT = SQRT
? *

Yes   No

Print
Ans

Stop

Calculate
AVER =
$\dfrac{SQRT + QUOT}{2}$

Let
SQRT = AVER

*An acceptable accuracy must be
established for QUOT = SQRT

Figure   7-4 Algorithm-
level flowchart for square
root.

7-2   LEVELS OF FLOWCHARTS

There are three levels of flowcharts generally used: (1) the concept level;
(2) the algorithm level; (3) the instruction level.

The concept-level flowchart is a system-type flowchart used to describe,
in a broad sense, the overall program. It contains the major sequence of
statements. Figure 7-3 is a concept-level flow diagram for determining if the
roots of the quadratic equation $x^2 - 6x + 8.75 = 0$ are real.

An algorithm is a well-defined set of rules or procedures by which a given
result is obtained. For example, an algorithm could describe a technique for
solving a specific function, such as multiplication by repeated additions. In
general each block of the concept-level flowchart is expanded to show the
individual steps that are required to achieve a desired result. The algorithm is
the method used in achieving the solution for each major function shown at
the concept level. Figure 7-4 illustrates an algorithm-level flowchart utilizing
the Newton-Raphson method for determining the square root of a number.

An instruction-level flowchart (see Fig. 7-5) is the most basic form of chart
available. Every function described is in the form of (an) equivalent instruc-
tion(s). Concept and algorithm flowcharts can be generated apart from any
specific microprocessor. However, to produce an instruction-level flowchart
the specific unit's instruction set must be known. The instruction-level

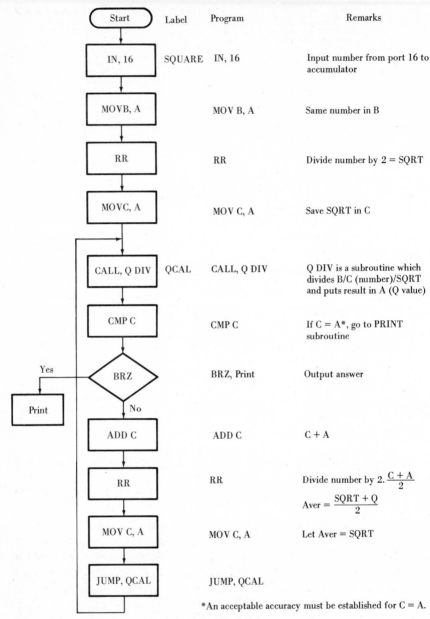

Figure 7-5 Instruction-level flowchart for determining the square root using the generic instruction set.

flowchart is then used to produce a program in assembly or machine-code language. When the program becomes quite large, instruction-level flowcharts can become quite unmanageable, since all instructions are specified at

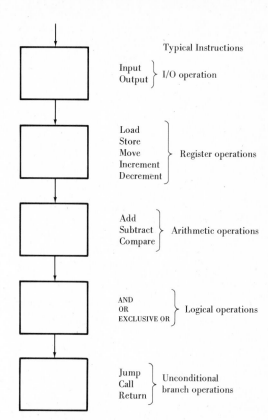

Figure 7-6 Instruction-level flowchart using the process symbols.

this level. Assembly language listings should be adequate and contain all the desired program statements and memory locations for data and addresses. Flowcharts are helpful when decisions and loops (discussed in Sec. 7-3) are utilized.

Typical instructions found within the process symbols are shown in the instruction-level flowchart of Fig. 7-6. It includes I/O, register, arithmetic, logic, and unconditional-branch operations. Figure 7-7 shows the use of the decision symbol to test the accumulator, the carry, and the flag bits. The decision symbol causes the program either to continue sequentially or to branch to another area of the program. These branches are called *conditional branches*.

Instruction-Level Programming Examples

The use of the process and decision symbols can be further illustrated by the two examples shown in Figs. 7-8 and 7-9.

In Fig. 7-8, a program is written which logically ANDS the contents of registers B and C and transfers the result to port 07.

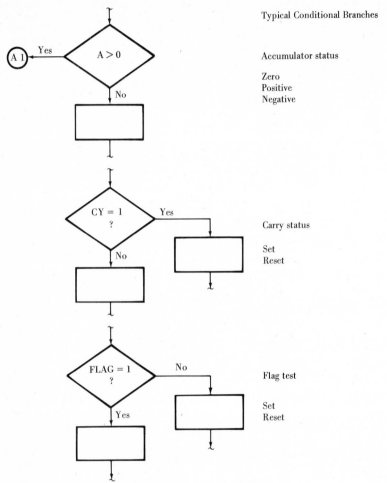

Typical Conditional Branches

Accumulator status

Zero
Positive
Negative

Carry status

Set
Reset

Flag test

Set
Reset

Figure 7-7 Conditional branches.

In Fig. 7-9, registers B and C are again logically ANDed. If the result of the logic operation is 0, the program branches to a program called Fail; otherwise the output is transmitted to port 07.

7-3 PROGRAMMING LOOPS

Suppose an entire 64K memory were filled with instructions which were executed only once. This extremely large program would take about a third of a second to complete, assuming an average of 5 μs to execute 1 byte. After this time the memory would have to be reloaded to execute additional programs. This approach to programming is inefficient, because invariably many of the instructions will be repeated in the same sequence over and over

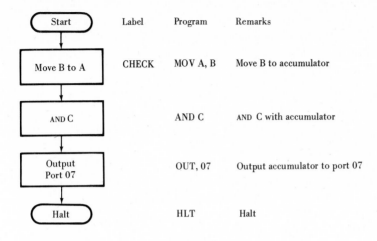

Figure 7-8 Use of process symbols.

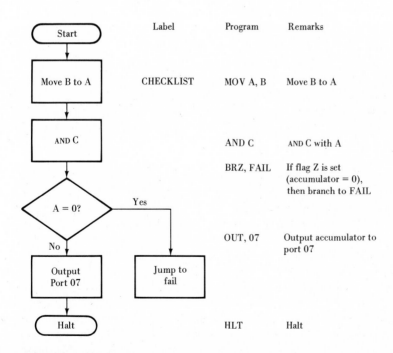

Figure 7-9 Use of decision symbols.

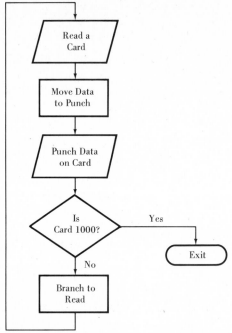

Figure 7-10 A Simple Loop Flowchart.

again, the only change being new operands. If calculations or sequences of operations involve the repetition of instructions in such a manner, then the programmer can avoid wasted storage space and effort by writing out one set of instructions. The last instruction in the set directs the microprocessor to branch back (or repeat) the process rather than writing a complete set of instructions for each new piece of data. This repetitive operation is called *looping.*

A simple flowchart utilizing looping is shown in Fig. 7-10, where an input card is read, its contents moved to the punch area, and the date punched on a blank card. In a 1,000-card input deck, this flowchart would be used repetitively until the one thousandth card was processed.

The necessary elements for the loop are a loop counter, which keeps track of the iteration through the loop, and the conditional branch instruction, which allows the program either to repeat or to "fall through" out of the loop to the next instruction in the program.

Loop Examples

Suppose we come to a point in a program where it is necessary to input 1 byte of data from an I/O port (see Fig. 7-11). A status control word is

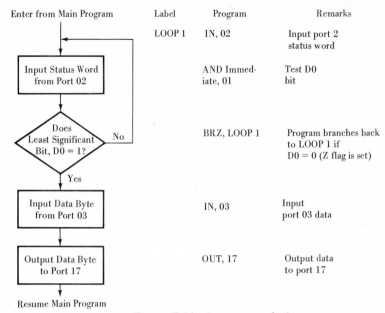

Figure 7-11 Loop example 1—
input and output 1 byte of data.

assigned to port 02 and the input data word to port 03. If there is valid input data, port 02 will transmit a status word with the least significant bit, $D0$, shown in Fig. 7-11, at logic 1. The microprocessor will continually loop-test $D0$ until the status word does contain a 1 at this location. Subsequent data received from port 03 is transmitted to its final destination, port 17, by the Output instruction.

Often it is required to go around a loop a fixed number of times. One method of accomplishing this is to set a register (register B) with the number of loops required and then to decrement it every time it passes through this loop until the register is at 0. Figure 7-12 shows how 5 bytes of data from port 03 are transmitted to the microprocessor and then subsequently stored in memory locations Data to Data + 4. Note that there are two loops in the programs. The small, inner loop used to test for status information was described in the previous example.

7-4 SUBROUTINES

Subroutines are programming segments that are generally written separately from the main program and whose primary function is to provide a well-defined mathematical or logic operation. Software is structured so that subroutines, if at all possible, are repeatedly used during the operation of the

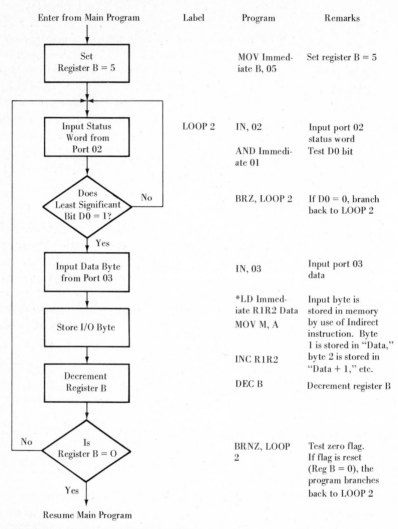

Enter from Main Program	Label	Program	Remarks
Set Register B = 5		MOV Immediate B, 05	Set register B = 5
Input Status Word from Port 02	LOOP 2	IN, 02	Input port 02 status word
		AND Immediate 01	Test D0 bit
Does Least Significant Bit D0 = 1? — No		BRZ, LOOP 2	If D0 = 0, branch back to LOOP 2
Yes			
Input Data Byte from Port 03		IN, 03	Input port 03 data
Store I/O Byte		*LD Immediate R1R2 Data MOV M, A	Input byte is stored in memory by use of Indirect instruction. Byte 1 is stored in "Data," byte 2 is stored in "Data + 1," etc.
		INC R1R2	
Decrement Register B		DEC B	Decrement register B
No — Is Register B = O		BRNZ, LOOP 2	Test zero flag. If flag is reset (Reg B = 0), the program branches back to LOOP 2
Yes			

Resume Main Program

*R1R2 represents a register pair (R1 and R2).

Figure 7-12 Loop example 2—store 5 data bytes.

main program (see Fig. 7-13). Typically, subroutines have particular use in mathematical processing of data. Common subroutines include Arctan and Binary-to-BCD or BCD-to-Binary. Sometimes subroutines themselves have subroutines, and so there can be several levels of subroutines. This programming technique is known as *nesting*.

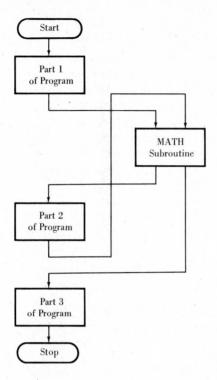

Figure 7-13   Utilization of math subroutine with main program.

In assembly language a subroutine will always be referenced by a label, such as the labels LOOP 1 and LOOP 2 shown in Figs. 7-11 and 7-12. An assembler also assigns a memory starting address for each label it encounters. When the main program requires a subroutine, it uses an instruction, such as Call, which saves (pushes) the contents of the program counter into the stack and forces the program counter to the Call address. When the subroutine is completed, it returns (pops) the registers and the program counter (via a Return instruction) from the stack. (See Sec. 5-7 for details on stacks and subroutine sequencing.)

Subroutine Examples

Figure 7-11 illustrated a program that inputs 1 byte of data from port 03 and outputs the data to port 17; it was part of the main program. Suppose we now wish to make this a subroutine. The only microprocessor registers used in the program are the accumulator (or register A) and the Status register, so only these registers need to be saved in the stack. The subroutine is shown in

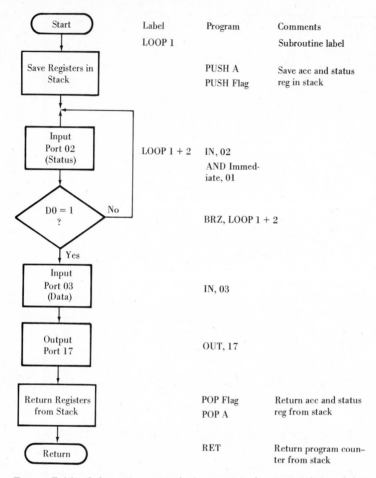

Label	Program	Comments
LOOP 1		Subroutine label
	PUSH A	Save acc and status
	PUSH Flag	reg in stack
LOOP 1 + 2	IN, 02	
	AND Immed- iate, 01	
	BRZ, LOOP 1 + 2	
	IN, 03	
	OUT, 17	
	POP Flag	Return acc and status
	POP A	reg from stack
	RET	Return program coun- ter from stack

Figure 7-14 Subroutine example 1—input and output 1 byte of data.

Fig. 7-14. At the end of the subroutine the accumulator, the Status register, and the program counter are returned to the main program. The instruction in the main program that initiates the subroutine is:

Call, LOOP 1

Common subroutines perform I/O, code conversion, and trig functions. A subroutine quite different from these is a time-delay subroutine. Its intent is to use up or literally waste time. Utilizing a subroutine is just one approach to performing this function. As an example of using subroutines, consider a 30-μs delay required by the main program. If the execution time of the Return (RET) and No Operation (NOP) are 10 and 4 μs, respectively, then a subroutine that offers the required time delay could be coded as follows:

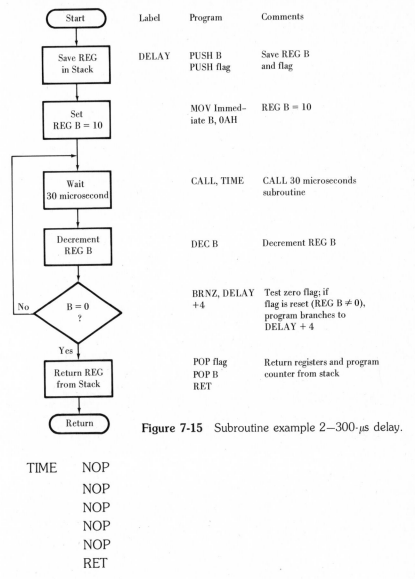

	Label	Program	Comments
Start			
Save REG in Stack	DELAY	PUSH B PUSH flag	Save REG B and flag
Set REG B = 10		MOV Immed- iate B, 0AH	REG B = 10
Wait 30 microsecond		CALL, TIME	CALL 30 microseconds subroutine
Decrement REG B		DEC B	Decrement REG B
B = 0 ?		BRNZ, DELAY +4	Test zero flag; if flag is reset (REG B ≠ 0), program branches to DELAY + 4
Return REG from Stack		POP flag POP B RET	Return registers and program counter from stack
Return			

Figure 7-15 Subroutine example 2—300-μs delay.

```
TIME    NOP
        NOP
        NOP
        NOP
        NOP
        RET
```

Each time the main program issues the instruction

Call, TIME

a delay of 30 μs is accomplished. Suppose it is required to generate a delay of about 300 μs in the main program. Figure 7-15 shows how this may be accomplished by using a loop and the time-delay subroutine. The process symbol of a flowchart might read:

```
┌─────────┐
│  WAIT   │
│ 300 μs  │
└─────────┘
```

Register B is used as a loop counter; it is decremented after each Call time-delay subroutine is executed. After 10 Calls, approximately 300 μs have elapsed and the program falls out of the time-delay loop. A more precise time it takes to execute the program can be calculated by summing the execution times of all the instructions which constitute the program. This includes 1 Move, 10 Call, 10 Decrement, 10 Branch If Not Zero, 2 Push, 2 Pop, and 1 Return instruction as well as the 300-μs time-delay subroutine.

The power of subroutines cannot be overemphasized. It should now be evident that subroutines have the following advantages:

- They save memory space by eliminating the need to rewrite the same sequence of instructions over and over again.
- They simplify programming by calling well-established subroutines.
- They reduce coding errors—if subroutines are not used, then every instruction has to be coded and tested before being accepted in its final form. Invariably the more instructions that are written, the greater the number of errors that will be generated. Conversely, the fewer instructions which are utilized, the fewer errors the program will have, and the easier it will be to find and correct them.

7-5 MACROS

Macros were defined in Chap. 6 as a group of instructions utilized many times yet sufficiently small not to be worthy of a subroutine. The advantage of macros are:

- A small group of instructions is replaced by one macro.
- Programming is simplified.
- The program is less error-prone.
- Macros create new instructions.

The main disadvantage is that macros still require storage space for the instruction each time they are used. It is advisable to use subroutines whenever possible, not macros.

7-6 EIGHT PROGRAMMING EXAMPLES

To illustrate the application of programs in microprocessing systems, a group of programs is presented. A description of the program, a flowchart, and an assembly-type format listing are included for all programs.

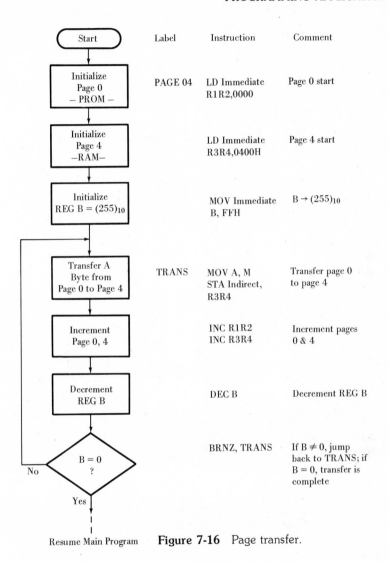

Label	Instruction	Comment
	Start	
PAGE 04	LD Immediate R1R2,0000	Page 0 start
	LD Immediate R3R4,0400H	Page 4 start
	MOV Immediate B, FFH	$B \rightarrow (255)_{10}$
TRANS	MOV A, M STA Indirect, R3R4	Transfer page 0 to page 4
	INC R1R2 INC R3R4	Increment pages 0 & 4
	DEC B	Decrement REG B
	BRNZ, TRANS	If $B \neq 0$, jump back to TRANS; if $B = 0$, transfer is complete

Flowchart blocks: Start; Initialize Page 0 – PROM –; Initialize Page 4 –RAM–; Initialize REG B = $(255)_{10}$; Transfer A Byte from Page 0 to Page 4; Increment Page 0, 4; Decrement REG B; B = 0 ? (No / Yes); Resume Main Program.

Figure 7-16 Page transfer.

APPLICATION EXAMPLE ONE

Page Transfer

An area of memory, called a page, is to transfer its contents to another area of memory. This can be very useful in diagnostic testing when a program residing in PROM is possibly in error. As shown in Fig. 7-16, the PROM program resides in page 0, memory locations 0000 to 00FFH, and is to be transferred to page 4, memory locations 0400 to 04FFH. The starting

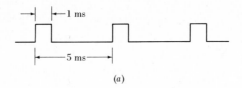

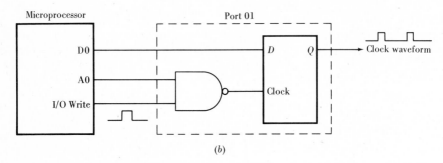

Figure 7-17 Clock generator. (a) Clock wave-form; (b) logic implementation.

addresses of page 0 and page 4 are loaded into the memory pointer register, R1R2 and another register pair, R3R4, respectively. Register B is loaded with 255_{10}, which represents the page length. A byte from page 0 is transferred temporarily to the accumulator and then placed in page 4. This process is continued until register B, decremented after each byte transfer, is at 0. When register B is at 0, a total of 256 bytes has been transferred from page 0 to page 4. Now the programmer may run the PROM program in RAM and alter its contents to produce an error-free program.

APPLICATION EXAMPLE TWO

Clock Generator

A clock generator can be implemented primarily by software techniques, as shown in this example. The required waveform, which has 1-ms pulse width and a 5-ms period, is shown in Fig. 7-17. The clock generator requires a NAND gate and a D flip-flop at port 01 to yield the desired waveshape. Port 01 is clocked when the A0 Address line equals 1 and the control line I/O Write is true. The accumulator is used to output a 1 at D0 on the data bus when an Output instruction is generated. When the accumulator is cleared followed by an Output instruction, the 0, or Off, portion of the waveshape is generated. Time delays following each Output instruction produce the appropriate pulse width and period of the signal. If it becomes necessary to change the clock pulse width or the frequency, a rather simple programming change is all that

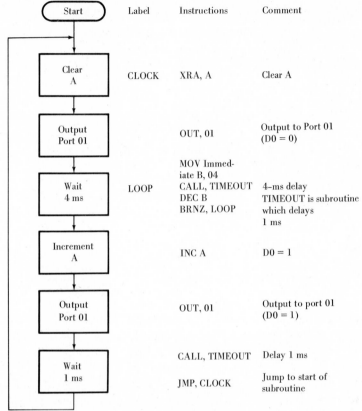

Label	Instructions	Comment

Start

Clear A — CLOCK — XRA, A — Clear A

Output Port 01 — OUT, 01 — Output to Port 01 (D0 = 0)

Wait 4 ms — LOOP — MOV Immediate B, 04 / CALL, TIMEOUT / DEC B / BRNZ, LOOP — 4-ms delay / TIMEOUT is subroutine which delays 1 ms

Increment A — INC A — D0 = 1

Output Port 01 — OUT, 01 — Output to port 01 (D0 = 1)

Wait 1 ms — CALL, TIMEOUT — Delay 1 ms / JMP, CLOCK — Jump to start of subroutine

Figure 7-18 Clock generator flowchart and program.

is required. An alternative hardware clock generator would require component and possibly wiring changes. The flowchart and program are found in Fig. 7-18.

APPLICATION EXAMPLE THREE

Error Detection

Devices are generally designed in two fashions: either "dumb" or "smart." A dumb device has no processing or decision capability of its own. It is designed to perform a specific function and it does it. A smart device, on the other hand, can perform other functions. Its capability is dependent on the overall requirements of the system. Suppose a smart I/O device is able to determine if it has malfunctioned. The malfunction could be an overflow caused by a previous input or output, or perhaps a mechanical or electrical failure, such as a temporary loss of power. If 10 of these smart I/Os were

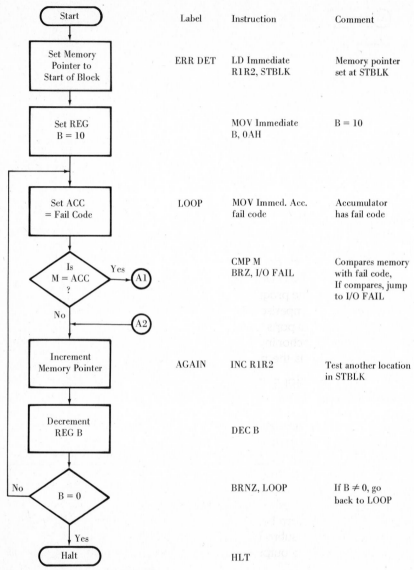

Label	Instruction	Comment
ERR DET	LD Immediate R1R2, STBLK	Memory pointer set at STBLK
	MOV Immediate B, 0AH	B = 10
LOOP	MOV Immed. Acc. fail code	Accumulator has fail code
	CMP M BRZ, I/O FAIL	Compares memory with fail code, If compares, jump to I/O FAIL
AGAIN	INC R1R2	Test another location in STBLK
	DEC B	
	BRNZ, LOOP	If B ≠ 0, go back to LOOP
	HLT	

Figure 7-19 I/O error detector.

designed into a microcomputing system, then a program to locate the I/Os that have malfunctioned can be written, as shown in Fig. 7-19.

When an I/O detects a failure it interrupts the microprocessor and loads a Fail code at a known address in memory. STBLK is the start of the block of 10 addresses in the memory that identify the I/Os. A failure of the first I/O

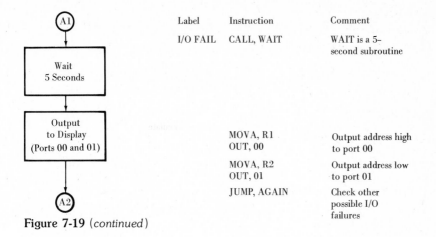

Label	Instruction	Comment
I/O FAIL	CALL, WAIT	WAIT is a 5–second subroutine
	MOVA, R1	Output address high
	OUT, 00	to port 00
	MOVA, R2	Output address low
	OUT, 01	to port 01
	JUMP, AGAIN	Check other possible I/O failures

Figure 7-19 (*continued*)

would cause the Fail code corresponding to the identification (ID) at STBLK, a failure of the second I/O would cause a Fail code corresponding to the ID at STBLK + 1, etc. The program compares the contents of STBLK with the Fail code. When a comparison is made, the program waits 5 seconds and then outputs to display ports 00 and 01. The addresses in STBLK are used to identify the malfunctioning I/O. Only after all 10 addresses of STBLK have been examined is the program completed.

APPLICATION EXAMPLE FOUR

Memory Tester

RAM memory chips can easily be tested by writing a pattern into memory and then reading back from the same memory location. A proper comparison causes the next location to be similarly tested. A software memory-test program and flowchart that utilizes alternating 1010 1010 (0AAH) and 0101 0101 (55H) test patterns is shown in Fig. 7-20. Initialization of start and end addresses and test patterns is first performed before the memory is tested. Should the pattern be different from that written, the program then branches to an error subroutine that traps the failed memory data and address location at two output ports and forces the program to a Halt.

APPLICATION EXAMPLE FIVE

Serial Input of Data

Input data can be transmitted to a microprocessor serially, one bit at a time, by detecting the start of the transmission and inserting the proper delays to clock in the data at the center of the bit time, where the bit is more likely to be stable. Figure 7-21 shows a typical TTY input with a start bit, 7 data bits, a parity bit (even), and 2 stop bits. The program is initialized by setting a bit

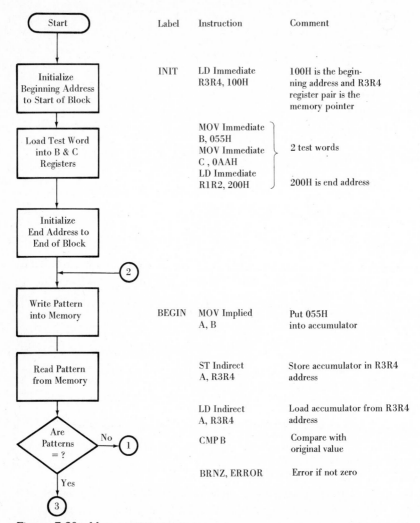

Figure 7-20 Memory test program.

counter to 8, since we wish to receive all 7 bits plus the parity bit. It also enables the internal Interrupt latch and then halts the microprocessor. If the input data is tied to the *D*0 line of the data bus and also to the Interrupt line, then an Interrupt will occur only when the negative-going edge of the start bit is detected. Detection of this bit initiates the program. The interrupt takes the microprocessor out of the Halt mode and causes the program to branch to INDATA. A 4.5-ms subroutine is used to establish the approximate center of the start bit. An additional 9.0-ms program loop enables the input data to be sampled into the microprocessor at the center of the bit time. The data

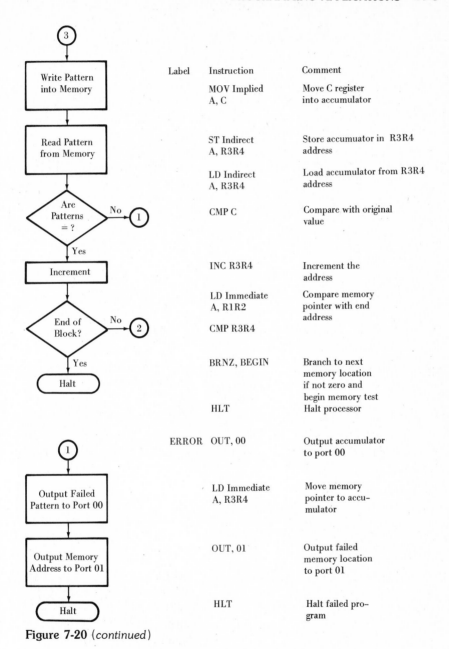

Label	Instruction	Comment
	MOV Implied A, C	Move C register into accumulator
	ST Indirect A, R3R4	Store accumuator in R3R4 address
	LD Indirect A, R3R4	Load accumulator from R3R4 address
	CMP C	Compare with original value
	INC R3R4	Increment the address
	LD Immediate A, R1R2	Compare memory pointer with end address
	CMP R3R4	
	BRNZ, BEGIN	Branch to next memory location if not zero and begin memory test
	HLT	Halt processor
ERROR	OUT, 00	Output accumulator to port 00
	LD Immediate A, R3R4	Move memory pointer to accu- mulator
	OUT, 01	Output failed memory location to port 01
	HLT	Halt failed pro- gram

Figure 7-20 (*continued*)

transfer is from the accumulator to the register R1. After another 9-ms delay, the second bit is stored in the register R1. After eight 9-ms delays, all 8 bits are stored in register R1 and the program is halted.

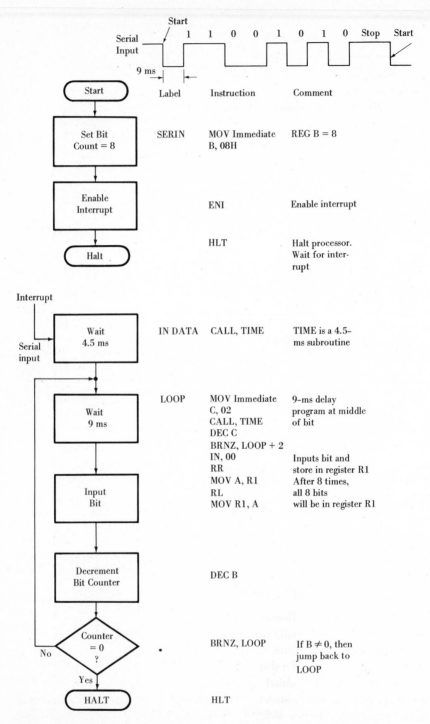

Figure 7-21 Input serial data.

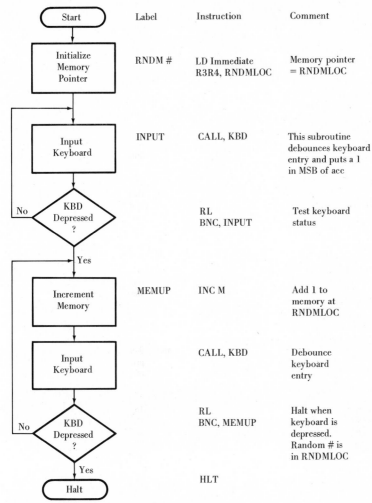

	Label	Instruction	Comment
Start			
Initialize Memory Pointer	RNDM #	LD Immediate R3R4, RNDMLOC	Memory pointer = RNDMLOC
Input Keyboard	INPUT	CALL, KBD	This subroutine debounces keyboard entry and puts a 1 in MSB of acc
KBD Depressed ?		RL BNC, INPUT	Test keyboard status
Increment Memory	MEMUP	INC M	Add 1 to memory at RNDMLOC
Input Keyboard		CALL, KBD	Debounce keyboard entry
KBD Depressed ?		RL BNC, MEMUP	Halt when keyboard is depressed. Random # is in RNDMLOC
Halt		HLT	

Figure 7-22 Random-number generator.

APPLICATION EXAMPLE SIX

Random-Number Generator

Many programs, especially programs that are written for games, require a random-number generator. One hardware random-number generator implementation consists of a shift register and an EXCLUSIVE OR logic circuit. The clock circuit can be enabled or disabled by an external device, such as a toggle switch. When the switch is enabled, the circuit operates with a 12-bit shift register to produce 4096 random numbers.

An alternative approach: A software random-number generator is shown in Fig. 7-22. The program places a random number at memory location RNDMLOC each time a keyboard entry is made twice. The keyboard generates a status/data word in which the most significant bit is a 1 when a certain key is depressed. The first entry of the keyboard causes the program to increment the data located RNDMLOC. The keyboard is tested again, and if the key is not depressed the data is incremented at a fast rate. The keyboard subroutine requires about 20 instructions, and if each instruction averages 3 μs, the random number is updated about every 63 μs (60 for the subroutine and 3 for the INC M instruction), or 16,000 times a second. When the entry is keyed a second time, the program is halted.

APPLICATION EXAMPLE SEVEN

Parity (Odd) Checker

In the transmission of an ASCII* word, 7 bits are considered data and 1 bit parity. If the parity is designated as odd parity, then the number of 1s in the 8-bit byte is either 1, 3, 5 or 7. Suppose the problem is to test an ASCII byte in memory and verify if it is correct; if it is not correct the program is to jump to a fail program. Figure 7-23 shows how this can be accomplished. The memory pointer locates the ASCII byte. Registers R3 and R4 are loaded with 00 and 08H, respectively. The least significant bit of the ASCII byte is shifted into the carry, and it is tested for a 1 or a 0. If it is a 1, then Register R3 is incremented. Register R4 is decremented regardless of the state of the bit in the carry position. After the 8 ASCII bits are checked, register R4 contains 00 and register R3 contains the number of 1s in the ASCII byte. The program then checks register R3 for a 01, 03, 05, or 07. If any of them appear, the ASCII byte was odd parity and the program is halted; however, if none of them appears, the program jumps to another program called Fail, indicating that the ASCII byte contained 0 or an even number of 1s.

APPLICATION EXAMPLE EIGHT

Outputting a Teletype Message: HELLO—HOW ARE YOU?

Interfacing a teletype (TTY), which is a serial unit, to a microprocessor requires the utilization of a serial-to-parallel converter, such as a UART (see Chap. 9). If the UART is assigned a status port of 23 and a data port of 31, then when the microprocessor is ready to output a character to the TTY it must first check the UART's status word to find out if the UART is ready to transmit to the TTY. When the status word is received at port 23H, the least significant bit is tested. If it is a 1, then the microprocessor outputs the character to the UART via port 31H, which in turn sends it to the TTY. After

---

*ASCII is a standard alphanumeric code defining a character set. See Chap. 9, Sec. 4 for further details.

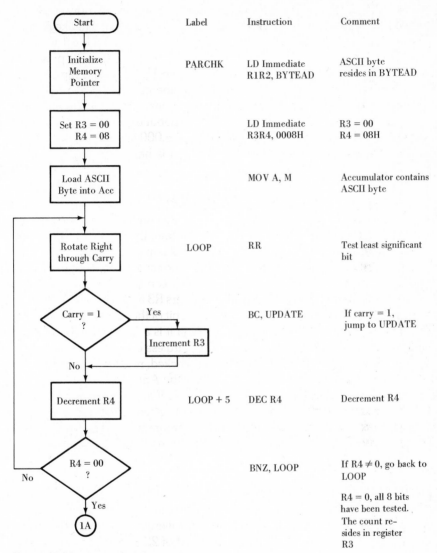

	Label	Instruction	Comment
Start			
Initialize Memory Pointer	PARCHK	LD Immediate R1R2, BYTEAD	ASCII byte resides in BYTEAD
Set R3 = 00 R4 = 08		LD Immediate R3R4, 0008H	R3 = 00 R4 = 08H
Load ASCII Byte into Acc		MOV A, M	Accumulator contains ASCII byte
Rotate Right through Carry	LOOP	RR	Test least significant bit
Carry = 1 ? Yes		BC, UPDATE	If carry = 1, jump to UPDATE
Increment R3			
No			
Decrement R4	LOOP + 5	DEC R4	Decrement R4
R4 = 00 ? No		BNZ, LOOP	If R4 ≠ 0, go back to LOOP
Yes 1A			R4 = 0, all 8 bits have been tested. The count resides in register R3

Figure 7-23 Parity (odd) checker.

20 characters (14H) are transmitted from memory locations Charst to Charst + 19, the program is halted, indicating that the entire message has been transmitted. The 20 ASCII characters are: H, E, L, L, O, −, H, O, W, SPACE, A, R, E, SPACE, Y, O, U, ?, CARRIAGE RETURN, LINE FEED.*

The flowchart and program are shown in Fig. 7-24.

*In Fig. 7-24, the characters are encoded using ASCII code.

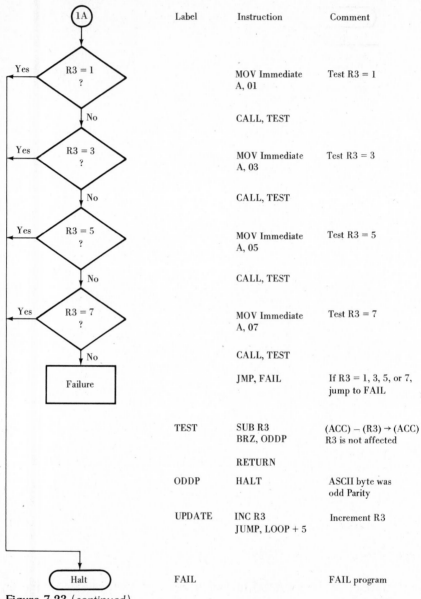

	Label	Instruction	Comment
R3 = 1 ?		MOV Immediate A, 01	Test R3 = 1
		CALL, TEST	
R3 = 3 ?		MOV Immediate A, 03	Test R3 = 3
		CALL, TEST	
R3 = 5 ?		MOV Immediate A, 05	Test R3 = 5
		CALL, TEST	
R3 = 7 ?		MOV Immediate A, 07	Test R3 = 7
		CALL, TEST	
Failure		JMP, FAIL	If R3 = 1, 3, 5, or 7, jump to FAIL
	TEST	SUB R3 BRZ, ODDP	(ACC) − (R3) → (ACC) R3 is not affected
		RETURN	
	ODDP	HALT	ASCII byte was odd Parity
	UPDATE	INC R3 JUMP, LOOP + 5	Increment R3
Halt	FAIL		FAIL program

Figure 7-23 (*continued*)

PROBLEMS

1. What are the major uses of a flowchart?
2. Develop an algorithm flowchart and program using standard charting

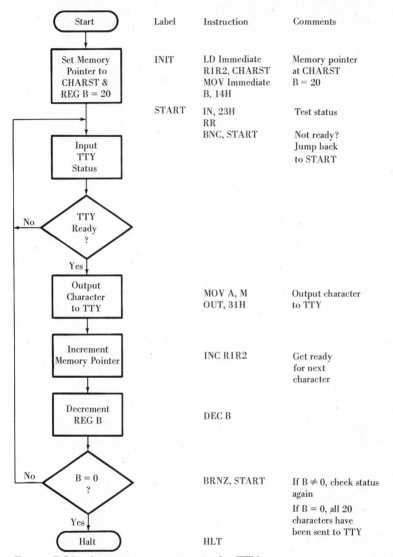

Label	Instruction	Comments
INIT	LD Immediate R1R2, CHARST MOV Immediate B, 14H	Memory pointer at CHARST B = 20
START	IN, 23H RR BNC, START	Test status Not ready? Jump back to START
	MOV A, M OUT, 31H	Output character to TTY
	INC R1R2	Get ready for next character
	DEC B	
	BRNZ, START	If B ≠ 0, check status again If B = 0, all 20 characters have been sent to TTY
	HLT	

Figure 7-24 Outputting a message to the TTY.

symbols that multiplies two numbers by successive additions. Test for any number being 0.

3. A vending machine dispenses a soft drink provided: (a) it receives exactly a quarter; (b) it has cups; (c) it has the soft drink mixture. If any of the above conditions is not true, the money is returned. Write a flowchart on the operation of this vending machine.

Label	Instruction	Comment	
CHARST	48H	H	Parity bit is
	45H	E	not used
	4CH	L	
	4CH	L	
	4FH	O	
	2DH	—	
	48H	H	
	4FH	O	
	57H	W	
	20H	SP	(space)
	41H	A	
	52H	R	
	45H	E	
	20H	SP	(space)
	59H	Y	
	4FH	O	
	55H	U	
	3FH	?	
	0DH	CR	(carriage return)
	0AH	LF	(line feed)

Figure 7-24 (*continued*)

4. Write an instruction-level flowchart and a program using the generic instruction set which adds the contents of memory location ALPHA to memory location BETA and puts the result in memory location GAMMA.

   (*a*) Use indirect memory instructions.

   (*b*) Use load and store direct instructions.

5. Develop an instruction-level flowchart and program that receives 6 input data bytes from port 1 and stores them in memory starting at location 4224H. Use R1 to store the count and register pair R2R3 as the memory pointer register. Assume port 1 is always ready.

6. Output port 16H consists of eight latched LEDs. Write a flowchart and a program that blinks all the LEDs at a 2-s rate (on for 1 s, off for 1 s). Use a 100-ms watt loop which exists in location labeled TIMEOUT.

7. Write a program to output the message: FINE AND YOU? The TTY status port is 23H and its status word is 1XXXXXXX. The TTY data port is 30H.

REFERENCES

1. Intel Corporation: *8080 Microcomputer User's Manual,* September 1975.
2. Spencer, D. D.: *Fundamentals of Digital Computers,* Howard W. Sams & Co., Inc., Indianapolis, 1969.
3. Stark, Peter A.: *Digital Computer Programming,* The Macmillan Company, New York, 1969.

Beyond the
Microprocessor Chip

The microprocessor, which was first described in Chap. 3, is normally used in conjunction with other supporting chips that enable a wide spectrum of applications, from dedicated control functions to data processors. Recent advances in technology have made possible the manufacture of higher-density chips, resulting in higher-integration-level devices. One such device is the microcomputer chip. With the ability to produce systems with a smaller parts count, solid-state device manufacturers have successfully developed 16-bit microcomputers which can directly compete with the minicomputer. Another approach widely used where high performance is mandated is the "bit-slice" unit, which contains most of the arithmetic registers of a microprocessor, except that the registers are either 2 or 4 bits wide. By grouping the bit slices, or "vertical slices," as they are also commonly called, to form a 16-bit arithmetic unit and then adding memory and control circuitry external to the chips, it is possible to make a very powerful data processor. This chapter will concern itself with those units which have exceeded the performance or integration level of the basic 8-bit microprocessor chip; that is, those units which go beyond the microprocessor.

8-1 THE MULTICHIP SYSTEM

Since the microprocessor chip does not contain any memory or I/O capability, it must rely on external chips to structure it into a microcomputing system. One widely used method is to dedicate three separate buses to provide the address, data, and control lines for those elements which are

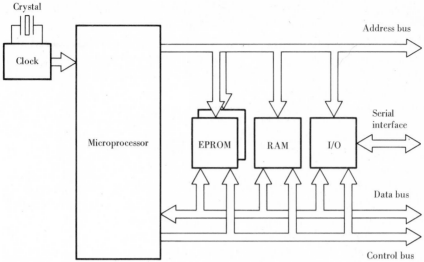

Figure 8-1 A typical microcomputer using multiple chips.

used to define a microcomputer system. A typical system, as shown in Fig. 8-1, consists of the microprocessor, RAM and EPROM memory units, and an I/O chip, which provides a serial interface. Tri-state logic on the buses assures that no loading problems will ensue within this configuration.

The basic operation when the multichip system is used consists of the same sequences of fetching and executing instructions as were discussed in Chaps. 3 and 5.

The data memory provides the operands during the execution cycle, while the I/O device converts the external serial interface into the parallel interface required by the data bus.

In the configuration shown in Fig. 8-1, chips of different technologies were chosen for data and instruction memories. EPROMs were selected to provide the user with the flexibility of modifying instruction programs while maintaining a nonvolatile memory. The clock driver chip supplies compatible voltage levels and the basic timing signals required by the microprocessor. An external crystal is used as the clock source.

The Microcomputer Chip

Although the multichip approach is providing large-scale integration techniques for building computers and other digital systems, the development of the microcomputer chip represents another major milestone in solid-state technology. The ability to produce a total computer on a chip has been long sought. Its development, however, is not a panacea, since many compromises in the design were made by manufacturers of the chips. Memory size, memory technology, processor architecture, and I/O structure are some of the key variables which designers have had to decide upon. In some chips, the memory of the microcomputer is not externally expandable and therefore limits the capability of the device. The development of the microcomputer and its utilization in a multichip-system environment does yield many advantages, however. These include:

· Fewer chips are used to design a system. Typically a seven-component system can be replaced by a single unit.

· There is greater reliability and higher system efficiency as a result of utilizing internal memories.

· Projected costs are lower because there are fewer parts.

· Chips are designed so that they can be used with existing families of peripheral devices.

· Last and most important, software is compatible with existing microprocessor products, which allows the technology to be updated while maintaining the original software.

A strategy utilized by some of the solid-state manufacturers has resulted in the marketing of a two-device (two-chip) configuration, which is highly competitive.

A two-chip system generally offers more program memory capability than the single-chip device. The single microcomputing chip has size constraints, as it must contain the microprocessor, the ROM, the RAM, timing, and some I/O capability. Many other available "dedicated" chips also exceed the capabilities of a two-chip system. That is, the density of dedicated RAM chips is in the 16K-to 64K-bit range, while the RAM density within a two-chip system is generally limited to less than 8K bits.

A two-chip system is shown in Fig. 8-2. The RAM, the microprocessor, and the clock are partitioned on one chip, while the ROM program memory, the parallel I/O lines, and the timer, used to generate time delays, reside on the second chip.

Most single- and dual-chip systems provide software compatibility with existing microprocessing units. These newer units contain many if not all of the original instructions grouped as a subset of a larger instruction set to help minimize software costs. In this manner, programs which were developed and validated and are operational with the original chip are directly usable with the new system. This technique is commonly referred to as *upward compatibility* of software. The newer chips, whether they are partitioned into one or two devices, have faster execution times. This is due to operating with faster clocks, better handling capability of data by the chip, and optimized instruction sets having no more than 2 bytes per instruction.

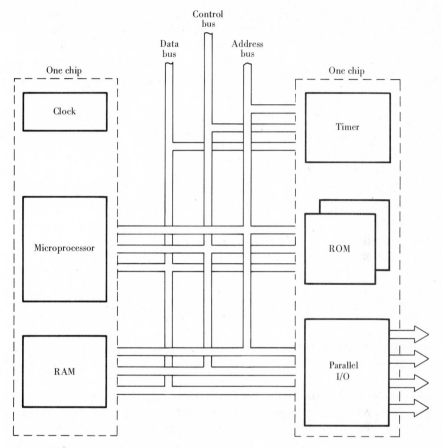

Figure 8-2 A two-chip microcomputer.

8-2 THE MICROCOMPUTER

The microcomputer chip combines into a single chip all the functions of a two-chip system. Figure 8-3 is a block diagram of a typical microcomputer. The parallel and serial I/O lines are programmable, allowing for greater flexibility. The timer can also be used as a counter to count external events, and since it is programmable, it can be preset to any value. Should the maximum count/time of the unit be exceeded, an Overflow flag and an Interrupt request are set. The on-board clock circuitry has an oscillator which uses an external clock source or crystal as a reference input. The memory is available in three forms: instructions can utilize EPROMs, for breadboard development, or ROMs. The data storage is provided by a RAM.

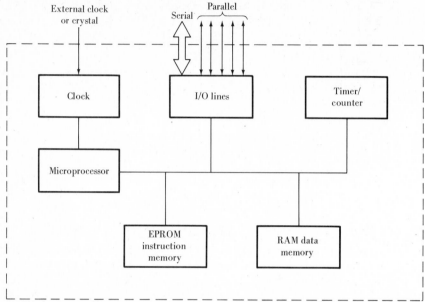

Figure 8-3 A typical single-chip system.

Internal Architecture of a Microcomputer Chip

The microcomputer can be partitioned into three sections, as shown in Fig. 8-4. The arithmetic section includes the accumulator and the arithmetic logic unit, which perform the logic and arithmetic operations. The instruction register and decoding/timing circuits provide the basic control of the chip. Data paths are enabled after the instruction is decoded. Several elements of the microcomputer, such as the accumulator, Carry flag, and Interrupt input, are tested during program execution by the conditional branch logic. If the condition is met, then the jump in the program does take place.

The major difference between a microprocessor and a microcomputer occurs in the register/memory and I/O interface section. While the microprocessor typically has dedicated registers, the microcomputer utilizes a RAM memory partitioned into two sections, each section functioning as a register bank. The RAM also contains a stack and a RAM scratch pad/data area. The two register banks provide "context switching" capability, which means that should an interrupt occur, the program can switch from one set of registers to the other without going through a "save register" routine. The register banks can also be used simultaneously if required. The registers are selected by use of another register which functions as a register pointer. The stack provides the capability of storing the program counter and status word whenever a subroutine or an interrupt is initiated. When either event occurs,

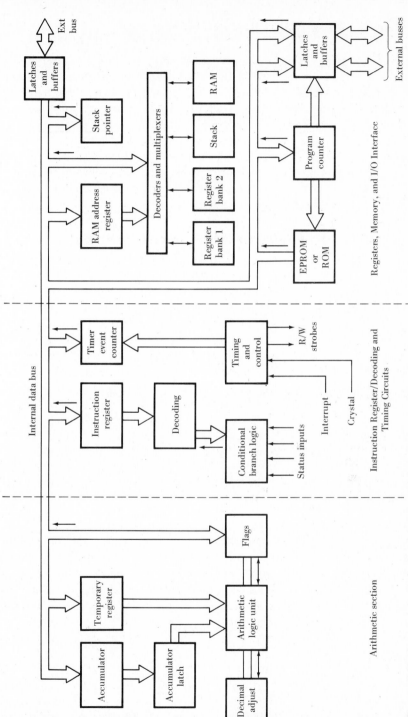

Figure 8-4 Internal architecture of a microcomputer.

the contents of the program counter and of other registers are stored in the stack. The remainder of the RAM memory is used to store data and/or serve as a scratch pad area. The instruction memory, which can be either a PROM or a ROM, is addressed by the program counter. The high-order bits are externally available, so that if additional program memory is required, it can be addressed by these bits. The microcomputer interface section is generally more extensive than that of a microprocessor. The microcomputer typically has three to four ports, with most ports being programmable and consisting of eight bidirectional lines. A half- or full-duplex serial communication interface is normally available on the microcomputer.

8-3 MICROPROGRAMMABLE PROCESSORS

Microprogrammable processors are computers that have a programmable rather than a fixed software instruction set. The development of the micro-programmable microprocessor is a result of a variety of high-performance applications, such as signal processors and digital controllers, requiring greater capability than that offered by the microprocessor. The approach taken by the semiconductor industry was to develop a microprogrammed processor whose performance would reach the boundaries of the minicomputer. To produce devices that were capable of fast operation, the units were originally designed with the same TTL bipolar technology as minicomputers. MOS technology used in early microprocessor developments was just too slow for the intended applications; its gate delay times were much greater than those of units which employed the bipolar technology. In addition, the MOS microprocessor data word length was initially 4 bits (later 8 bits), producing an inefficient word length where the high-performance applications were required.

The microprogrammable microprocessor has an architecture quite different from that of "conventional" MOS processors. Its unique features are:

1. The user specifies the instruction set; this implies that the processor's instructions are customized to applications and stored in a PROM or ROM. A later section of this chapter will treat this subject in more depth.

2. The arithmetic unit is partitioned into several small chips, each device containing identical functions.

As an example, we shall see how it is possible to develop a high-speed, 16-bit bipolar arithmetic unit with registers, logic, and control as its main functions.

The partitioning of the arithmetic unit into several identical smaller units is required because of two present-day technology limitations:

1. High performance generally cannot be derived without dissipating a great deal of power. Since most LSI devices are limited to 1 or 2 watts (W),

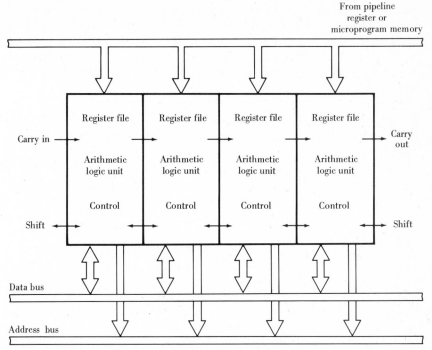

Figure 8-5   Arithmetic section of a microprogrammable bit-slice microprocessor.

the function must be segmented into smaller chips. As an example, if a function requires 10 W, one design approach that may be considered is to partition the function into five smaller devices, each chip using 2 W.

2.   Bipolar circuits are fabricated on a greater silicon area than MOS. A complete 16-bit arithmetic unit of bipolar TTL technology is today not possible on one chip; however, it is not unreasonable to implement this function with MOS technology. If bipolar technology is used, it is reasonable to implement this function with units of 2 or 4 or possibly 8 bits each.

The partitioning of the arithmetic unit is accomplished by segmenting the unit vertically into "slices," with each smaller unit containing a slice of the whole. Figure 8-5 represents a typical 16-bit arithmetic section of a microprogramming unit, with each slice containing 4 bits. If the slices were to be limited to 2 bits in width, then eight slices would be needed. Four-bit-wide chips are predominantly used. Longer word lengths are made possible by merely grouping the slices together to any width that is a multiple of the basic size. A 32-bit processor requires eight 4-bit slices or sixteen 2-bit slices. Present bit slices are 2 and 4 bits wide, and with advances in producing higher-density chips, an 8-bit slice is eminent. Although a 2- or 4-bit-slice chip cannot operate efficiently by itself, several of these units grouped in parallel can perform high-speed processing.

There is limited communication between the chips at the Shift and Carry interface. The control section of the CPU is excluded from the vertical partitioning. Separate devices will be used to implement these functions.

Microprogramming System Overview

The basic functional block diagram is shown in Fig. 8-6. It consists of separate arithmetic and control units implemented by the vertical bit slices and multiple control chips, respectively. The main memory is also made up of individual devices grouped together to form the total memory configuration required. The data and address buses interface with the I/O unit.

The basic function of the control unit in all microprocessors is to enable appropriate data paths for the execution of the instructions. The control unit is generally very complex, as it must accept and generate many types of signals to allow the operations to be performed. The more complex the function, the more "irregular" the chip cell pattern which implements the function and hence the more costly the device. By contrast, memories are highly "regular," since the same cell pattern (the flip-flop or its derivative) is used as the basic storage element over and over again. This enables regular patterns of LSI devices, such as memories, to be denser than irregular units.

In the microprogrammable microprocessor, the highly irregular control unit is replaced by a memory unit called a *microprogram memory* (or *control store*) and a second unit called a *control sequencer*. Together they regulate the execution of instructions from the microprogram memory. The sequencer functions as a program counter, providing the memory address of the next (micro)instruction. Its value is based on internal and external status data. Until recently, it was not economically feasible to replace the control section of a computer by memory, since the cost of memory was higher than that of any other functional element of the system; but with the large increase in production of memories and with developments in technology, the price of ROMs and PROMs has come down significantly.

Several definitions which can help describe the overall architecture of microprogramming units are now in order.

Microprogram Memory A memory whose functional output is used to control the microprocessor elements. The microprogram memory contains conventional PROMs and ROMs, but the structure of the memory word is quite different; data widths of the units are twice to four times those of conventional units. A common instruction memory size used with a 16-bit microprocessor is $4K \times 16$; a typical microprogram memory size can be $4K \times 48$ bits. A greater explanation of how the memory word is structured will be given later in this chapter.

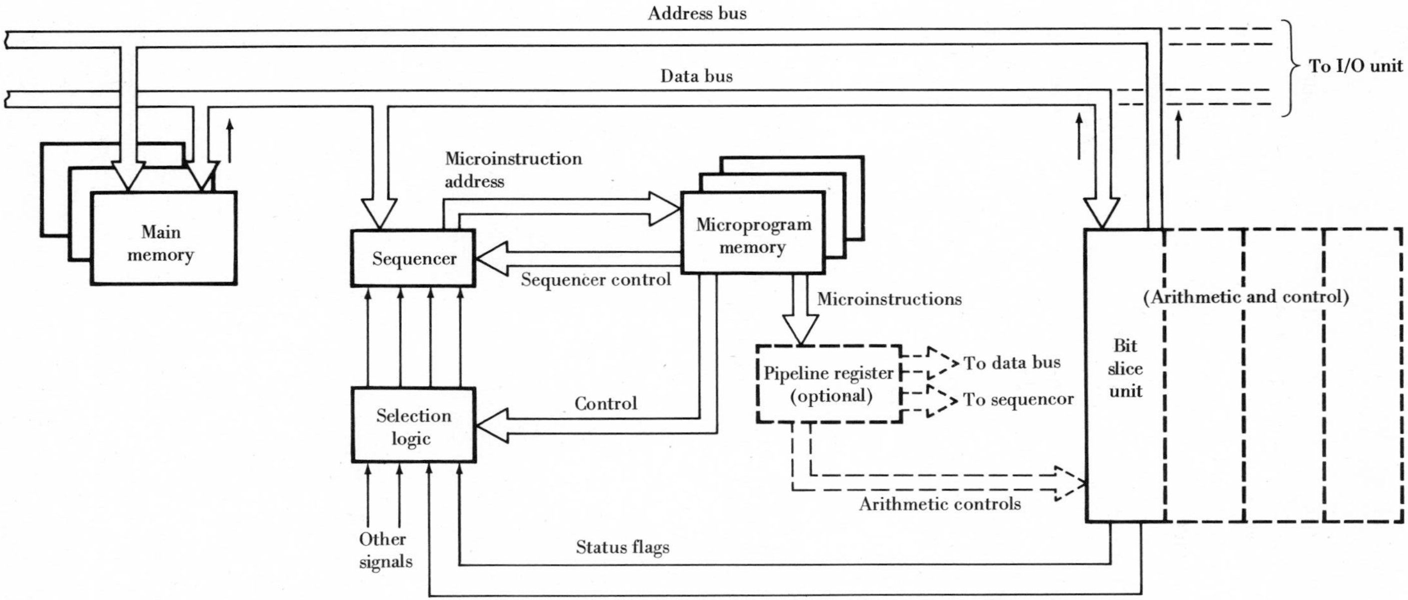

Figure 8-6 A microprogrammable microprocessor chip set.

Microinstruction A command of the microprogrammed memory, which generally specifies internal operations to be performed. Prior to the execution of macroinstructions there are many "housekeeping" operations in the form of microinstructions that have to be performed. Some microinstructions are Fetch, Decode, Test, and Increment.

Macroinstructions A conventional microprocessor has an instruction memory containing program instructions. The functional equivalent in a microprogrammable computer is the macromemory containing macroinstructions. There is no physical difference between the instruction memory and the macroinstruction memory. In a conventional microprocessor, the control section controls the instruction flow; in a microprogrammable unit, the macromemory uses microinstructions to perform tasks. Microinstructions are intended to be very basic and brief; there are many microinstructions per macroinstruction. Figure 8-7 illustrates a typical macroinstruction of Add Memory to Register which has been coded into five corresponding microinstructions.

System Operation

The overall instruction sequence in microprogramming can be summarized by the following sequence (see Fig. 8-6):

1. Macroinstructions are fetched from main memory under the control of microinstructions.

2. The OP code of the macroinstruction is interpreted by the sequencer and then executed as a series of microinstructions.

3. The operand portion of the macro is routed to the arithmetic bit-slice unit for computation or address manipulation of main memory.

4. Control pulses are effectively generated by microinstruction memory performing internal functions necessary to interpret the macroinstruction.

5. The sequencer determines the next address of the microinstruction (microprogram) memory based on status control signals and status flags.

6. The pipeline register is frequently used to improve overall performance and speed. Improvement is accomplished by initiating the next address fetch of the microinstruction before the current microinstruction is completed. Further detail on this approach will be presented in the next section.

Instruction Look-Ahead and Pipelining

An optional technique used to enhance speed is *pipelining,* a method which permits the instruction fetch of the next cycle to begin (*instruction look-ahead*) before the current instruction execution has been completed. The system is characterized by a pipeline register located (as shown in Fig. 8-6) at the output of the microprogram memory. The pipeline register contains the

Macroinstruction

Add Memory to Register   Add (R1), R0

where R1 is the Destination Register
R0 is the Source Memory Address

Microinstruction 1—Fetch Microinstruction from Memory
· The contents of the program counter is applied to the bus. A Data In bus cycle is initiated.
· The processor waits for memory to reply with data.
· Data from bus is applied to the arithmetic scratch pad area. It is loaded into the instruction register.

Microinstruction 2—Decode Macroinstruction
· Increments program counter by 2.
· Branches to the microroutine starting address.

Microinstruction 3—Fetch Source Operand from Memory
· The content of R0 as contained in the arithmetic unit is applied to the bus. A Data In bus cycle is initiated.
· The processor waits for memory to reply with data.
· Data from the bus is applied to the arithmetic scratch pad area. It is loaded into an internal scratch pad register.

Microinstruction 4—Test for Destination Mode 0
· For mode 0, perform Add; else branch on destination register mode.

Microinstruction 5—Add the Contents of R1 to the Contents of the Internal Scratch Pad Register
· Add R1 to the internal scratch pad register.
· Put results in R1.
· Clock the condition codes to the program status word.
· Test for pending service request; if none is requested, go to the next instruction fetch.

Figure 8-7 A macroinstruction compared with the equivalent microinstructions.

result of the previous microinstruction, a portion of the current microinstruction, and some data for the next microinstruction.

All processor instruction times have previously been defined in the text as the time required to execute an instruction fetch followed by the execution time of the instruction. Because of pipelining, the microcycle is defined by the time of either an instruction fetch or an instruction execution, whichever is longer, rather than by the sum.

Pipelining is highly advantageous when instructions follow one another on a regular basis. When a branch instruction occurs, the processor can no longer utilize the Look-ahead instruction and so this must be discarded. As an example, imagine a program segment consisting of seven instructions followed by a Branch on Negative Accumulator instruction. Through the use of look-ahead, fetch instruction 2 is initiated before instruction 1 is completed. Similarly, instruction 3 is fetched before instruction 2 is completed, etc. Instruction 7 is similarly initiated before instruction 6 is completed; but when the same technique is utilized for the next instruction, complications arise. Note that instruction 8 is the Branch instruction and that the instruction should not be initiated until the results of the previous instruction are completed. This will properly determine whether to branch or to continue sequentially with the next program step. It is easier to logically implement instruction fetches in the manner just described than to inhibit initially the branch-type instructions until the results of the previous instruction are derived. Most programs have sequential fetches to branches on the order of 5 to 1 or higher, allowing this technique to show merit as a means of enhancing faster throughput.

The Control Unit

The major elements of the microprogram control unit are the microprogram sequencer and the microprogram memory. A diagram of the control unit is shown in Fig. 8-8. The sequencer is a circuit whose primary function is to generate the next microprogram address. The sequencer has the ability to jump past the next sequential microinstruction memory, depending on factors such as status information or I/O data. The sequencer can be a single-chip device, or when implemented as a group of devices, it will provide the address range needed to sequence longer microprogram memories.

There are several next-address generation techniques employed by the sequencer. The sequencer may perform any of the following functions:

1. Increment the program address counter to provide a Continue signal which generates the next sequential address

2. Load a branch address from the microprogram memory into the program address counter

3. Accept an external conditional/unconditional jump address, which is loaded into the program address counter

The sequencer, by including within its architecture a stack and a stack pointer, allows for jumps to or returns from subroutines. The sequencer can

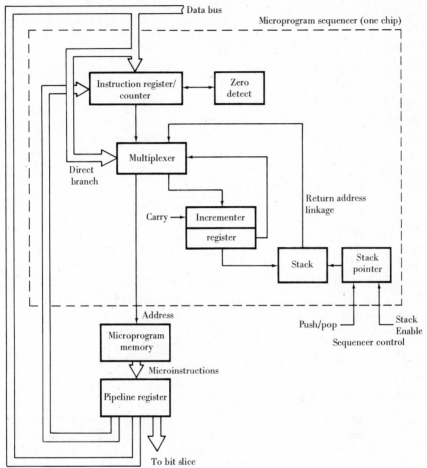

Figure 8-8 A microprogram control unit.

also count iterations of a loop of instructions. Typical instructions of the sequencer are Continue, Branch, Conditional Branch, and Loop Count.

The microprogram memory is implemented in ROM or PROM technology. Each microinstruction word of the microprogram memory is divided into many fields, all words typically having one of several microinstruction formats. Each format, by use of its fields, allows control of processing functions, sequence control and test, and determination of the next microinstruction to be executed. The basic field widths are variable and it is not uncommon to find sizes of memory field varying from 8 bits down to 1 bit. The number of fields depends on many design factors, as well as on the user's requirements.

Microinstruction Word Format

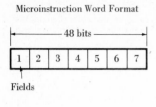

Fields

Microprogram Memory

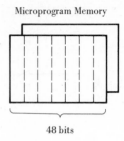

48 bits

Field Definition

Field	Typical no. of bits	Assignment
1	10	ALU control. Determines the source, destination, function, and carry in state of bit slice devices
2	10	R and S register control. Specifies the addresses or determines the selection of source and destination addresses for scratch pad registers
3	9	Sequencer control. Determines function, branch micro test enabling and test condition select and polarity
4	4	Status word control. Determines the selection, condition, and clocking of the status word control
5	2	Data path control of the multiplexer switch
6	5	Bus control. Provides the control to execute the bus signals. The bus control also has control over the processor clock, causing it to halt or reactivate based on bus transmission
7	8	The remaining 8 bits are formatted to provide a direct microbranch address or control over shift/rotate instructions

Figure 8-9 A microinstruction word format.

A diagram of a typical microinstruction word is shown in Fig. 8-9. In this example, the format of the microinstruction word has seven fields with different functional assignments and field widths as indicated. The micro-instruction shown in this example contains 48 bits, which is 3 times as wide as the 16-bit macroinstruction. The reason for this is that at the microlevel many parallel operations are performed on the existing instruction and in preparation for the next instruction. This enhances throughput, since the processor does not have to wait for sequential operations to be performed as in the case of MOS processors.

Architecture of the Bit-Slice Chip

The bit-slice chip in a simplified 4-bit configuration is shown in Fig. 8-10. All data paths within the device are 4 bits wide. The chip has a 16-word × 4-bit

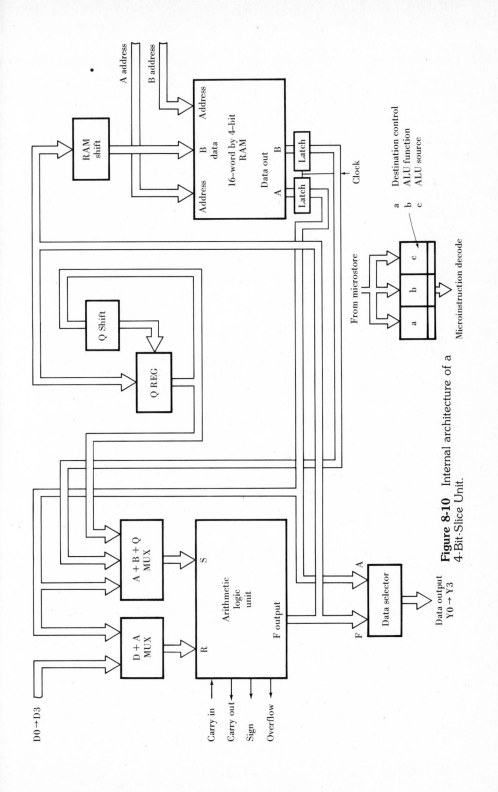

Figure 8-10 Internal architecture of a 4-Bit-Slice Unit.

RAM, which enables the system to use 8 words or all 16 words as general (data) registers. When 8 words are used as general registers, the remainder of the RAM is used as a scratch pad memory. The RAM, or file (as it is commonly known), is accessible by two separate ports, each port being controlled by a 4-bit address field input: a 0001 address input from either port (address A or B) will access register 1, while register 8 has an assigned code of 1000. Access to the registers from two ports allows for simultaneous use of the registers. Latches at the RAM outputs hold the RAM data while the clock input is low, thus eliminating any possible race condition that might occur while new data is being written into the RAM. A RAM Write Enable signal controls the Write operation.

The arithmetic logic unit can perform arithmetic and logic operations on two 4-bit operands called R and S. Typical operations include the Add, Subtract, AND, OR, EXCLUSIVE OR, and NOR functions. More recent chips contain built-in logic capable of performing multiplication and division. The Q register is a multipurpose register used as an accumulator extension and/or for multiplication and division operations.

The operation of the chip is based on the microinstruction word. One of the fields determines the ALU operation using the R and S inputs of the ALU (see Fig. 8-10). Another field determines which multiplexed input shall be used as the source operand. A third field determines the destination output operand, which can be either from the ALU output F or from the RAM data output A. This field also controls the shifting and loading assignments of the RAM and the Q register. Figure 8-11 represents typical ALU function and

ALU Function Assignment

I_5	I_4	I_3	FUNCTION	
0	0	0	Add	R plus S
0	0	1	Subtract	$S - R$
0	1	0	Subtract	$R - S$
0	1	1	OR	$R + S$
1	0	0	AND	$R \cdot S$
1	0	1	AND	$R \cdot S$
1	1	0	EX OR	$R \oplus S$
1	1	1	EX NOR	$\overline{R \oplus S}$

ALU Source Assignment

I_2	I_1	I_0	R^*	S^*
0	0	0	A	Q
0	0	1	A	B
0	1	0	0	Q
0	1	1	0	B
1	0	0	0	A
1	0	1	D	A
1	1	0	D	Q
1	1	1	D	0

*A 0 in either of these columns indicates that a logic level of 0 is used as the value of R or S as indicated.   •

Figure 8-11 Function and source assignments for the 2901A chip.

source assignments for the 2901A microprocessor chip. These assignments are part of field 1 of the microinstruction word shown in Fig. 8-9. There are several other signals which are generated within the chip; typical signals are the Carry, the Overflow, and the Sign bit.

There are many internal paths within the chip, as illustrated in Fig. 8-10. The R and S designations are source operands used in performing a function within the ALU. Each operand has several paths which when selected will act as the source for R or S. The direct, or D, input is used to insert or modify data within the general registers. The R input multiplexes the D or the A input, while the S input multiplexes the A, B, or Q input.

The RAM has two means of selecting registers but only one data source, the B input. B data may or may not be shifted, depending on the instruction, before entering the RAM. Similarly, if the Q register is used, it is optional, based on the instruction, to shift the Q data. Data outputs from the RAM, A and B, are multiplexed into the ALU. The chip output can also be selected from the ALU or from the A data output of the RAM.

Implications of Microprogramming

The most important characteristic of microprogramming units is their flexibility. Not only are all these classes of machines provided with data word expandability, but the user also has the ability to specify the instruction set for the unit. In a hard-wire control logic unit, typical of most MOS processing units, the vendor provides the instruction set that the user applies to the programs. However, this allows no flexibility for modifying any of the specified instructions. In a microprogrammable machine the control memory is programmable with ROMs or PROMs. The bit patterns which provide the control can be altered so that new paths and new controls can be generated if desired. The macroinstruction should be considered as a series of microinstructions over which the user has some control in specifying fields. The basic operations of fetching the instructions from memory and deriving the next instruction are part of the overhead fields of the microprogramming unit. The user's fields determine the instructions and controls necessary to implement them.

The most important application of the user's being able to generate the instruction set occurs when dealing with emulation. Emulation is a mimic technique in which the microprogrammed processor is made to behave like another computer by utilizing the instruction set of the machine to be emulated. For example, the microprogrammable macroinstructions of a 2901 can form the instruction set of another device, such as the PDP-8, 8080, or 6800. Thus the microprogrammable microcomputer is emulating the other machine. A common application for emulation occurs when an established computer system needs to be updated. The microprogrammable unit will provide hardware technological advances while maintaining the existing software in the form of the identical machine language code of the older computer. Enormous savings are generally realized by utilizing the established operational and support programs, along with the benefits of increased speed and reliability associated with the new devices.

Microprogrammable processors implemented with bit-slice chips offer many advantages, including customized instructions and higher throughput, over the MOS fixed-control units. However, as it involves two programming levels (macro and micro), the generation of the software is somewhat expensive relative to conventional units. In addition, the user requires an in-depth knowledge of the internal logic and timing of the unit. Support software is being developed at a much slower rate than for units with the conventional, fixed architecture. Microprogrammable units represent the most advanced form of microprocessing and should accordingly be utilized only in those applications which warrant them.

PROBLEMS

1. Describe the functional partitioning of a two-chip microcomputer.
2. What are the basic elements of a typical single-chip microcomputer?
3. A microprogrammable bit-slice processor is used in a design rather than a microprocessor.
    a. Discuss the main reasons for this choice.
    b. What technology is used?
    c. Discuss how a 32-bit (4-byte) word length is possible.
4. Discuss the function of a
    a. Microprogram memory
    b. Microinstruction
    c. Macroinstruction
5. What is the purpose of a Pipeline register? How is pipelining achieved?
6. What is a microprogram sequencer? What function does it perform?
7. Describe typical operations performed by the ALU of the bit-slice chip.
8. A bit-slice processor can be microprogrammed to mimic an "off the shelf" microprocessor.
    a. What is this technique called?
    b. What are its main advantages?
    c. Can it simulate the speed of the microprocessor? Why is this so?

REFERENCES

1. Alexandridis: "Bit Slice Microprocessor Architecture," *Computer,* vol. 11, June 1978, p. 56.

2. Muething: "Designing the Maximum Performance into Bit Slice Minicomputers," *Electronics,* vol. 49, September 30, 1976.

3. Raytheon Corporation: 2901 Data Sheet.

4. Sussman, Meyer, and Reitman: "The Low End of the PDP-11M Military Computer Family—The LSI-11M," *Military Electronic Defence Expo '77.*

5. Wiles, Musa, Ritter, Booney, and Gunter: "Compatibility Cures Growing Pain of Microcomputing Family," *Electronics,* vol. 51, no. 3, February 2, 1978, p. 95.

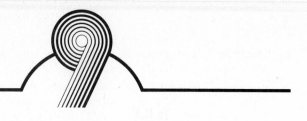

The Microprocessor Interface

The major microprocessor interface is with the memory, which acts as both the source and the destination of data. A typical microprocessor has 16 address lines which make 65,536 addresses available to the memory. Data is transmitted bidirectionally, typically via an 8-bit-wide data bus. The microprocessor generates control signals, such as Memory Read and Memory Write, to control the memory interface, thereby controlling the direction of the data bus.

Another major interface exists between peripheral equipment, or input-output (I/O) devices, and the microprocessor. Such devices may range from the fairly complex, such as:

- Floppy disk—input-output
- High-speed paper tape reader—input
- High-speed punch—output
- Video terminal (CRT and keyboard)—output-input
- Analog-to-digital converter (ADC)—input
- Digital-to-analog converter (DAC)—output
- PROM programmer—input-output
- High-speed printer—output
- Teletype (TTY)—input-output
- Cassette recorder—input-output
- Special-purpose LSI chips—input-output

to the rather simple, less complex:

- Key pad—input
- Toggle switch—input
- Light-emitting diode (LED)—output

These devices represent the real world, or outside world, data communication channels.

9-1 DATA TRANSFER TECHNIQUES

The transfer of I/O information can be handled by two methods: program control and direct memory access (DMA). The data transfer path of the program control method is through the microprocessor, while the DMA approach bypasses the microprocessor.

Some microprocessors have both methods available, and here it is up to the user to determine which method is most applicable.

Program Control I/O

Program control I/O is the most economical method of data transfer, since it allows the software to control the interface. The microprocessor transfers information by using for the movement of data either the accumulator or a register, which may act as a temporary storage device for data later to be transferred to the memory. The process of accessing the I/O in a programmed instruction, placing it in the accumulator or register, and then transferring it to memory may waste valuable time required for real time processing, and this is the primary weakness of this method.

Isolated I/O and *memory-mapped I/O* are two techniques under program control which involve assignment and transfer of I/O information.

Isolated I/O

Isolated I/O is a technique concerned with the transmission of data between an I/O port and the accumulator of a microprocessor. The microprocessor interface usually consists of an 8-bit bidirectional data bus, 8 out of 16 address lines which access up to 256 I/Os, and two control lines, I/O read and I/O write. A typical isolated I/O microcomputer system is shown in Fig. 9-1. In order to generate the I/O control lines and the I/O address, the microprocessor must provide input and output instructions. These are generally 2-byte instructions, where the first byte is the OP code (defines the instruction) and the second byte provides the port address of the device.

Byte 1   OP Code

Byte 2   Device Address

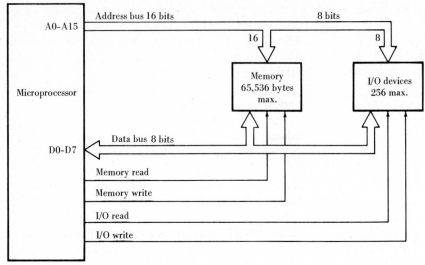

Figure 9-1 Isolated I/O.

As an example, suppose there are two I/Os, where I/O device 01 is an input port and I/O device 02 is an Output port, and port 01 data is to be transferred to port 02. A simple microprocessor program that will accomplish this is:

IN, 01
OUT, 02

The Input instruction

· Causes the port device number specified by the second byte of the instruction to be output on the address bus. In this case A0 is 1 and A1 through A7 are 0.

· Generates a Read pulse used to transfer the data from the I/O to the microprocessor.

· Loads the input data from the bus into the accumulator.

The Output instruction

· Causes the port device number specified by the second byte of the instruction to be output on the address bus. In this case A1 is 1 and A0 and A2 through A7 are logic 0.

· Transfers the accumulator contents on the data bus.

· Generates a Write pulse used to transfer data from the microprocessor to the I/O.

An example of a typical isolated I/O circuit implementation is shown in Fig. 9-2. Output port 2 consists of an 8-bit or octal latch and a simple light-emitting diode (LED) circuit. The microprocessor data bus is latched into port 2 when both A1 and the I/O Write pulse are at logic 1. An LED will be on whenever a 1 is latched. Input port 1 contains an 8-bit tri-state buffer which is enabled when A0 and I/O Read are at logic 1. With eight or fewer I/Os, each of the eight address lines A0 through A7 can be dedicated to a particular I/O. When the system requires more than eight I/Os, it will be necessary to add a hardware decoder logic circuit.

Memory-Mapped I/O

In memory-mapped I/O, I/O peripherals are treated as memory locations. Data is transferred via the data bus in exactly the same manner as memory is written or read. The I/O is assigned a memory address, which could permit up to 2^{16}, or 65,536, I/O devices. This, however, is impractical, since it would result in no memory assignment and hence no programs. The approach taken in using memory-mapped I/O is to dedicate some address assignments to I/O and to keep the remaining addresses for memory. The great advantage of memory-mapped I/O is the ability and ease of programming with the entire microprocessor memory instructions available. Data transfers do not necessarily go through the accumulator but can go through any register within the microprocessor. Memory-mapped I/O differs from isolated I/O in that no separate I/O control lines are used and all 16 address lines serve I/O as well as memory (see Fig. 9-3).

Suppose, for example, data is to be transferred from an output port to an input port by the memory-mapped I/O technique. A program to accomplish this is shown in Fig. 9-4a. The MOV B, M instruction causes the contents of the memory pointer registers R1R2 to go out on the address bus and then transfer the operand specified by the registers to the microprocessor B register. Port 8000 is selected when A15 is logic 1 and A0 through A14 are 0 (see Fig. 9-4c). Port 4000 is selected when A14 is 1 and A15 and A0 through A13 are 0. A15 and A14 are the I/O-select addresses, while A0 through A13 are the memory-select addresses. This means that the maximum memory assigned in the memory-mapped system is 2^{14} (A0 to A13), or 16K bytes of memory. Figure 9-4b shows the memory-mapped I/O transfer. Note that no I/O control lines are necessary, since there are no Input or Output instructions required. Address bits A15 and A14 used in the selection of ports 8000 and 4000 are logic oᴿed, so that memory is disabled when either A15 or A14 is logic 1.

In the memory-mapped technique, all 65,536 memory bytes available for memory assignment are time-shared between memory and I/O. In the example, 16K bytes are assigned to memory, while the remainder are

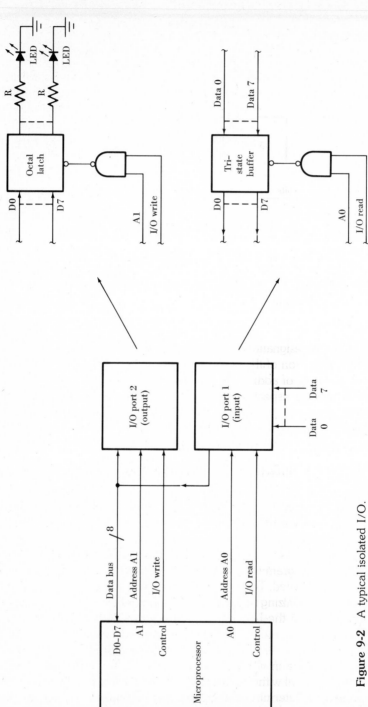

Figure 9-2 A typical isolated I/O.

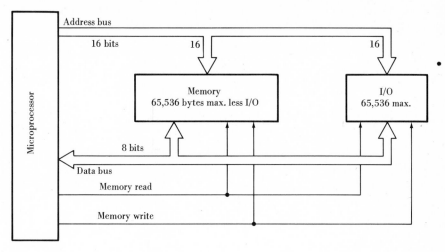

Figure 9-3 Memory-mapped I/O.

potential I/O port designations. Alternative design techniques are available which permit utilization of the memory-mapped I/O concept without sacrificing large amounts of address space to be dedicated to I/O assignments. These methods are especially helpful when the system requires large amounts of memory and a limited number of I/Os. Because of its flexibility and general compatibility with all microprocessing systems, memory-mapped I/O is the most widely used technique.

9-2 SYNCHRONIZING DATA TRANSFERS

The programmed I/O technique represents a software method of transferring I/O data. Whenever an Input or Output instruction is executed in the program, data from the I/O will be transferred. If the data is not available or present at the interface when the instruction is executed and subsequent instructions require the initial data for further processing, then failure conditions in the program will develop. Such an occurrence should not go unnoticed or be tolerated. To help circumvent this potential problem, several data transfer synchronizing techniques are available to enable more efficient communications with the I/O. Among them are polling and interrupts.

Polling

Polling is a technique in which multiple I/O devices time-share a microprocessor I/O channel without contention. The microprocessor performs a *polling routine* to determine which I/O device (either input or output) requires service. Since I/O devices are normally identified by port addresses

OP Code	Operand	Comment Field
LD Immediate R1R2	8000H	Set memory pointer (R1 & R2 registers) to 8000
MOV	B, M	Port 8000 data → register B
LD Immediate R1R2	4000H	
MOV	M, B	Register B → port 4000

(a)

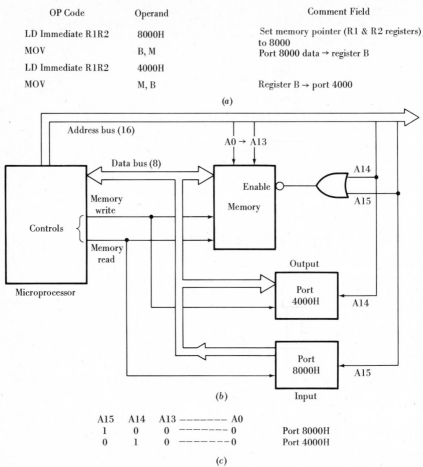

(b)

A15	A14	A13 ————— A0	
1	0	0 ———— 0	Port 8000H
0	1	0 ——— 0	Port 4000H

(c)

Figure 9-4 Memory-mapped I/O transfer.

that are unique for each I/O device, another means is needed to identify the I/O device requiring service. This is accomplished by having the I/O device generate a status word on a second port. The status word is transmitted to the microprocessor in the same manner as data, via the data bus. A typical program that illustrates status word assignment is shown in Fig. 9-5, together with its block diagram.

The Input Port 01 instruction, which utilizes a 1 (A0 = 1) address assignment code, is gated with an I/O Read pulse. The gate output enables the tri-state buffer producing D0 on the data bus. D0 is logic 0 if the input to the buffer is at 0 but goes to logic 1 when the buffer is at logic 1. After execution of the Input Port 01 instruction, the data bus bit D0 is in the microprocessor accumulator and contains either a 0, indicating that the I/O device is not

Label	OP Code	Operand	Comment
DEVICE IN	IN,	01	Input status word
	RR		Rotate accumulator right through carry; (D0 → Carry)
	BNC	DEVICE IN	Jump back to start if carry is not set
	IN,	02	Input data word

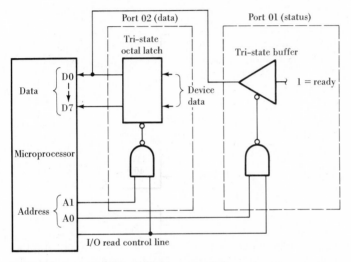

Figure 9-5 I/O device with status and data ports.

ready, or a 1 to indicate that the I/O is ready. The Rotate Right (RR) instruction tests D0 by shifting it into the Carry flag. If D0 is a 1, then executing the RR instruction causes the Carry flag to be set to a 1. The Branch When There Is No Carry instruction (BNC) simply jumps the program back to the start (Device In) if the carry is not set, or it executes an Input Port 02 instruction, with 2 (A1 = 1) as its address code, if the carry is set. A1, when gated with an I/O Read, results in valid device data to the microprocessor by enabling the tri-state octal latch. In this example, two I/O ports have been identified, as shown below:

		D7	D6	D5	D4	D3	D2	D1	D0
Port 01	Status	X	X	X	X	X	X	X	1
Port 02	Data	X	X	X	X	X	X	X	X

where X = "don't care"

If the status word were XXX1XXXX or D4 = 1, then four Rotate Left instructions would be required.

Label	OP Code	Operand	Comment Field
(a) DEVICE IN	IN	01	Input status word
	AND Immediate	10H	Mask out all bits except D4
	BRZ	DEVICE IN	Jump back to DEVICE IN if zero flag is set
	IN	02	Input data word
(b)	MOV Immediate B	0AAH	0AAH → Register B
DEVICE IN	IN	01	Input status word
	CMP B		If B = accumulator, then zero flag is set; otherwise it is reset
	BRNZ	DEVICE IN	Jump back to DEVICE IN if zero flag is not set
	IN	02	Input data word

Figure 9-6 Status tests.

A better instruction to utilize, because it is generally less time-consuming, is the AND Immediate Mode (AND) instruction. This instruction logic ANDs the second byte of the instruction, 10H, with the accumulator. If the status bit D4 is logic 0, the AND instruction causes the Zero flag to set; however, if D4 is logic 1, then the Zero flag is reset. The program is shown in Fig. 9-6a.

A final method of testing status words is to compare the input status word with the assigned word residing in a microprocessor register or memory. Suppose the assigned status word is 10101010. The program that tests the words is shown in Fig. 9-6b.

When two devices transmit information over the same channel, each device is assigned a different status word. Two devices—for example, an input device, I/O device 1, and an output device, I/O device 2—can have their ports specified in the following manner:

I/O Device 1		D7	D6	D5	D4	D3	D2	D1	D0
Port 23	Status	1	X	X	X	X	X	X	X
Port 20	Data	X	X	X	X	X	X	X	X
I/O Device 2									
Port 15	Status	X	X	X	X	1	X	X	X
Port 50	Data	X	X	X	X	X	X	X	X

Label	OP Code	Operand	Comment Field
DEV 1	IN	23H	Input port 23 status
	RL		Test bit D7
	BNC	DEV 1	Jump to DEV 1 if carry is not set
	IN	20H	Input port 20 data
	MOV	B, A	Save DEV 1 data in register B
DEV 2	IN	15H	Input port 15 status
	AND Immediate	08H	Test bit D3
	BRZ	DEV 2	Jump to DEV 2 if zero flag is set
	MOV	A, B	Put DEV 1 data in accumulator
	OUT	50H	Output to port 50

Figure 9-7 I/O device transfer.

A program that will transmit one byte of input data from device 1 to device 2 is, shown in Fig. 9-7.

The Polling Routine The assignment of status word addresses to I/O devices permits ports to be uniquely identified. Since the data bus channel is time-shared, a program called the polling routine is used to eliminate any potential contention that may develop among I/O devices. If the polling routine always starts at the same I/O device and that device always has the highest priority, the routine is called *priority polling*. When the polling routine starts where the last I/O device was polled, so that no device is more important than the others, the technique is called *round-robin polling* (see Fig. 9-8). Some microprocessors use a polling technique called *daisy chaining*, where the priority of the I/O device is determined by the presence or absence of a control signal, usually called the Grant signal. This signal originates at the microprocessor (see Fig. 9-9). The Grant signal propagates down, starting at the highest priority I/O and ending at the lowest priority I/O. An I/O in need of service must wait for the Grant signal before raising its Request line (a line common to all I/O devices). All the devices must be designed to monitor the state of the Request line, so that once an I/O has been serviced it must wait until all other pending I/O device requests have been completed before it can be serviced again.

In some cases the microprocessor must wait for an I/O device to be ready. For example, suppose an I/O device such as a casette recorder has to load a program or data into memory when the main program accesses it. This

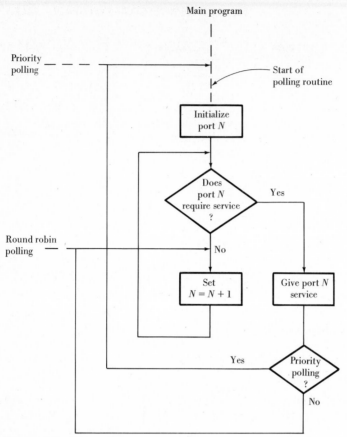

Figure 9-8 The polling routine.

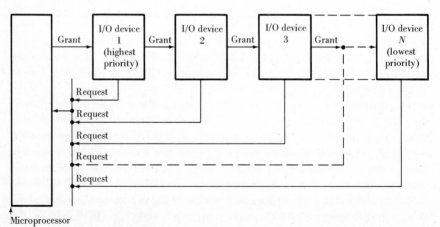

Figure 9-9 Daisy chaining.

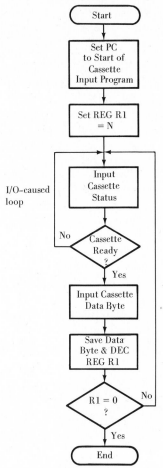

Figure 9-10 Input cassette recorder flowchart.

program or data may be vital to the microprocessor system. Should the cassette recorder not be ready due to some malfunction in its electronics, the microprocessor will be tied up in a loop (see Fig. 9-10). This may waste valuable microprocessor time and, in fact, may effectively halt any further processing. Some microprocessor systems employ a real time clock technique which causes the program to break the loop and return to a known place in the main program if the I/O device is not ready within a specified time. The real time clock technique can be implemented by hardware or software; if it is in software it will take up valuable memory space. In order to increase the microprocessor system efficiency and avoid causing loops in the I/O, a method whereby the I/O device requests service when it is ready is needed. This method is called *interrupt control*.

The Interrupt

There are two types of interrupts: internal and external. An external interrupt is one from an I/O device. An internal interrupt is a status latch or flag within the microprocessor which can be enabled or disabled by special Interrupt instructions. When the internal interrupt is disabled, generally no external interrupt will be serviced by the microprocessor. However, should the internal interrupt structure be enabled, the system can then respond to external interrupts. When an interrupt occurs, the processor will acknowledge the interrupt by disabling the internal interrupt status latch to prevent further interrupts from being serviced. Some microprocessors have a special nonmaskable interrupt line that overrides the status of the internal interrupt latch and accepts the interrupt. When an I/O device has valid data or requires an output from the microprocessor, it simply raises its interrupt line. In a typical communication, the microprocessor will generally respond as follows:

1. Complete its current instruction
2. Test the state of the internal Interrupt flag
   a. If it is disabled, the microprocessor will go on to its next instruction.
   b. If it is enabled, the microprocessor will generate an Interrupt Acknowledge and disable the internal Interrupt flag to allow for no further interrupts (except nonmaskable interrupts), thus synchronizing the interrupt sequence.
3. Save the program counter in the stack
4. Set the program counter to the interrupt program

Nonmaskable Interrupts   Microprocessors that have a nonmaskable interrupt line allow high-priority interrupts to be serviced independently of the state of the internal Interrupt flag. Should the nonmaskable interrupt line be activated by an I/O device, the instruction in progress is allowed to be completed and then certain registers, status flags, and the program counter are stored in the stack. The Interrupt routine may be located via an indirect addressing scheme in which a fixed address points to a location in R/W memory which itself is the address of the Interrupt program. A typical nonmaskable interrupt is from a power monitor source.

The Interrupt Program   The Interrupt program is similar to a subroutine. It must save status and register data and thereby preserve the pre-interrupt contents of the microprocessor. Since the external interrupt causes the internal interrupt status flag to be disabled, the stored Interrupt program must enable the internal interrupt status flag by use of an instruction. If the flag is enabled prior to the end of the Interrupt program, then even while the Interrupt program is being executed, the microprocessor can be reinter-

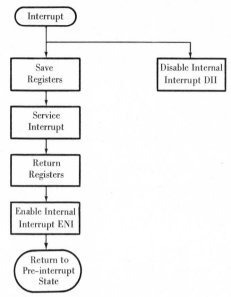

Figure 9-11 Interrupt program sequence.

rupted. It is therefore customary to utilize the Enable Interrupt (ENI) instruction at the end of the Interrupt program to permit new external interrupts to enter the system. A typical Interrupt program sequence is shown in Fig. 9-11.

Multiple Interrupts Microprocessor devices are usually pin-limited and therefore have at best a few signal pins dedicated for Interrupts. When many I/O devices are required to interface with the microprocessing system, the I/O devices have their Request lines logic oʀed, as shown in Fig. 9-12. This causes the Interrupt line to be enabled when any of the I/O devices requests service. It is the task of the Interrupt program to "find" the I/O device that caused the Interrupt by polling the I/O devices. For example, suppose three I/O devices, device 1, device 2, and device 3 of Fig. 9-12, are used in a given microprocessing system and one of these I/O devices is requesting service. The external Interrupt line is enabled, and the microprocessor will follow the Interrupt procedure previously described. Each I/O device will have a unique status word which the microprocessor checks to determine if it was the interrupting device. Suppose these I/O devices are defined as follows:

I/O Device 1
    Status port   20H
    Status word   XXXXXXX1
    Data port   21H

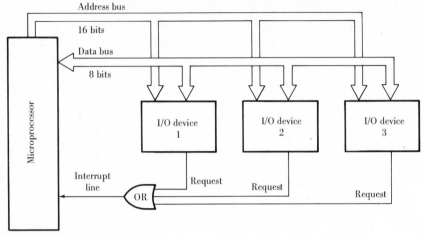

Figure 9-12 Multiple interrupts.

I/O Device 2
    Status port   52H
    Status word   XXXXXX1X
    Data port   55H
I/O Device 3
    Status port   13H
    Status word   XXXXX1XX
    Data port   11H

The program flowchart and program are shown in Figs. 9-13 and 9-14. The Interrupt program stores 1 byte of data from I/O device 1, 2, or 3 in memory locations 2016H, 2031H, and 2056H, respectively. Note that placement of the Enable Interrupt instruction assures that no further interrupts, except the nommaskable interrupt, will be processed until the Interrupt program is completed.

Vectored Interrupt

Polling, by its very nature, requires the microprocessor to spend time in finding the interrupting I/O. Most microprocessors utilize a technique in which the interrupting I/O does not have to be identified by the software but has a uniquely defined memory address assigned to it. This technique is called *vectored interrupt*. A vectored interrupt causes the PC to jump to an Interrupt program (as described previously) that defines a unique I/O. The advantage of vectored interrupt over polled interrupt is that the I/O is serviced immediately, provided the internal Interrupt flag is enabled.

Figure 9-15 shows a comparison of polled and vectored interrupt. Here three devices, a TTY, a CRT, and a keyboard, which require polling can interrupt the microprocessor using the multiple interrupt technique. When the keyboard device interrupts the program, the program branches to the

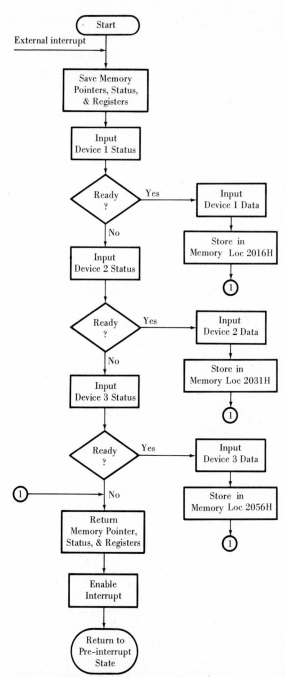

Figure 9-13 Interrupt program flowchart.

Label	OP Code	Operand	Comment Field
DEV POL	PUSH Accumulator		Store accumulator
	PUSH Flag Register		Store flag register
	PUSH R1R2		Store memory pointer
	IN	20H	Device 1 test
	AND Immediate	01	
	BRNZ	Found 1	
	IN	52H	Device 2 test
	AND Immediate	02	
	BRNZ	Found 2	
	IN	13H	Device 3 test
	AND Immediate	04	
	BRNZ	Found 3	
END	POP	R1R2	Return program to
	POP	Flag Register	preinterrupt
	POP	Accumulator	state
	ENI		
	RET		
Found 1	LD Immediate R1R2	2016H	Stores byte in
	IN	21H	memory location
	MOV	M, A	2016H
	JMP	END	
Found 2	LD Immediate R1R2	2031H	Store byte in
	IN	55H	memory location
	MOV	M, A	2031H
	JMP	END	
Found 3	LD Immediate R1R2	2056H	Store byte in
	IN	11H	memory location
	MOV	M, A	2056H
	JMP	END	

Figure 9-14 Interrupt program.

Interrupt program, which polls each I/O device. When the interrupting device has been identified as the keyboard, the keyboard program is run, and then the program returns to its pre-interrupt status. When the power supply monitor circuitry of Fig. 9-15 detects a possible loss of critical power,

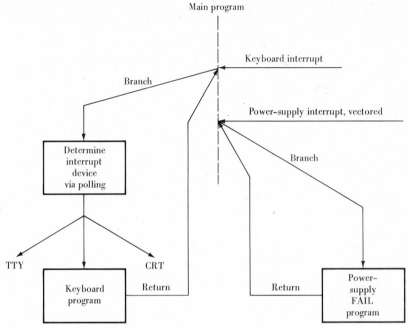

Figure 9-15 Polled vs. vector interrupt.

it sends a vectored interrupt to the microprocessor. The program immediately branches to the power supply fail program, which usually saves all critical registers and the data in an area of nonvolatile memory, such as a core memory or an area of Read/Write memory that is powered by an independent source. Vectored interrupts save valuable microprocessing time and alleviate the need for polling.

Microprocessors have many different interrupt vectoring schemes. The 8080 microprocessor, for example, has up to eight vectored interrupts but only one interrupt line. This is accomplished by allowing the interrupting I/O device to force a data byte onto the data bus, which the 8080 interprets as an instruction, usually a Restart instruction. This 8-bit restart instruction includes a 3-bit field which, when decoded by the 8080, forces the program counter to one of eight possible memory locations. At these addresses are the first instruction of the routine designed to service the interrupting device.

The priority of a given I/O device is determined by the Interrupt program. If the program is of a high priority, the Enable Interrupt instruction (ENI) is placed at the end of the program. Low-priority I/O devices have the Enable Interrupt instruction at the start of their Interrupt program, thereby allowing themselves to be interrupted. LSI programmable interrupt controllers are available which minimize software and hardware design in handling multi-level priority interrupts.

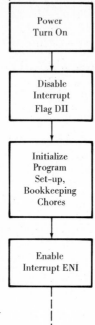

Figure 9-16 Start sequence—
use of Disable Interrupt.

The Disable Interrupt instruction (DII), as shown in Fig. 9-16, is used during the initial start-up of a program sequence when the initial state of the internal Interrupt flag is unknown and no interrupting devices are allowed. Other applications in which the DII is used are occasions when keyboard input routines and stack pointer loads are performed. When these "book-keeping chores" are completed, use of the Enable Interrupt instruction in a program allows the interrupt system to be enabled.

When programs depend on interrupts to initialize a system, then a possible start-up procedure is to first reset the microprocessor, set the PC to a known value, usually 0000, and then perform the following program sequence:

PC	Inst.
0000	ENI
0001	Halt

Any interrupt is then allowed, and its Interrupt program runs.

9-3 DIRECT MEMORY ACCESS

Direct Memory Access, or DMA, is a method usually reserved for transferring blocks of data to and from memory at high speed. Devices that utilize DMA

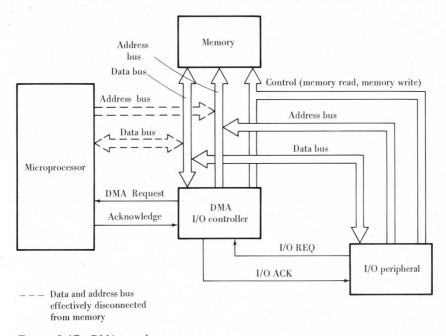

Figure 9-17   DMA interface.

are usually mass-storage devices, such as floppy disks or cassettes. Special hardware in the form of a DMA controller is used to control the transfer of information from the I/O peripheral. The DMA controller logic includes an address register, which stores the starting memory address location, and a word counter, which holds a count equivalent to the number of words that are to be transferred. Both the address and the count and an indication whether the transfer is an input or an output must precede the DMA transfer. DMA requests are handled in a way similar to the handling of interrupt requests: a request is generated by an I/O device asynchronous with the microprocessor. A typical DMA interface is shown in Fig. 9-17.

The steps in a DMA transfer are:

1.   The DMA controller sends a Request on the microprocessor DMA line.

2.   The microprocessor responds with a DMA Acknowledge signal and places the address, data, and control buses in a high-impedance state (tri-stated).

3.   *a.*   To read from memory: The DMA controller sends the address and a Memory Read strobe.

   b.   To write into memory: The DMA controller sends the address, the data, and a Memory Write strobe.

4. After each memory byte is transferred, the address register gets incremented and the word counter gets decremented.

5. After the memory transfer is complete, the DMA controller removes its DMA Request, thereby giving control of the buses to the microprocessor.

The DMA Request is synchronized internally by the microprocessor. The DMA Acknowledge is generated by the microprocessor either after the completion of a machine cycle or prior to the end of a machine cycle that contains states other than memory fetches. The microprocessor will always complete the machine cycle in progress and start with the next machine cycle after the DMA controller request has been terminated. A short time after the DMA Acknowledge is generated, the microprocessor tri-states its data and address buses, placing the DMA controller in control of the buses. Frequent DMA accesses can reduce the overall throughput of the system. The DMA controller can, however, be designed to detect the presence of the states or clock cycles just prior to the end of the microprocessor's machine cycle and to use these states to access memory directly. This design technique is called *cycle stealing.* Cycle stealing does not change the speed or throughput of the microprocessing system.

Although the DMA controller is usually fairly complex from a hardware standpoint, it is possible to design a simple but slow direct memory access I/O like the one represented in Fig. 9-18. Its purpose is to allow manual access of the memory. The device consists of switches, tri-state buffers, LEDs, and resistors. The following sequences are performed for writing and reading memory.

Writing

1. Writing a byte into memory is accomplished by setting up switches A0 to A15 and D0 to D7 for the desired address and data.

2. DMA request line will be logic 1 as a result of the opening of switch S3, which is normally closed.

3. The microprocessor responds with a DMA Acknowledge, which causes the tri-state buffers to be activated and illuminates the LED for a visual indication.

4. Depressing momentary switch S1 causes the Write control lines to go to logic 0, writing the data bytes D0 to D7 into memory at the address specified by A0 to A15. The LEDs at D0 to D7 also give a visual readout of the data byte selected.

Reading

1. Reading out from memory is accomplished in the same manner except that switch S2, memory Read, is momentarily depressed and switches D0 to D7 are opened.

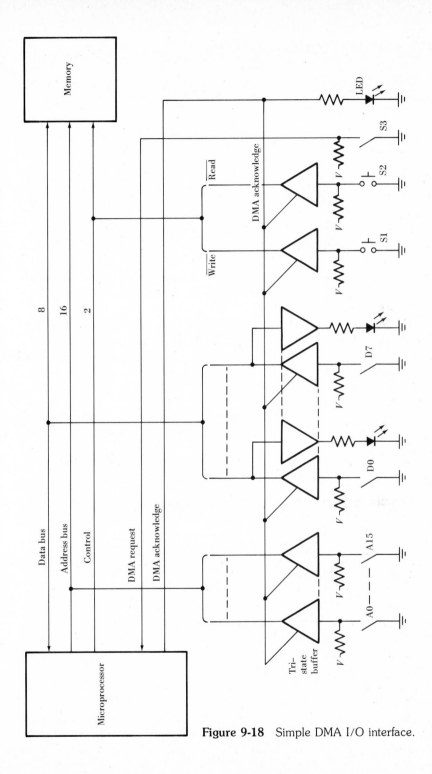

Figure 9-18 Simple DMA I/O interface.

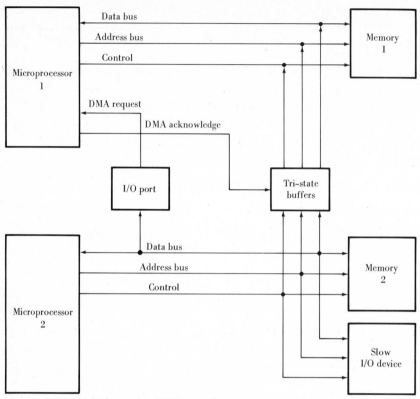

Figure 9-19 Multiprocessor DMA transfer.

2. Upon completion of the DMA, S3 is closed and the DMA Acknowledge is extinguished. This places the tri-state buffers in the high-impedance mode and returns control of the buses to the microprocessor.

A DMA I/O can be designed to interface with a slow I/O device to allow a large number of bytes to load into the DMA I/O's registers. When the DMA I/O register bank is full, a DMA Request is transmitted to the microprocessor, which then initiates storage of the data into memory at a fast rate. This obviously increases the throughput of the system, but the penalty is a fairly complex DMA I/O hardware design. LSI direct memory access I/O devices are becoming available, and these may remove the need for designing DMA devices. A method of interfacing a slow I/O device without using a hardware DMA I/O would be to utilize a multiprocessor DMA transfer technique, as shown in Fig. 9-19. Microprocessor 2 takes the place of the DMA device and transfers the slow I/O device's data to memory 2. Microprocessor 2 outputs data to a latched port under program control. The output of the latched I/O port enables the DMA control line of microprocessor 1. The DMA Acknowledge causes the tri-state buffer to be enabled and allows microprocessor 2 to control memory 1. Although the DMA transfer is relatively slow, since microprocessor 2 controls the transfer, valuable time is still saved, since a large block of data from the slow I/O device is already stored in memory 2. For example, if the slow I/O device inputs a byte of data in 100 ms, 50 bytes would take 5 s. After all 50 bytes are in memory 2, the DMA request is generated by microprocessor 2. If microprocessor 2 is running at 2 megahertz (MHz), it will take about 2 μs to complete a four-state instruction. If it requires 100 bytes, including loops to transfer the data from memory 2 to memory 1, then the total transfer time will be 200 μs.

9-4 INPUT-OUTPUT DEVICES

Teletypewriters

The most common peripheral, or I/O, device is the teletypewriter, and of those models now available, the most popular and economical is the ASR-33 (automatic send-receive) manufactured by the Teletype Corporation. This particular model consists of the following units:

1. Keyboard   **3.** Paper tape punch
2. Printer   **4.** Paper tape reader

The ASR-33 Teletype is shown in Fig. 9-20. The controls shown have the following functions:

Paper Tape Punch Control	REL Pushbutton	Disengages the tape in the punch to allow for tape removal or tape loading.
	BSP Pushbutton	Backspaces the tape in the punch by one space.
	ON Pushbutton	Engages the tape punch and allows the punching of tape.
	OFF Pushbutton	Disengages the tape punch.
Tape Reader Control	START Switch Position	Begins tape reading.
	STOP Switch Position	Stops tape reading.
	FREE Switch Position	Releases the sprocket wheel, allowing tape to be manually moved within the reader.
Mode Knob	OFF Knob Position	Turns Teletype off.
	LOCAL Knob Position	Teletype is on but not connected to the signal lines of a processor.
	LINE Knob Position	Teletype is on and connected to a processor.

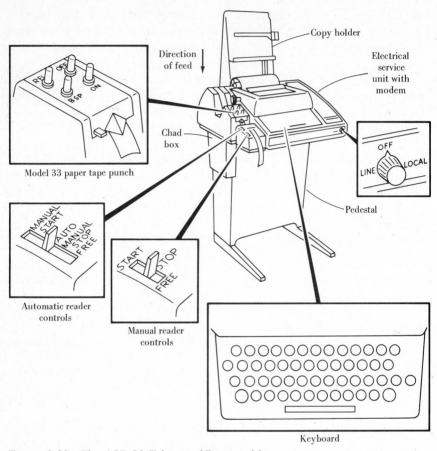

Figure 9-20 The ASR-33 Teletype. (*Reprinted by permission of Intel Corporation, Copyright 197_.*)

ASR-33 Keyboard The keyboard of an ASR-33 Teletype is similar to that of a standard typewriter, except that some nonprinting characters used as control characters are included. The more frequently used control characters are:

Return Terminates a line of symbolic program (carriage return).

Line Feed Follows carriage return to advance printer one line.

CTRL/REPT/P Used for leader/trailer of binary program paper tapes. Keys must be released in reverse order.

Rubout Used for deleting characters. It punches all channels on paper tape.

Printer   The printer produces a typed copy of input and output. In the Line position the printer types only the output from the processor. In the Local position the printer types the keyboard characters.

Tape Punch   The tape punch when engaged punches paper tape from either the keyboard or the processor, as determined by the setting of the Local or Line knob.

Tape Reader   The tape reader when engaged reads the characters that are punched on paper tape and is used to input data to a processor.

ASCII   The ASR-33 Teletype is a low-speed device that transmits and receives at a maximum rate of 10 characters per second. The most common alphanumeric code used to represent characters is the American Standard Code for Information Interchange, or ASCII. Six-bit or 7-bit ASCII is used for data representation. Six-bit ASCII, called half-ASCII, represents up to 64 characters, which include:

- The uppercase alphabet
- The numerals 0 to 9
- Various symbols
- Control characters

The 7-bit ASCII code, called full ASCII, includes the lowercase alphabet and can represent up to 128 characters. An eighth bit is often added to the 7-bit code as a parity bit to determine whether the character has been transmitted correctly.

Table 9-1 shows the full ASCII format. The ASR-33 transmits and receives in an 11-bit serial data format, as shown in Fig. 9-21. It consists of:

- A start bit, always at logic 0, to determine the start of a transmission.
- Seven data bits to determine the character. The least significant bit is transferred first. Octal 123, for example, represents an uppercase S.
- One parity bit—odd parity, as shown in Fig. 9-21.
- Two stop bits, necessary to allow time for mechanical devices to settle and be ready for the next data transmission.

The transmission rate is expressed in *baud*. The baud rate is equal to the reciprocal of the minimum bit time. Most transmissions use a 50 percent duty cycle so that all the bits have equal bit times. The bit time of an ASR-33 transmission is 9.09 ms. This means that the baud rate of the teletype is $\frac{1}{9.09 \text{ ms}}$, or 110 baud. Since 11 bits are required to determine a character, the transmission time of one character is 11 × 9.09 ms, about 100 ms, and the transmission rate is therefore 10 characters per second.

TABLE 9-1 Complete ASCII

CHARACTER	BINARY BIT 7 TO BIT 0	OCTAL	DECIMAL	HEXADECIMAL	CHARACTER	BINARY BIT 7 TO BIT 0	OCTAL	DECIMAL	HEXADECIMAL	CHARACTER	BINARY BIT 7 TO BIT 0	OCTAL	DECIMAL	HEXADECIMAL
NUL	00000000	000	000	00	4	00110100	064	052	34	h	01101000	150	104	68
SOH	00000001	001	001	01	5	00110101	065	053	35	i	01101001	151	105	69
STX	00000010	002	002	02	6	00110110	066	054	36	j	01101010	152	106	6A
ETX	00000011	003	003	03	7	00110111	067	055	37	k	01101011	153	107	6B
EOT	00000100	004	004	04	8	00111000	070	056	38	l	01101100	154	108	6C
ENQ	00000101	005	005	05	9	00111001	071	057	39	m	01101101	155	109	6D
ACK	00000110	006	006	06	:	00111010	072	058	3A	n	01101110	156	110	6E
BEL	00000111	007	007	07	;	00111011	073	059	3B	o	01101111	157	111	6F
BS	00001000	010	008	08	<	00111100	074	060	3C	p	01110000	160	112	70
HT	00001001	011	009	09	=	00111101	075	061	3D	q	01110001	161	113	71
LF	00001010	012	010	0A	>	00111110	076	062	3E	r	01110010	162	114	72
VT	00001011	013	011	0B	?	00111111	077	063	3F	s	01110011	163	115	73
FF	00001100	014	012	0C	@	01000000	100	064	40	t	01110100	164	116	74
CR	00001101	015	013	0D	A	01000001	101	065	41	u	01110101	165	117	75
SO	00001110	016	014	0E	B	01000010	102	066	42	v	01110110	166	118	76
SI	00001111	017	015	0F	C	01000011	103	067	43	w	01110111	167	119	77
DLE	00010000	020	016	10	D	01000100	104	068	44	x	01111000	170	120	78
DC1	00010001	021	017	11	E	01000101	105	069	45	y	01111001	171	121	79
DC2	00010010	022	018	12	F	01000110	106	070	46	z	01111010	172	122	7A
DC3	00010011	023	019	13	G	01000111	107	071	47	{	01111011	173	123	7B
DC4	00010100	024	020	14	H	01001000	110	072	48	¦	01111100	174	124	7C
NAK	00010101	025	021	15	I	01001001	111	073	49	}	01111101	175	125	7D
SYN	00010110	026	022	16	J	01001010	112	074	4A	~	01111110	176	126	7E
ETB	00010111	027	023	17	K	01001011	113	075	4B	DEL	01111111	177	127	7F
CAN	00011000	030	024	18	L	01001100	114	076	4C					
EM	00011001	031	025	19	M	01001101	115	077	4D					
SUB	00011010	032	026	1A	N	01001110	116	078	4E					
ESC	00011011	033	027	1B	O	01001111	117	079	4F					
FS	00011100	034	028	1C	P	01010000	120	080	50					
GS	00011101	035	029	1D	Q	01010001	121	081	51					
RS	00011110	036	030	1E	R	01010010	122	082	52					
US	00011111	037	031	1F	S	01010011	123	083	53					
SP	00100000	040	032	20	T	01010100	124	084	54					
!	00100001	041	033	21	U	01010101	125	085	55					
"	00100010	042	034	22	V	01010110	126	086	56					
#	00100011	043	035	23	W	01010111	127	087	57					
$	00100100	044	036	24	X	01011000	130	088	58					
%	00100101	045	037	25	Y	01011001	131	089	59					
&	00100110	046	038	26	Z	01011010	132	090	5A					
'	00100111	047	039	27	[	01011011	133	091	5B					
(	00101000	050	040	28	\	01011100	134	092	5C					
)	00101001	051	041	29	]	01011101	135	093	5D					
.	00101010	052	042	2A	∧	01011110	136	094	5E					
+	00101011	053	043	2B	—	01011111	137	095	5F					
,	00101100	054	044	2C	`	01100000	140	096	60					
—	00101101	055	045	2D	a	01100001	141	097	61					
.	00101110	056	046	2E	b	01100010	142	098	62					
/	00101111	057	047	2F	c	01100011	143	099	63					
0	00110000	060	048	30	d	01100100	144	100	64					
1	00110001	061	049	31	e	01100101	145	101	65					
2	00110010	062	050	32	f	01100110	146	102	66					
3	00110011	063	051	33	g	01100111	147	103	67					

Abbreviations for Control Characters:

NUL — null, or all zeros
SOH — start of heading
STX — start of text
ETX — end of text
EOT — end of transmission
ENQ — enquiry
ACK — acknowledge
BEL — bell
BS — backspace
HT — horizontal tabulation
LF — line feed
VT — vertical tabulation
FF — form feed
CR — carriage return
SO — shift out
SI — shift in
DLE — data link escape
DC1 — device control 1
DC2 — device control 2
DC3 — device control 3
DC4 — device control 4
NAK — negative acknowledge
SYN — synchronous idle
ETB — end of transmission block
CAN — cancel
EM — end of medium
SUB — substitute
ESC — escape
FS — file separator
GS — group separator
RS — record separator
US — unit separator
SP — space
DEL — delete

Note: The bit 7 in the binary column is sometimes used as a parity bit.

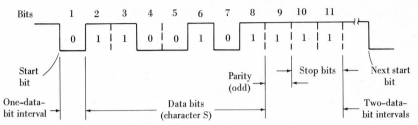

Figure 9-21 The ASR-33 serial data format.

Transmission Techniques

A data link enables a device such as the ASR-33 to communicate with other terminals or controlling elements. Data links may be classified according to the direction in which the data is transmitted. Links or paths where data is capable of being transmitted in either direction but not simultaneously are called *half-duplex* links (see Fig. 9-22a). In a *full-duplex* link (Fig. 9-22b), data is transmitted over separate data paths simultaneously. An example of the half-duplex system, as commonly used, is the teletype system. A popular full-duplex system is a telecommunications interface between two units that converts digital signals to modulated analog signals in units called *modems*. Modems will be described in a subsequent section.

Serial Transmission Forms

There are several hardware interfaces which have been established to provide a form of standardization in the transmission of data. Two of the

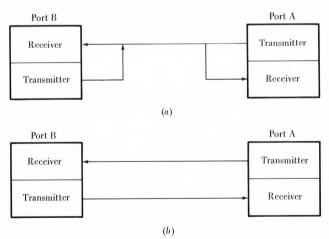

Figure 9-22 Half- and full-duplex transmission links. (a) Half-duplex data link; (b) full-duplex data link.

most popular are the EIA RS-232C and the current loop interface. The EIA (*Electronic Industries Association*) form provides a voltage interface between the data terminal equipment (*Receive*) and the data communications equipment (*Send*). Typical data in RS-232C format is shown in Fig. 9-23a. RS-232C line drivers convert the TTL levels to RS-232C levels. An EIA RS-232C line receiver is typically an MSI circuit that converts the waveshape to TTL levels. The advantage of using this bipolar Non-Return to Zero (NRZ) signal is that it is more immune to noise over long distance than TTL. The maximum cable length for the RS-232C is 50 feet.

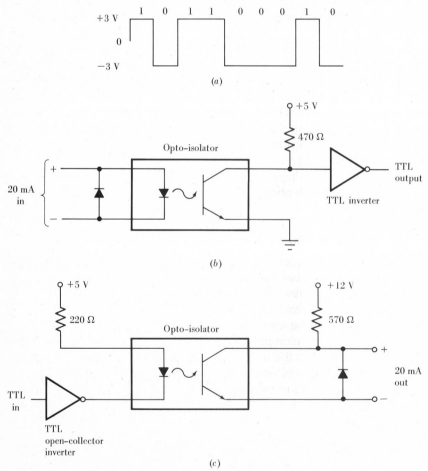

Figure 9-23 Transmission forms. (*a*) RS-232C voltage format; (*b*) current loop—20-mA-to-TTL interface; (*c*) current loop—TTL-to-20-mA interface.

The RS-232C has a maximum transmission capability of about 20,000 bits per second. To accommodate higher rates, a new standard from EIA, designated RS-449, will permit data rates of up to 2 megabits. It is anticipated that the RS-449 will eventually replace the RS-232C.

Current Loops Most digital systems use a *voltage* source for interfacing between devices. However, when interfacing devices are a large distance apart, the voltage is reduced on the receiving end and the transmission is very susceptible to noise. If a *current* source, commonly called a *current loop,* is used, distances of up to several hundred feet can be realized with very little signal loss. Current loop interfaces are often used with mechanical devices. Typically, the computer end of the circuit is a non-current loop (TTL) circuit, while the terminal end is a current loop circuit. The ASR-33 uses either a 20-milliampere (mA) or a 60-mA current loop. Common circuits used to convert a 20-mA current loop to TTL levels and TTL levels to a current loop are shown in Fig. 9-23. These circuits use opto-isolators, which are inexpensive devices containing a light source (LED) and a phototransistor. The presence of a 20-mA source is logic 1 and the absence of that source is logic 0. In Fig. 9-23b, a 20-mA source turns on the LED and the phototransistor, causing the input to the TTL inverter to go to logic 0 and the output to go to logic 1.

In Fig. 9-23c, a TTL logic 1 at the input of the TTL open-collector inverter causes the LED and the phototransistor to turn on, allowing about 20 mA to be transmitted.

UART Serial Interface

A UART (*universal asynchronous receiver/transmitter*) is a programmable LSI device that interfaces the microprocessor to devices such as modems and teletypes that require a serial data format. It also converts serial data to parallel for use in the microprocessor (see Fig. 9-24). The UART receives control signals from the microprocessor and outputs a status word to the microprocessor. The microprocessor assigns a port address to the UART and enables or disables the unit. Control lines are decoded in the UART to determine the direction of the data bus, to permit the data bus to be used for control or status word transmission, or to disable the UART by tri-stating the data lines to the microprocessor. The control word programs the UART and defines:

- Selectable baud rates (1x, 16x, 64x, where x is the basic baud frequency)
- Programmable character length (5 to 7 bits)
- Programmable number of stop bits (1 or 2)
- Error detection by use of even or odd parity

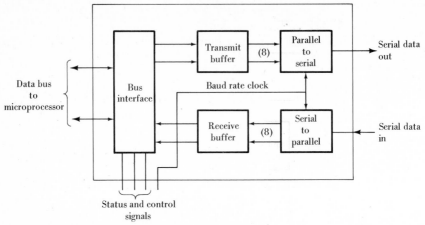

Figure 9-24 Functional block diagram of a UART.

Since the serial input to a UART is asynchronous, the UART requires a multiple of the incoming baud rate to determine the middle of the bit time. In UARTs that don't have programmable baud rates, a 16x clock is usually required at the receiver.

Modems

A modem (an acronym for *modu*lator/*demo*dulator) is a device that modulates dc digital signals, thus converting them to ac audio analog signals. A modem output is suitable for transmission over a communications link, such as the telephone lines. At the receiving end of the link, another modem (the demodulator) reconverts the signals to their original digital form, making them suitable for a terminal or a computer input. Figure 9-25*a* shows a two-modem system with each unit having the capability of transmitting and receiving. Modems are required in a telecommunications application whenever one digital device must communicate with another at a distance greater than 50 feet. If modems were not used, the dc pulses (representing binary 1s and 0s) would be degraded by the electrical characteristics of the transmission line. The result is that the information would be lost or misinterpreted.

There are two basic forms of modems: those handling asynchronous data and those handling synchronous data. Teletype and acoustic couplers are two major uses of asynchronous modems. Asynchronous modems are low-speed units, with transmission speeds under 2000 bits per second. Synchronous modems make use of internal clock sources within the modem instead of the start and stop bits associated with the character transmission of asynchronous modems (see Fig. 9-25*b*). The elimination of the start and stop bits on every character of a synchronous modem increases throughput and

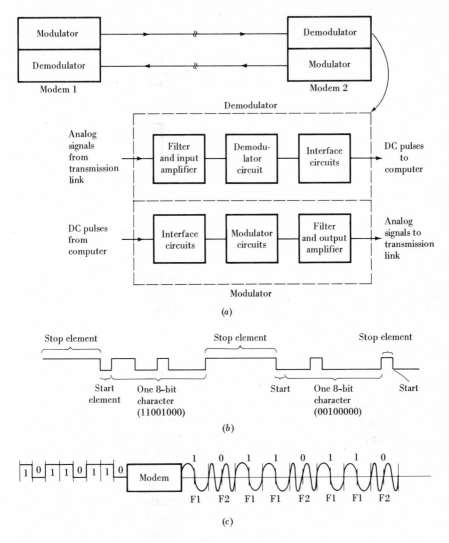

Figure 9-25 Modems. (*a*) Communication link using modems; (*b*) asynchronous data transmission; (*c*) frequency shift keying.

allows higher transmission speeds. Although more efficient, a synchronous modem is also somewhat more costly. Synchronous medium- and high-speed modems are capable of speeds up to 9600 bits per second.

There are three basic modulation techniques: frequency modulation (FM), amplitude modulation (AM), and phase modulation (PM). The most

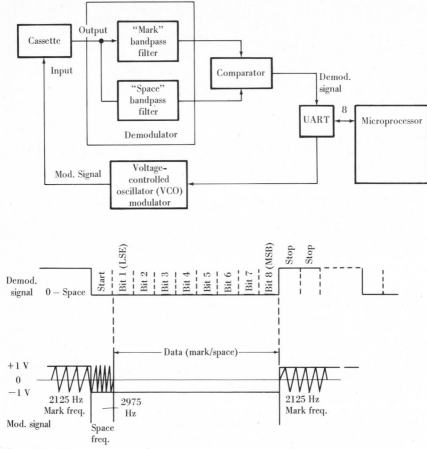

Figure 9-26 Cassette/microprocessor interface.

popular form of frequency modulation is *frequency-shift keying* (FSK). In this system, the carrier frequency (assume 1700 Hz) is modulated by plus or minus 500 Hz to represent binary 0 or binary 1. Thus a frequency of 1200 Hz generally represents a binary 1; 2200 Hz, a binary 0. See Fig. 9-25c.

Magnetic Tape Cassettes

The magnetic tape cassette is a nonvolatile storage medium with a typical capacity between 5 and 10 million bits. It is widely used in small systems as a mass-memory device from which to load RAM. Thus it is a functional replacement for the paper tape reader and paper tape punch. Its low cost, compact size, and ease of loading and unloading, coupled with a straightforward microprocessor interface, as shown in Fig. 9-26, are the major reasons for its acceptance. Some disadvantages include its relatively high error rate, which is approximately 1 bit of error per 10^6 bits recorded. The cassette is also relatively slow, typically operating at 300 baud, and must be manually controlled. However, it is the best storage medium for the hobbyist and in small-scale applications, since it can be used in a standard audio recorder/reproducer and can store a large number of programs.

A typical cassette-microprocessor interface is shown in Fig. 9-26. The cassette input-output signal is FSK where a "mark" is represented by 2125 Hz and a "space" by 2975 Hz.

Suppose the microprocessor wishes to input cassette data. The program must first test the status of the UART to determine whether a cassette data byte is available. If it is, the microprocessor will input the data byte. The correct procedure to input cassette data would be as follows:

1. Set up the program to input cassette data; this step is commonly known as "bootstrapping."

2. Place the cassette in the play mode.

3. Run the program.

4. Turn off the cassette after completion of the data transfer.

5. Disable the bootstrap program and return to normal program sequences.

The interface circuitry required to convert FSK to logic 1 and 0 for the UART will consist of a demodulator containing two bandpass filters that pass only the two frequencies of concern (2125 Hz and 2975 Hz). The comparator generates a logic 1 and logic 0 for the mark and space frequencies, respectively.

The output of data from the microprocessor to the cassette is accomplished as follows:

1. Place the cassette in the Record mode.

2. Bootstrap the cassette output program.

3. Run the program.

4. Turn off the cassette after completion of the data transfer.

5. Disable the Bootstrap program and return to normal programming sequences.

The circuitry required to convert logic 1s and 0s from the UART to FSK for the cassette recorder consists of a modulator containing a voltage-controlled oscillator, where one voltage (logic 1) generates the mark frequency and the other voltage (logic 0) generates the space frequency.

The Parallel-Interface Chip

Unlike the UART, which is almost a standard acronym used by most manufacturers, the LSI parallel interface chip is known by different acronyms: PIO,

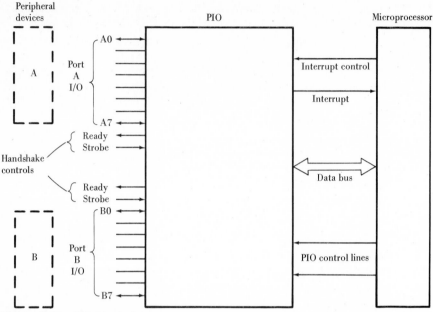

Figure 9-27 PIO block diagram.

PIA, PPI,* etc. The PIO is programmable as either input or output, typically contains two or more ports, and is used primarily as an interface device between the microprocessor and a peripheral unit such as a printer or keyboard. The architecture of most PIO units is somewhat similar, in that they have the following capabilities:

· Two or more independent 8-bit bidirectional peripheral interface ports with a specific sequence or protocol for data transfer control
· An interrupt control logic section which, based on the occurrence of a status condition of the device, generates an interrupt to the microprocessor
· Programmable byte modes for each port (input or output)
· Tri-state outputs

A typical PIO block diagram is shown in Fig. 9-27; each port has a bidirectional data bus tied to the device. The communication controls between the peripheral device and the I/O port are the "handshake" signals Strobe and Ready. In other systems, the signals are called Request and Acknowledge. The term *handshake* is used because the signals communicate with one another in a known sequence. For example, consider the following sequence utilizing Port A and shown in Fig. 9-28.

*PIO = Parallel I/O. PIA = Peripheral interface adapter. PPI = Programmable peripheral interface.

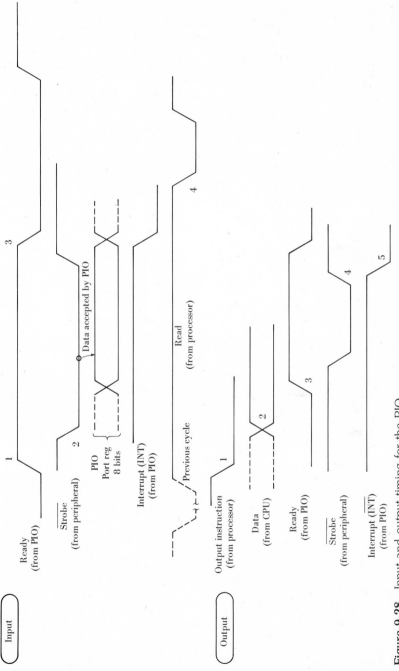

Figure 9-28 Input and output timing for the PIO.

Input Mode

1. The Ready signal from the PIO goes active when the port A input register is empty and is ready to accept data from the peripheral device.

2. The peripheral initiates the cycle using the $\overline{\text{Strobe}}$ line after the CPU has performed a Data Read. A low level on this line loads data into the port input register. The rising edge of this signal activates the interrupt request line ($\overline{\text{INT}}$) if the Interrupt Enable is set and this is the highest requesting device.

3. The next falling edge of the clock will reset the Ready line to an inactive state, signifying that the input register is full and further loading must be inhibited until the CPU reads the data.

4. The CPU, during its interrupt service routine, will read the data from the interrupting port, raising the Ready line to indicate that new data can be loaded into the PIO.

Output Mode

1. The Output mode is initiated by the execution of an Output instruction by the CPU.

2. Data is transferred from the CPU data bus to the port A output register.

3. The Ready line from the PIO goes high to indicate that the output register data is stable and is ready to transfer to the peripheral device.

4. The Ready signal will remain active until a positive edge is received from the $\overline{\text{Strobe}}$ line indicating that the peripheral has taken the data.

5. The rising edge of the $\overline{\text{Strobe}}$ generates an interrupt (if it has been enabled) and causes the Ready line to go inactive.

Standard Buses

There are several bus standards available for microprocessing and scientific-oriented systems. Standardization of the bus enhances system design, since it reduces the number of interface designs, provides ease of adaptability, and has logistics and maintenance benefits. Thus a unit which is properly designed and has met the standard bus requirements ideally needs only to be connected to the system to become operational. The issue which has evolved in the microprocessing world is to determine which bus system to utilize as the industry standard. There are three major bus systems on the market: the IEEE-488, the Intel Multibus, and the S-100 bus system. There are also three levels of standardization in bus systems:

1. Functional

2. Mechanical pin layout

3. Electrical signal and timing relationship

The IEEE bus was originally developed by Hewlett-Packard. Hewlett-Packard's success caused the Institute of Electrical and Electronic Engineers (IEEE) to adopt it as its standard. Other names for the bus are the HP-IB (Hewlett-Packard Interface Bus), the GPIB (General-Purpose Interface Bus), and the ANSI (American National Standards Institute) bus. Up to 15 devices (peripherals or instruments) can be connected to the bus, with the devices separated by a distance of no more than 2 meters (m). The total length of the bus is limited to 20 m. The bus has a maximum of 1 megabyte of data transmission capability, with realistic rates of 250 to 500 kilobytes per second over the full transmission path. The bus contains eight bidirectional data lines, which are also used for addresses, and eight control lines, which include handshaking signals. There are a total of 24 pins on the IEEE connector. Each device on the bus is controlled by a bus controller, and the command inputs to the devices are in ASCII code. There are four types of devices that interface to the bus. They are:

1. Devices such as counters, which are able only to transmit (talk).

2. Devices such as signal generators, which are able only to receive (listen).

3. Devices such as digital multimeters, which are able both to transmit and to receive data.

4. A controller, which can range from a desk-top calculator to a micro-processor and whose function is to control, transmit, or receive information.

The Multibus is an Intel product widely used in Intel's own line of micro-computers, RAMS, and peripherals. The Multibus has gained considerable support from other manufacturers of products compatible with Intel equipment. The Multibus system has three basic buses: data, address, and control. The Multibus connector consists of 86 pins with 16 data lines available, thus permitting full use of the bus when utilizing the newer 16-bit microprocessors. Since the newer microprocessors have the capability of directly addressing 1 megabyte, 20 pins are assigned as address lines. Control signals include memory control, I/O control, Interrupt lines and handshaking signals. The Multibus has a transmission speed exceeding 1 megabyte and the capability of connecting multiple boards, which can include up to 16 processors, thus making it superior to the IEEE bus system. When more than one processor is included in the system, special multibus signals enable one processor to control the other processors. Thus the controlling processor is called the *master* and the controlled processors are the *slaves,* and the system is said to have a master-slave configuration.

The S-100 bus was originally developed for the Altair/IMSAI 8800 microprocessing system, which used the 8080 unit. Initially intended for the hobbyist market, its popularity increased, and as a result it came to be utilized for interfacing with many different memory, I/O, and special peripheral units. The S-100 connector has 100 pins with 16 unidirectional data lines, eight for inputs and eight for outputs. The bus also contains 16 address lines and eight interrupt lines. Some problems have developed with this bus system, the primary difficulty being that many pin positions on the connector were left initially unassigned by Altair, permitting suppliers of cards to utilize the unassigned pins for their own signals, thus preventing a true standardization within the S-100 bus structure.

The Floppy Disk

The floppy disk, also known as the flexible disk or diskette, is the most important mass-memory system developed in recent years. It is a data entry system replacing the punched cards which once dominated the industry. The disk, consisting of oxide-coated Mylar, resembles a thin, flexible 45-rpm record and is housed in a square, flexible protective plastic jacket or cartridge (see Fig. 9-29a). The disk rotates within the cartridge, with a read/write head making physical contact on the disk surface. The three holes in the cartridge are the large center opening for the drive hub, a slit to permit access by the read/write head, and a small sector hole to provide access to the index hole.

The index mark serves as the physical beginning of all tracks. The data on the disk is recorded in tracks, with each track divided into sectors. The recording head of the disk drive moves radially over the disk to select one of the 77 tracks of the system. The track format is shown in Fig. 9-29b. A typical 8-in single disk has a transfer rate of 250K bits per second and an access time of 200 ms. A single IBM diskette can store nearly 250,000 bytes, a product of 77 tracks, 26 sectors per track, and 128 bytes per sector, on a single side, or as much data as is contained in three thousand 80-column punch cards. In order to increase storage capacity, floppy disk manufacturers are also producing double-density diskettes and dual- and triple-drive units containing multiple diskettes that can store data on both sides.

Floppy disk units usually consist of a combination of a stepper motor and a rack-and-pinion drive. The electronics of a floppy disk unit is a disk controller consisting of an LSI integrated circuit, which is an integral part of the system. The unit provides formatting verification and data accessing controls for bidirectional transfer of information between the main memory (through DMA) and the magnetically stored data on the diskette. The controller is designed to operate independent of the microprocessor/microcomputer of the system.

Paper Tape Reader and Punch

The paper tape reader and punch was mentioned previously in relation to the teletype. Using an ASR-33 Teletype that punches and reads at 10

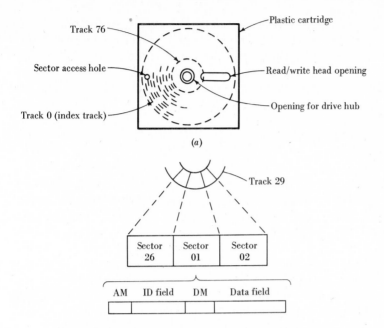

Address Mark (AM) — Identifies bytes between this address mark and the following data or delete mark as the ID field of the sector.

ID Field — Identifies the record contained in the data field by sector number and track number.

Data Mark or Delete Mark — A data mark indicates the data field contains a good record; a delete mark indicates the data field contains a deleted record.

Data Field — Contains a maximum of 128_{10}. If less than 128_{10} data bytes comprise the record, the data field is completed with fill bytes.

(b)

Figure 9-29 Floppy disk. (a) Outline drawing of a floppy disk; (b) track format.

characters per second, it would take approximately 30 minutes to read a Basic interpreter program from paper tape.

Readers and punches are separate units that are often physically mounted in the same structure. The reader feeds the punched tape over an array of photodiodes, which detect the presence or absence of a hole and cause a logic 1 or logic 0, respectively, to be generated. Typical readers can read paper tape at 300 characters per second; therefore, a Basic interpreter program can be loaded in 1 minute. High-speed readers capable of operating at 1000 characters per second are also available. Punches, which are obviously slower because of the mechanical requirement of punching a hole for a logic 1, typically punch at a rate of 50 characters per second, while high-speed punches operate at 150 characters per second. The paper tape can be either reeled, in which case tape drives are required for high speed, or "fan-folded," where the paper tape is folded in a fan-type arrangement and is placed in a rectangular container.

9-5 INTERFACING·TRENDS

Future trends of LSI devices include more sophisticated I/O peripheral chips and converter units. Converters (analog-to-digital and digital-to-analog) have in recent years been produced with ever-increasing conversion-bit accuracy. There are two major forms of converters: the hybrid and the monolithic. Hybrid means that two or more device types are contained in a single package. A monolithic unit is a device constructed from a single silicon substrate. Hybrid units exceed 8 bits; present units are 12 and 16 bits. Monolithic units are 8 bits; they are microprocessor-compatible, which means that bus-compatible latches for storing data are part of the device. The converters are also available as hybrid multichip systems (one analog and one digital device), extending the resolution to 12 bits.

An alternative approach of developing LSI-compatible microprocessor analog-to-digital converters is to include the conversion on the chip itself. This approach minimizes all interfaces so that a digitized value corresponding to the analog signal is entered as data in the microprocessor. The integrated converters will further enhance the capability of microcomputing systems and increase their role in the future.

PROBLEMS

1. Given the instruction OUT, 08H:
   a. Which I/O technique does it use?
   b. What is the port address, and which Address lines (A0 to A15) go to logic 1?
   c. What control signal is necessary to effect this data transfer?
   d. What microprocessor register does the data always come from?
   e. From your answers, sketch a microprocessor-I/O interface.
2. The instruction MOV M, C performs the same function as the output instruction in Prob. 1.
   a. Which I/O technique is used?
   b. What control signal is necessary to effect this data transfer?
   c. What microprocessor register does this data come from?
   d. Discuss how the port address is specified.
   e. What is the primary advantage of this technique?
   f. A microprocessor has a maximum address capability of 65,536 bytes (A0 to A15). If address line A15 is always used to indicate an I/O device transfer, how many bytes are left for program data?

g. Sketch a microprocessor-I/O interface using this technique when the I/O port address is 1002.

3. Write a polling program that transfers device 1 data to device 2.

		D7	D6	D5	D4	D3	D2	D1	D0
I/O Device 1	Status Port 04	X	X	X	X	X	X	1	X
	Data Port 16	X	X	X	X	X	X	X	X
I/O Device 2	Status Port 08	1	X	X	X	X	X	X	X
	Data Port 32	X	X	X	X	X	X	X	X

4. What are two microprocessor synchronizing techniques used to communicate with I/Os? Discuss the efficiency of both techniques.

5. a. Discuss the sequence within the microprocessor system that takes place when an interrupt occurs.
   b. What happens if the interrupt is a nonmaskable interrupt?
   c. Define vectored interrupt. What is the main advantage of having vectored interrupt capability?

6. Write a high-priority interrupt subroutine for the program in Prob. 3.

7. a. What method is used to transfer blocks of data at a relatively high speed?
   b. Explain how this transfer is synchronized by the microprocessor.

8. a. Discuss the basic functions of an ASR-33 teletype.
   b. What is the purpose of stop bits?

9. If the baud rate of an I/O device is 300 baud:
   a. What is the minimum bit time?
   b. How many characters per second are transmitted if 11 serial bits is equal to the character?
   c. Solve (a) and (b) for 9600 baud and 10 serial bits.

10. a. Using the ASCII table, determine the hexadecimal code for the following characters:
    - 0
    - 1
    - 9
    - A
    - B
    - F
    - ?
    - CR
    - LF
    b. Write a subroutine to input these nine characters (0 1 9 A B F ? CR LF) from a serial I/O into memory locations 1000 to 1008. A

UART which interfaces the serial I/O has an input status word of
* 01 at port 20 and data word at port 21.

c.   Discuss how to convert the decimal numbers 0 to 9 and letters A
to F in ASCII to hexadecimal for output to a hexadecimal display.

11.   a.   Discuss the possible errors in transmission using a half-duplex link.
b.   What characteristics of a full-duplex link reduce errors of transmission exhibited in a half-duplex link?

12.   a.   What are the two common transmission forms used to interface
peripherals?
b.   Discuss the advantages of both transmission forms compared with
a TTL transmission.

13.   a.   What type of device is used to transmit and receive analog information over communication links such as telephone lines?
b.   Why is it used instead of a digital transmission link?

14.   a.   What are the basic functions of a UART?
b.   What characteristics make the UART an extremely popular interface device?

15.   Discuss the characteristics of the LSI parallel-interface device.

REFERENCES

1.   Blakeslee, T. R.: *Digital Design with Standard MSI and LSI,* John Wiley and
Sons, Inc., New York, 1975.

2.   Intel Corporation: *8080 Microcomputer Systems User's Manual,* September
1975.

3.   Mostek: *MK3881 Parallel I/O Controller,* 1978.

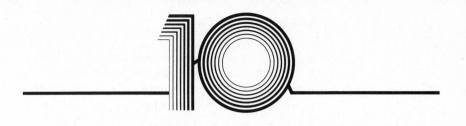

Application and Selection

The microprocessor is the single most important electronic development since the transistor and, like the transistor, has revolutionized all industries in its wide range of applications. Its popularity has been established by its low cost, small area, low power consumption, and high reliability. These characteristics have encouraged newer applications in industry as well as in the home. Ready-made software packages are being made available to simplify programming and reduce the cost of systems. Chapter 10 will present several representative examples of the use of the microprocessor. Equally important to recognizing their potential use is gaining a knowledge of techniques for selecting the microprocessor system that best meets the user's requirements. To accomplish this, we will discuss selection criteria at the system, hardware, and software levels that can be used to generate tradeoff data on competing candidate systems.

10-1 APPLICATION OVERVIEW

To be widely used, microprocessors must not only provide all the favorable design features inherent in LSI, but must also be cost-competitive for a particular application. As an example, a microprocessor that is being considered for a game must be of sufficiently low cost to make it economically feasible for the manufacturer to utilize it.

Figure 10-1 partitions the wide range of applications into seven categories and illustrates that as the level of complexity increases in the use of microprocessors, the cost of the units also increases. Note that microprocessors used for games and home applications do not require chips that have large

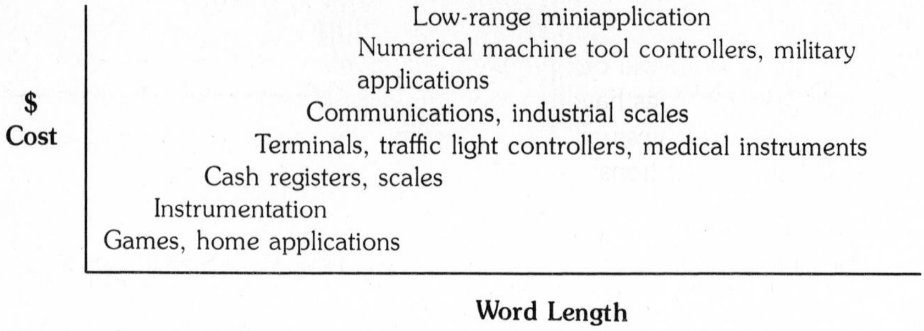

Low-range miniapplication
Numerical machine tool controllers, military
applications
Communications, industrial scales
Terminals, traffic light controllers, medical instruments
Cash registers, scales
Instrumentation
Games, home applications

$
Cost

Word Length

Figure 10-1 Applications of microprocessors.

data word lengths. Typically, 4-bit units are used in this category. As the cost increases in developing more sophisticated microprocessor base systems, data word length units of 8 and 16 bits are used.

Microprocessor systems have the potential of operating as "number crunchers," or very fast numeric units. The gradual evolution of high-speed technologies that can support fast processing has limited this form of application. Most applications, however, have looked to the microprocessor as a controller, or as an element that regulates the output by pre-storing the process in the form of instructions and sampling the input data in real time. The importance of the speed and response time of a microprocessor in these typical controller applications will be addressed later in this chapter. An initial overview, however, will first be given to general applications of microprocessors in the home, work, travel, leisure, and general health environments.

Home Application

Microprocessors in the home will one day be as commonplace as television sets. A listing of possible home applications is given below:

1. Home applications: files, recipes, tax records, checking accounts, bank accounts, important telephone listings, home business accounts, and inventory control

2. Entertainment: video games, tape/TV controller, and intellectually stimulating games, such as chess, backgammon, and bridge

3. Security: monitoring windows and doors, digital combination locks

4. Education: instructional programs

5. Miscellaneous:
   a. Cooking: temperature controller
   b. Heating: monitoring and controlling furnace temperature and pressure
   c. Electrical: monitoring electrical output current in all rooms and dimming lights when not in use

Work

The microprocessor will offer small businesses advantages similar to those which large companies have been enjoying from using minicomputers and larger computers. The small business will be able to use a microcomputer in the following applications:

- Inventory control
- Personnel records
- Timekeeping
- Billing
- Accounts receivable
- Payroll

Current microprocessor applications for use in larger businesses are:

- Point-of-sale terminals
- Automatic typesetting
- Smart instruments
- Automatic timeclocks
- Medical systems
- Optical character recognition
- Avionics (electronic aviation systems)
- Automated test stations
- Industrial control
- Remote utility meter reading systems

Travel

The microprocessor will make our modes of transportation more efficient and reliable than ever before. The microprocessor will reduce traffic fatalities by having remote traffic controllers monitor traffic. The microprocessor within an automobile will provide the following functions:

- Remote traffic control
- Monitoring the complete electrical system
- Minitoring tire pressures
- No-lock (anti-skid) braking
- Antitheft ignition systems
- Improving fuel economy by calculating the optimum air/fuel mixture and controlling the setting
- Reducing pollution
- Transmitting emergency conditions to police

Leisure Activities

Sporting events and games are utilizing the microprocessor to enrich our leisure activities. Possible uses are in:

- Automatic bowling scorers
- Automatic fencing hits and scorers
- Controlled scoreboard displays

Health

Low-cost microprocessing systems will allow a medical office to have complete up-to-date medical records of individuals. Transferring medical records from one area to another using telephone networks will take a matter of seconds. A pulse-measuring device will be available at a small cost so that each individual can monitor his or her own pulse rate. Medical test equipment will give accurate and reliable information to medical personnel.

10-2 APPLICATION EXAMPLES

Having provided an overview into the general applications of microprocessors, we will now develop more detailed applications in several categories. Each of the following examples will include flowcharts to describe the sequence of events.

EXAMPLE 1—PATIENT MONITORING SYSTEM

A microprocessor is used to continuously monitor the status of each patient's vital signs, including heart rate, blood pressure, pulse rate, EKG, respiration, and body temperature. The system provides data to an EKG recorder and a printer, which outputs the patient's identification and health status. Should

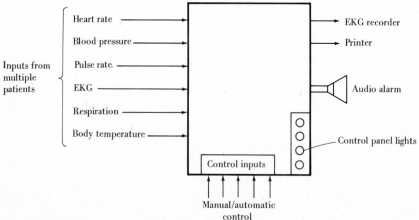

Figure 10-2 Patient monitoring system.

any test indicate abnormal conditions, then the failed parameters will be transmitted to the output warning port, which provides an audio alarm and a control panel indication of the patient's status at the nurse's station. See Fig. 10-2.

The flowchart for an intensive-care monitoring system is shown in Fig. 10-3. As shown in the flowchart, all patients are monitored continuously.

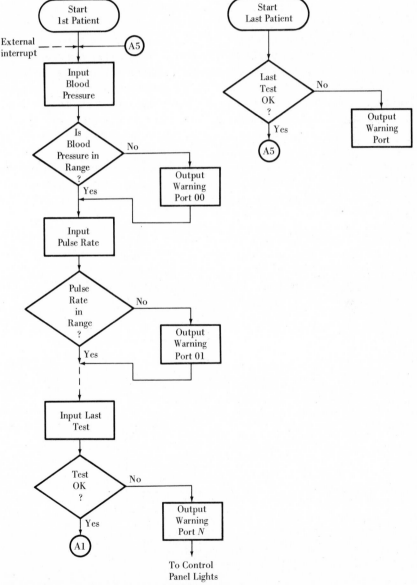

Figure 10-3 Intensive-care monitoring system.

After performing the last test on the first patient, the program will jump to A1, where another subroutine representing the second patient is executed. When the last patient has been monitored, the program jumps to A5, which is the start of the first patient subroutine.

EXAMPLE 2—AUTOMOTIVE APPLICATION: SOBRIETY TESTER

One of the primary causes of traffic accidents and fatalities is the diminished reaction time of the driver of an automobile who has been consuming alcoholic beverages. A drunk driver can be stopped if the ignition switch is disabled; thus a safety system would require that upon entering a vehicle the driver first place the key into the ignition switch and turn the key one position to the right to enable the start of the program (see Fig. 10-4). The keyboard I/O consists of a keypad and keyboard encoder. The ignition I/O contains simple relay logic and buffers. A display I/O is required to display a random number, which will be used to test the retention powers of the driver. Operation of the sobriety tester is shown by the flowchart in Fig. 10-5. Power turn-on causes the microprocessor to reset the program counter to 0000, which is the start of the sobriety program. The driver's personal keyword is entered and tested. A random number is generated if the keyword is in agreement with the keyboard entry. The random number is flashed on the display twice, 2 seconds on and 2 seconds off. The driver then depresses the keyboard again to enter the random number. If the random number agrees

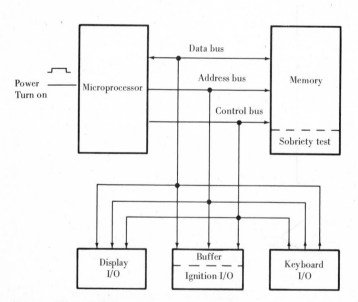

Figure 10-4 Sobriety tester application.

with the keyboard entry, the ignition I/O is enabled and the ignition switch is turned on, allowing the driver to start the vehicle. Should either the keyword or the random number be incorrectly inserted, then the program loops back to the input of the keyword again.

EXAMPLE 3—A PLANT MONITOR APPLICATION

A simplified microcomputer application of a plant monitor is shown in Fig. 10-6. Here 16 possible analog inputs representing temperature, pressure, air composition, power, etc., are transmitted to an analog multiplexer (MUX).

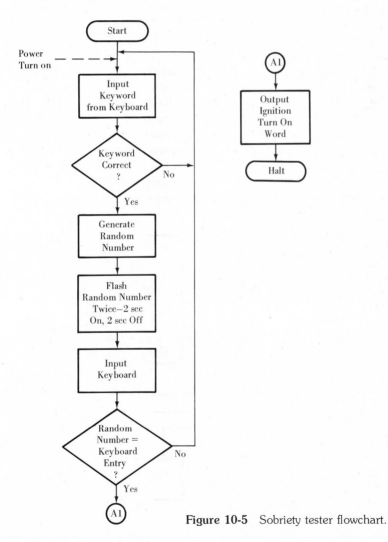

Figure 10-5 Sobriety tester flowchart.

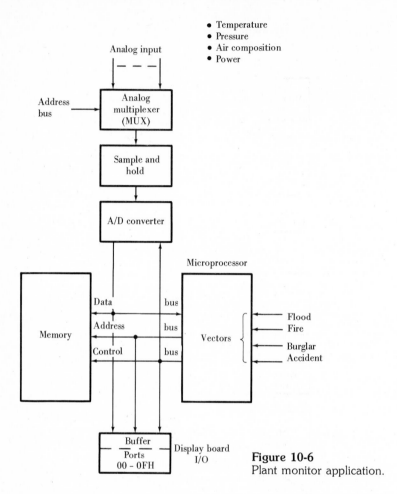

Figure 10-6
Plant monitor application.

The output of the MUX is sampled and held and presented to the input of an analog-to-digital converter. The microprocessor supplies the address for the MUX and routes the data to the appropriate port in the display I/O. Four vectored inputs are available in the microprocessor to cause the program to immediately jump to the interrupting device program. Actions such as turning on the sprinkler system when fire is detected and/or sounding a plant alarm would be commenced immediately.

The flowchart for the plant monitor is shown in Fig. 10-7. The microprocessor initializes the analog MUX and then halts. When the digital data from the analog-to-digital converter is valid, the analog-to-digital converter outputs a Conversion Complete pulse. This pulse interrupts the microprocessor, allowing data to be input, and then outputs it to the I/O port, which is

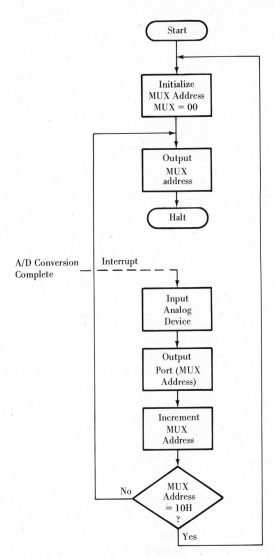

Figure 10-7
Plant monitor flowchart.

the same address as the MUX. The MUX address is incremented and the microprocessor checks to see if it was the last address, 10H. If it is 10H, then the MUX address is set to 00 to indicate the start of another cycle.

10-3 SELECTING A MICROPROCESSOR SYSTEM

Selection of the proper and most cost-effective system for a specific application may at first seem like a simple task, but there are many pitfalls which, if encountered, can cost time and money should the wrong selection be made. There are several major categories which are important in microprocessor selection. These include hardware, software, and system considerations.

Hardware

Word Length   This is one of the most important features to be considered. Microprocessors are available in fixed word lengths from less than 4 bits to 16 bits. Microprogrammable units have arithmetic bit slices in increments of 2 or 4 bits, which provide expandable word length capability, such as 24 or 32 bits. The criteria for determining word length include many factors, such as computational accuracy and data word input and output bit requirements.

Registers   Processors that are designed with general-purpose registers have inherently greater capability than units with dedicated registers. The general-purpose registers are used for addressing, indexing, and status and as multiple accumulators. The accumulators provide locations in the CPU in which an operand can be temporarily stored and then retrieved quickly when needed. Accumulators simplify programming and conserve main memory by eliminating memory buffering of data. Multiple accumulators are especially important for ROM programs that contain no writable memory. Microprocessors that do not have general registers should have index and base registers available for address modification. If they do not, cumbersome programming steps will be required to perform these functions. In comparing microprocessors, be especially aware of the number of accessible registers which are available to the user, not just the total number of registers.

Most of the newer microprocessing units, particularly microprogrammable devices, have advanced hardware features integrated into the chip. Included in this category are circuits which implement the Multiply function in hardware. With such a unit, the Multiply execution time will be reduced by at least one-half of the time required to execute the instruction in firmware.

Stacks   Stacks can be used for nested subroutines,* interrupts, and temporary storage of data when programs reside in ROMs. There are two basic forms of stacks, software and hardware stacks. The software stack is a RAM with no fixed limit in size, sometimes known as an *infinite* or *variable stack*. The hardware stack consists of registers built into the chip with obviously limited size. With a ROM program microprocessor, the hardware stack can eliminate the need to use a scratch pad RAM. However, if your application

---

*Refers to one subroutine on top of another, usually occurring when the interrupt subroutines are themselves being interrupted.

requires nested subroutines, a microprocessor with a variable stack size must be selected.

Instruction Set and Addressing Modes   If the application requires a large manipulation of data, look for microprocessor units that have a versatile instruction set in this category. Some units provide instructions that permit single-bit manipulation of the accumulator, while in other units operations to a single bit can be accomplished on any register or location in memory. Instructions in this category permit I/O status data, for example, to be recognized by a Bit Set, Bit Reset, or Test instruction. The common approach is to input the I/O status data into the accumulator and perform n shifts until the bit is detected in the sign bit position. If there is a requirement to process input data which is formatted in BCD, then it is necessary to determine which units have a decimal instruction set. In such an application, the instruction set should contain a BCD Addition or a Decimal Adjust instruction. Where the application requires a great number of arithmetic functions with high resolution, it is advantageous to consider units that have double-precision arithmetic functions. Many microprocessor manufacturers define their total instruction set by counting the instruction only once, regardless of how many addressing modes it has. Other manufacturers count the same instruction as many times as there are addressing modes for it. To be consistent, convert to one approach all the microprocessing units being considered. Note that although it is desirable to have a microprocessor unit with a large instruction set (for example, over 100 instructions), in general most applications require 50 percent or less of the total of such an instruction set.

Addressing modes play an important part in determining the most suitable microprocessing unit for an application. Addressing modes provide the capability and flexibility of storing and retrieving operand data in a manner which best suits the programmer. For example, if a large quantity of data is to be stored and time is critical, the use of a direct mode which fetches the operand in the minimum number of machine cycles is desirable. If the direct address mode does not have this capability, then perhaps another address mode, such as indirect, can be substituted. However, the user must determine if the use of indirect addressing requires a significant number of machine cycles, thereby resulting in greater execution time.

Indexing mode capability is never sufficiently emphasized. It is quite important to have this addressing mode capability, particularly in hardware. In many instances, users who do not initially intend to perform many operations may later use this mode extensively as original programs are modified, or as new applications involving the movement of blocks of data are added. One index register is useful, but more than one is even more useful, since it is more convenient to keep track of tables simultaneously than to load the same index register with different data. Consequently, a careful review of all addressing mode capabilities of competing units should be performed and a determination made of the penalties in execution time which may result from their use.

Voltage Requirements   Early microprocessors required three voltage sources, whereas the newer-generation microprocessors require only one voltage source.

Clock   Microprocessors can also be considered to be static or dynamic. When a device is static, then the clock can be held at a high state for any length of time without losing any information. For troubleshooting, the clock can be slowed down or even single-pulsed into the system. Dynamic microprocessor units require overlapping clock signals and cannot be manipulated as the static units can.

Controls and Buffers   Determine whether the units under consideration contain TTL-compatible inputs or whether they require interface buffers. Early microprocessors required hardware such as a status latch and a bus controller to control interfaces. Newer units integrate the control functions within the microprocessor by providing more tri-state control lines and programmable interfaces.

Speed   The user must determine the speed requirements of the system. If the microprocessor is being used for the purpose of learning basic microprocessing fundamentals, then chances are slight that speed will be an important criterion in the selection of the unit. Speed is important in many applications for a very simple reason, the faster you execute a program, the more time is available to perform other functions. The utilization of a microprocessor unit in a real time application, such as process control, where the microprocessor controls a manufacturing process, requires not only fast responses in terms of computations from the unit but also a well-structured I/O and interrupt system which can respond rapidly to changing parameters. In such applications, where the success of the system is dependent upon operating speed, a well-thought-out approach to evaluating microprocessing systems is required.

Processing speed will now be covered from several viewpoints:

1.   A description of the technique for identifying instruction execution times, so that relative instruction comparisons of microprocessors can be performed.

2.   Benchmarks. These are test programs developed by competing manufacturers which meet the requirements likely to be imposed by the user in the evaluation.

3.   The particular chip technology. Processing speed is highly dependent on the technology selected for the chip. The most important speed-related parameter, the speed-power product, is discussed.

The most frequently used term in determining the speed of a microprocessor device is *throughput.* Throughput is universally used to express the speed performance of a unit. The faster the throughput of a unit, the more programs it performs in a given time. Throughput is a term that quantizes (or determines a numerical value for) how fast these programs are processed. Throughput is expressed in operations or instructions performed per unit of time. A microprocessor may have the throughput capability of performing 200,000 operations per second (OPs), or 200 KOPs (where $K = 10^3$). We will assume that when a processor is performing an operation it is executing an instruction, making the terms synonymous. Discussions will follow later as to the method of arriving at the throughput of a microprocessor. Note that with continuing technological improvements, the anticipated increase in throughput capability is estimated to be approximately 20 percent per year.

Microprocessors have execution times which vary according to the complexity of the instruction and the number of Fetches from memory that are required. Some units, such as the 8080, utilize up to 5 machine cycles or 17 clock cycles to fetch and execute an instruction. The instruction execution time is computed by the following relation:

Instruction execution time = number of clock cycles × clock period

For example, when a 2-MHz clock (500-ns) is used, the execution time for a 17–clock-cycle instruction will be 8.5 μs (17 × 500 ns = 8.5 μs). Instructions with shorter execution times require fewer machine cycles and correspondingly fewer clock cycles. Newer-generation units with better architecture and longer word lengths require a smaller number of machine cycles to perform the same function. A typical newer unit utilizes 2 machine cycles to input the instruction, decode, execute, increment the program counter, and output the address to memory. Some of these functions can be initiated before the previous function is completed, thereby reducing the overall execution time of the instruction.

A summary of the instruction set, in tabular form, can be found in most microprocessing reference manuals. This is a useful guide for quickly determining the execution time of any instruction, since the number of machine cycles or clock cycles for each instruction is usually specified therein. The formula we have given for instruction execution time is used when the instruction is specified in clock cycles. When the instruction is given in machine cycles, then it must be determined whether the number of clock cycles per machine cycle for the instruction is fixed or variable. This number

TABLE 10-1   Benchmark Comparisons

	VENDOR A		VENDOR B	
PROGRAM	MEMORY STORAGE IN WORDS	EXECUTION TIME IN MICROSECONDS (AVERAGE)	MEMORY STORAGE IN WORDS	EXECUTION TIME IN MICROSECONDS (AVERAGE)
1. Arithmetic	400	920(2.3)	450	1057(2.35)
2. Data Movement	350	980(2.8)	330	960(2.91)
3. I/O Operation	225	585(2.1)	250	700(2.8)
Average		(2.54)		(2.64)

could be a variable, depending on the design of the unit. When the number is a variable, the sum of all clock cycles constituting the machine cycles is needed to determine the execution time of the instruction. Once the execution time of an instruction has been determined, a direct comparison of that exact instruction can be made for competing microprocessing systems.

A further assessment of microprocessor speed can be made by the use of *benchmarks*. Benchmarks are a series of test programs used to evaluate the effectiveness of the microprocessing system under consideration. If Company *A* and Company *B* are vying for your application, then as a minimum several benchmark programs should be employed in the evaluation. The programs can be coded by the user or the vendor and used in the candidate microprocessing systems. The objective of benchmarks is to determine the total "run," or execution time, of the benchmark program rather than to compare, without application in mind, the individual execution times of similar instructions.

Table 10-1 shows the results of three different benchmark programs used to evaluate the performance of two competing manufacturers' products. The results indicate that in two of the three categories, Vendor *A* has the more efficient product in terms of memory allocation. However, even though Vendor *B*'s second program uses less memory, his average instruction time is slower than Vendor *A*'s benchmark for that program. The average instruction time is determined by the following equation:

$$\text{Average instruction time} = \frac{\text{total execution time}}{\text{total memory storage}}$$

In Table 10-1, we have chosen to select three benchmark programs that are representative of the type of programs the microprocessors will be executing. Since they describe typical programs, the benchmarks can be averaged to obtain an overall processing time for each microprocessor. The processor from Vendor *A* has a 2.54-μs average instruction or execution time. Note, however, that the more programs one uses in benchmark evaluations for a particular processor, the more accurate the average instruction that is derived. Once the average execution time of an instruction has been determined, the throughput of the processor can be calculated by the following equation:

$$\text{Throughput in operations per second} = \frac{1}{\text{Average instruction execution time}}$$

In the table, since the average instruction time is approximately 2.5 μs, the throughput of the system is about 400,000 operations per second, or 400 KOPs.

In addition to evaluating processing speeds, benchmarks enable the user to determine the exact number of storage words used in performing a function. Storage allocation is an important parameter in benchmark programming, since it provides the user with a guide for determining which unit requires fewer programming words. Units that utilize more space to perform allocated functions will have less reserve memory available to accommodate future requirements. A larger storage allocation may also require additional memory modules, which will impact on the cost of these systems.

There are many different benchmark programs that can be utilized for evaluating microprocessing systems. However, it is important to select only programs which will closely follow the environment that the microprocessor will be in. If the arithmetic capability is to be thoroughly exercised and there is to be very little I/O interaction, then it is important to develop benchmarks that primarily evaluate the arithmetic instructions of the device.

Some of the basic categories of benchmarks are as follows:

- Movement and manipulation of data
- Performing arithmetic operations
- Saving and restoring status upon receipt of Interrupts
- Monitoring of peripheral devices
- Searching for specific data in memory

The ground rules for specifying benchmarks can be made quite simple: The user specifies the overall function to be performed. Instructions and address modes are generally not specified. The person developing the benchmark has the prerogative of utilizing any instruction and address mode available in the instruction set. The benchmark results from different processors will probably not be the same, since microprocessors have different architectures, and therefore the approaches to executing even identical instructions are quite different. When you evaluate benchmarks, there are several other important points to note. Programs can be written to optimize speed or memory but generally not both simultaneously; the user must determine the most important criteria and then disseminate this information to those developing the benchmarks. If the user is attempting to personally develop a benchmark on two machines, one on which he has little background and one with which he is intimately familiar, then unless he thoroughly studies the first unit, the results should favor the second microprocessor. An alternative approach is to permit vendors to benchmark the program, giving each of them the same ground rules and then having the user objectively evaluate the results. Benchmarks are not the ultimate method of determining speed performance, yet they are useful, especially when applied to microprocessor programming of similar functions.

The microprocessors under consideration should show an approximate total of 50 percent throughput utilization so that any other projected programs can be included without being constrained in time. When sufficient margin is not allowed in the initial estimate, serious throughput limitations can later develop, possibly forcing degradation in performance or the need for complete redesign with a faster unit.

There are several important technological characteristics that must be recognized as prime parameters influencing high-speed processing units. Foremost is the speed-power product of the microprocessor unit. Speed-power product (SPP), as the name implies, is the product of the basic delay through a typical gate of the LSI microprocessor chip and the average power dissipated by the gate. SPP, however, is not limited to the microprocessor. Any device consisting of gates has the SPP parameter listed in the specification sheet. Expressed as an equation,

$$\text{Speed-power product} = \text{gate delay} \times \text{gate power}$$

When the gate delay is in nanoseconds ($s \times 10^{-9}$) and the gate power dissipation in milliwatts ($W \times 10^{-3}$), then the SPP is expressed in picojoules ($J \times 10^{-12}$).

The speed-power product is a performance parameter. The basic approach to high-speed processing is to attempt to run things faster, which unfortunately dissipates more power. Technologies that have low gate delays inherently produce high-speed circuits, but if they dissipate larger amounts of power to achieve a desired speed, then the SPP of the device will not be very low. Thus a typical emitter-coupled logic (ECL) unit, which may have an excellent (low) gate delay, may not have as high an SPP as an I^2L device, since ECL also has a high power dissipation. The user alone can best determine how to utilize the SPP parameter; selecting a unit with a low SPP may not result in the overall fastest microprocessing unit, but it does give the user a good compromise between the two parameters which constitute SPP.

Software

Software has become the major cost factor in procuring and utilizing micro-processing systems, and so all alternative software approaches which competing systems have to offer must be carefully evaluated. Preceding the evaluation, the user must first determine the total size of programs and select the level of programming language most compatible with the application. The choices include high-level, assembly, or machine-code language. Machine-code language, as pointed out in Chap. 6, should be used only when the total size of the program is small, e.g., under 200 words. There are issues, also covered in Chap. 6, on the advantages of assembly language over high-level language, and vice versa. Once the language level selection is made, the user can proceed with the software evaluation. If the programs are to be coded in a high-level language, it is important to know how efficiently the language supports each microprocessing system. Fortran, for example, although widely accepted as an application language and used in large computing systems, does not yet provide the user with the performance and efficient memory utilization of a microprocessor design language such as PL/M. Thus selecting a language which is not most suitable can add 50 percent or more to the size of a program. A program which takes up the additional memory may require more memory modules and more volume and dissipate more power. The added memory results in more instructions and increases the time required to execute the program.

There are alternatives available to the user at all levels of software design. Will the user require a software development system, or just the basic "bare bones" approach in assembling the program? Do the candidate systems offer the same complement of peripheral equipment, such as floppy disks and CRT monitors, or do the systems require the use of older, slower peripherals, such as a paper tape system and a teletype? Before deciding in favor of a slower system, consider the potential time that can be saved by using the faster peripherals in the system. Given a choice, most users would rather spend time developing software than utilizing slow input-output devices that reduce their overall available time with the programs.

There are several forms of assemblers which may be optional with the type of system being considered. A relocatable assembler in conjunction with a link editor offers a choice of permitting relocation of programs to different places in memory. There are some restrictions on relocation, such as not assigning programs in memory locations reserved for vector interrupts and stacks, but the relocatable assembler is much more flexible than its absolute counterpart. With a relocatable assembler, programs are reassembled less often and program modules are easily linked.

Several other key software programs must also be examined. If resident monitors are to be used, a determination must be made as to how efficient they are in memory utilization. Monitor programs, as you may recall, are an important software tool for debugging. Check to see which of the following capabilities the competing monitors will provide:

· Can major registers of the microprocessor, as well as the memory, be examined and modified?

· Does the monitor have a Breakpoint mode?

· What steps are necessary in the competing systems for programming PROMs?

Development systems provide the greatest cost to the user. Determine if the software development system is available as a cross or resident system. If a cross system is offered, is it compatible with your existing processing system? For meaningful comparisons between development systems, they should both be either cross or resident. It is not easy to translate the cost of an in-house timesharing system to that of a resident system, since those items which are different in cost must be identified separately. When a cross system is considered, determine the language of the cross-assembler. When a company provides Fortran for portability, note that the program must be recompiled in assembly language. This procedure adds to the software costs.

System Considerations

An important system consideration in implementing the processing function involves determining whether a microprocessor, a microcomputer, or a microprogrammable unit should be utilized to meet the system requirements. Microprocessors and microcomputers have essentially the same architecture in terms of control logic and fixed instruction set, while the microprogramming unit is substantially different. A microprogrammable unit adds a new level of complexity to software, since two forms of software, the macro and the micro, are required. Software support of microprogrammable units is costlier and has been slow reaching the development level of computers which have a fixed instruction set. Additionally, increased software development time is required for programming microprogrammable units. However, many benefits can be derived by selecting a microprogrammable unit. These include the following:

· The word length is not restricted to the fixed data word sizes. For example, development of a 6-bit or 20-bit word length unit is possible if bit-slice chips are used.

· Special instructions customized for the user's applications can be developed for microprogramming units.

· Based on architecture and technology, microprogrammable units are inherently higher-performance units.

· Emulation of an existing instruction set provides a powerful technique for saving present operating software while making technological updates possible with newer hardware. Thus a higher level of integration and greater reliability are possible.

PROBLEMS

1. Discuss an application that can utilize a microprocessor, a microcomputer, or a bit-slice processor (not discussed in this chapter). Draw a flowchart.

2. When you select a microprocessor for a particular application, it is advisable to develop a benchmark program.
   a. What purpose do benchmarks serve?
   b. What are the basic categories of benchmarks?

3. If the average instruction execution time of a program is 4 μs (microseconds), what is the processor's throughput?

4. What is meant by the speed-power product?

5. Discuss the advantages of having the following software:
   a. Relocatable assembler
   b. Monitor
   c. Development systems

REFERENCES

1. Intel Corporation: *SBC 80/System 80 Microcomputer Systems Configuration Guide,* 1978.

APPENDIX A
Powers of 2

2^n	n	2^{-n}
1	0	1.0
2	1	0.5
4	2	0.25
8	3	0.125
16	4	0.062 5
32	5	0.031 25
64	6	0.015 625
128	7	0.007 812 5
256	8	0.003 906 25
512	9	0.001 953 125
1 024	10	0.000 976 562 5
2 048	11	0.000 488 281 25
4 096	12	0.000 244 140 625
8 192	13	0.000 122 070 312 5
16 384	14	0.000 061 035 156 25
32 768	15	0.000 030 517 578 125
65 536	16	0.000 015 258 789 062 5
131 072	17	0.000 007 629 394 531 25
262 144	18	0.000 003 814 697 265 625
524 288	19	0.000 001 907 348 632 812 5
1 048 576	20	0.000 000 953 674 316 406 25
2 097 152	21	0.000 000 476 837 158 203 125
4 194 304	22	0.000 000 238 418 579 101 562 5
8 388 608	23	0.000 000 119 209 289 550 781 25
16 777 216	24	0.000 000 059 604 644 775 390 625
33 554 432	25	0.000 000 029 802 322 387 695 312 5
67 108 864	26	0.000 000 014 901 161 193 847 656 25
134 217 728	27	0.000 000 007 450 580 596 923 828 125
268 435 456	28	0.000 000 003 725 290 298 461 914 062 5
536 870 912	29	0.000 000 001 862 645 149 230 957 031 25
1 073 741 824	30	0.000 000 000 931 322 574 615 478 515 625
2 147 483 648	31	0.000 000 000 465 661 287 307 739 257 812 5
4 294 967 296	32	0.000 000 000 232 830 643 653 869 628 906 25
8 589 934 592	33	0.000 000 000 116 415 321 826 934 814 453 125
17 179 869 184	34	0.000 000 000 058 207 660 913 467 407 226 562 5
34 359 738 368	35	0.000 000 000 029 103 830 456 733 703 613 281 25
68 719 476 736	36	0.000 000 000 014 551 915 228 366 851 806 640 625
137 438 953 472	37	0.000 000 000 007 275 957 614 183 425 903 320 312 5
274 877 906 944	38	0.000 000 000 003 637 978 807 091 712 951 660 156 25
549 755 813 888	39	0.000 000 000 001 818 989 403 545 856 475 830 078 125
1 099 511 627 776	40	0.000 000 000 000 909 494 701 772 928 237 915 039 062 5
2 199 023 255 552	41	0.000 000 000 000 454 747 350 886 464 118 957 519 531 25
4 398 046 511 104	42	0.000 000 000 000 227 373 675 443 232 059 478 759 765 625
8 796 093 022 208	43	0.000 000 000 000 113 686 837 721 616 029 739 379 882 812 5
17 592 186 044 416	44	0.000 000 000 000 056 843 418 860 808 014 869 689 941 406 25
35 184 372 088 832	45	0.000 000 000 000 028 421 709 430 404 007 434 844 970 703 125
70 368 744 177 664	46	0.000 000 000 000 014 210 854 715 202 003 717 422 485 351 562 5
140 737 488 355 328	47	0.000 000 000 000 007 105 427 357 601 001 858 711 242 675 781 25
281 474 976 710 656	48	0.000 000 000 000 003 552 713 678 800 500 929 355 621 337 890 625
562 949 953 421 312	49	0.000 000 000 000 001 776 356 849 400 250 464 677 810 668 945 312 5

APPENDIX B
Hexadecimal-to-Octal Conversion

	0	1	2	3	4	5	6	7	8	9	A	B	C	D	E	F
0	000	001	002	003	004	005	006	007	010	011	012	013	014	015	016	017
1	020	021	022	023	024	025	026	027	030	031	032	033	034	035	036	037
2	040	041	042	043	044	045	046	047	050	051	052	053	054	055	056	057
3	060	061	062	063	064	065	066	067	070	071	072	073	074	075	076	077
4	100	101	102	103	104	105	106	107	110	111	112	113	114	115	116	117
5	120	121	122	123	124	125	126	127	130	131	132	133	134	135	136	137
6	140	141	142	143	144	145	146	147	150	151	152	153	154	155	156	157
7	160	161	162	163	164	165	166	167	170	171	172	173	174	175	176	177
8	200	201	202	203	204	205	206	207	210	211	212	213	214	215	216	217
9	220	221	222	223	224	225	226	227	230	231	232	233	234	235	236	237
A	240	241	242	243	244	245	246	247	250	251	252	253	254	255	256	257
B	260	261	262	263	264	265	266	267	270	271	272	273	274	275	276	277
C	300	301	302	303	304	305	306	307	310	311	312	313	314	315	316	317
D	320	321	322	323	324	325	326	327	330	331	332	333	334	335	336	337
E	340	341	342	343	344	345	346	347	350	351	352	353	354	355	356	357
F	360	361	362	363	364	365	366	367	370	371	372	373	374	375	376	377

Index